SUTTON MODERN BRI[...]

THATCHERISM
AND BRITISH POLITICS
1975–1999

SUTTON MODERN BRITISH HISTORY

General Editor: Keith Laybourn,
Professor of History, University of Huddersfield

1. The Rise of Socialism in Britain, *c.* 1881–1951
Keith Laybourn

2. Workhouse Children: Infant and Child Paupers under the
Worcestershire Poor Law, 1780–1871
Frank Compton

3. Social Conditions, Status and Community, *c.* 1860–1920
Edited by *Keith Laybourn*

4. The Making of the British Middle Class? Studies of Regional and
Cultural Diversity since the Eighteenth Century
Edited by *Alan Kidd and David Nicholls*

5. The Age of Appeasement: The Evolution of British Foreign Policy
in the 1930s
Peijian Shen

6. Thatcherism and British Politics, 1975–1999
Brendan Evans

Forthcoming Titles

The National Union of Mineworkers and British Politics, 1944–1995
Andrew J. Taylor

The Age of Unease: Government and Reform in Britain, 1782–1832
Michael Turner

The Republic in Modern England, 1850–1940
Edited by *David Nash and Antony Taylor*

Fascism in Modern Britain
Richard C. Thurlow

SUTTON MODERN BRITISH HISTORY

THATCHERISM
AND BRITISH POLITICS
1975–1999

BRENDAN EVANS

SUTTON PUBLISHING

First published in 1999 by
Sutton Publishing Limited · Phoenix Mill
Thrupp · Stroud · Gloucestershire · GL5 2BU

British Library Cataloguing in Publication Data
A catalogue record for this book is available from the British Library

ISBN 07509 1572 2 (hb)
ISBN 07509 1573 0 (pb)

Cover photograph: Margaret Thatcher and the then Conservative Party Chairman,
Norman Tebbit, at an electoral press conference in 1987 (Hulton Getty).

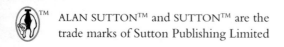
^{TM} ALAN SUTTON™ and SUTTON™ are the
trade marks of Sutton Publishing Limited

Typeset in 11/14 pt Sabon.
Typesetting and origination by
Sutton Publishing Limited
Printed in Great Britain by
Redwood Books, Trowbridge, Wiltshire.

CONTENTS

ABBREVIATIONS

ASI	Adam Smith Institute
BCCI	Bank of Credit and Commerce International
CBI	Confederation of British Industry
CCO	Conservative Central Office
CEGB	Central Electricity Generating Board
CND	Campaign for Nuclear Disarmament
CPC	Conservative Political Centre
CPRS	Central Policy Review Staff
CPS	Centre for Policy Studies
CRD	Conservative Research Department
CSD	Civil Service Department
DES	Department of Education and Science
ED	Employment Department
EMS	European Monetary System
EMU	European Monetary Union
ERM	Exchange Rate Mechanism
ET	Employment Training
GCHQ	Government Communications Headquarters
HEFCE	Higher Education Funding Council for England
IEA	Institute for Economic Affairs
IGC	Inter-Governmental Conference
IMF	International Monetary Fund
IoD	Institute of Directors
MSC	Manpower Services Commission
MTFS	Medium Term Financial Strategy
NCB	National Coal Board
NUM	National Union of Mineworkers
OPEC	Organisation of Petroleum Exporting Countries
PFI	Private Finance Initiative
PSBR	Public Sector Borrowing Rate
RPI	Retail Price Index
TEC	Training and Enterprise Council
UDC	Urban Development Corporation
UDM	Union of Democratic Mineworkers
YC	Young Conservatives
YTS	Youth Training Scheme

PREFACE

The years from 1975 to 1997 form a significant and discrete period in the history of the Conservative Party and the British nation alike. It encompassed two Conservative leaders who had major effects, both positive and negative, on the fortunes of both their party and country. The focus in this study is unapologetically upon the two Prime Ministers and leaders during the period under review, respectively Margaret Thatcher and John Major. This is justified both in terms of the Conservative Party, and also from the perspective of the British constitution. With respect to the Conservative Party it is evident that the leader is dominant, and nothing important ever becomes Conservative policy without the assent of the leader. When that leader is also the Prime Minister there is a further increase in power. The British constitution places few formal checks on the Prime Minister's power and some compare the position to that of a medieval monarch. This power is intensified further when, as happened from 1979 to 1997, one party is in continuous office. As a leading expert on British government expresses it, 'it is true that the impression of executive dominance was not nearly as marked under John Major as under Margaret Thatcher; but it remained the case even after 1990 that the government seemed subject to few formal checks on its policies.'[1]

To analyse the politics of the United Kingdom in these years from the perspective of two individuals may appear a distortion. In the Conservative Party there are other power centres than the leader, and due weight will be allocated to them in this analysis. In the country's political system there are also other actors who wield power and they too will not be neglected. Above all there is the validity of the maxim of Harold Macmillan that it is 'events' which really constrain the power of governments. It would be unrealistic, however, to ignore the central and decisive importance, both positive and negative, of the role played by Thatcher and Major. The assumption here is similar to that expressed by Karl Marx, who in considering the role of the human element in politics, asserted, 'men make history, but not in circumstances of their choosing'.

Why is 1975 a significant date in postwar British politics? In 1975, despite the two recent Labour Party general election victories, Labour appeared to be in an electoral decline and the Labour government was encountering mounting political difficulties. This reality was captured at the time by the view that Britain had become an 'anti-model' for other countries; and immediately afterwards by the description of the later 1970s as the time when 'the writing was on the wall.' Many aspects of British society appeared to be in difficulty, the aspirations of significant sections of the population, from middle managers to small businesses and public sector workers were not being met, and the economy seemed to be irredeemably sick. The choice of 1997 as the end of the period discussed here requires little justification, given the devastating defeat inflicted on the previously dominant Conservative government by the British electorate. The election on 1 May 1997 proved to be a Waterloo for the Conservative Party, when it secured a miserable 31 per cent of the vote, the elimination of its representation in Wales and Scotland and a weak position in parliament facing a Labour majority of 181.

Thatcher's emergence as Conservative Party leader in February 1975, despite the element of novelty and risk which it implied, carried with it a strong conviction that it represented the next wave in British politics; and her electoral victory in May 1979 inaugurated a continuous eighteen year era of Conservative rule by her and her chosen successor, John Major. If 1975 was the year that the Conservative Party appeared to change through the impact of its new leader, it was in 1979 that the country directly experienced the impact. 1979 ranks with 1906 and 1945 in Britain, and 1932 in the United States and Sweden, as a decisive turning point. The Liberal government of 1906 and the Labour government of 1945 both changed the course of British politics in the direction of radical social welfare policies, which soon became absorbed as part of a new national political consensus. Thatcher's victory in 1979 attempted to establish a rejection of the politics of social welfare as well as of policies of economic intervention to maintain full employment. Her governments were successful in defeating socialism as a serious political force, but the degree to which she was able to undermine policies aimed at enhancing social welfare and maintaining full employment are debated in this analysis. Equally, in the United States and Sweden, the year 1932 launched the two eras of liberal and social democratic domination respectively.

Thatcherism has become a sufficiently widely studied phenomenon that it is necessary to justify yet another analysis; although the quantity of books on the subject rectifies a tendency among political historians to study Labour Party history, despite the Conservative Party's dominance over British politics for nearly two centuries. Less frequently examined is the phenomenon of Thatcherism in the context of both Conservative and British political history. Such a focus is the purpose of this work, and it includes a comparative discussion of both the Thatcher and Major governments, an analysis of the Thatcherite legacy and the theoretical debate about the precise character of Thatcherism. Yet in evaluating its nature, the view expressed in an undergraduate essay that 'Thatcherism is merely the Conservative Party led by Mrs Thatcher' has much to commend it.

Since Thatcherism is a recent episode, and a highly contentious one both inside and outside the Conservative Party, it is impossible to view it in true historical perspective and with objectivity. Yet it is inappropriate for political historians to neglect recent events which necessarily have a greater and more direct impact on our current experiences than the politics of the Middle Ages, for example. It is also necessary to challenge potent myths which might otherwise pass into the historical consciousness: a particular danger when there has been an explicit attempt to 'manage' history, as with the Thatcher Memoirs, the work of the Thatcher Foundation and the efforts of her journalistic sympathisers who were extravagant and prolific in the press in the Major years. No study of Thatcherism in British politics can achieve complete objectivity, although it is possible to attempt to achieve it.

One example of an established myth that should be challenged is that the Thatcher leadership, until her downfall in 1990, was a golden age contrasted with the betrayals of both previous and subsequent Conservative governments. The myth contends that Heath reneged on a worthy attempt to pursue a Conservative agenda by his policy U-turns in 1972, in violation of the manifesto on which he was elected; and that the return to Conservative purity in the Thatcher years was interrupted by 'the betrayal' of her ousting in 1990. After her removal, according to this same myth, the legacy of strong leadership that she bequeathed was carelessly abandoned by her successor's vacillation and incompetence. While there is truth in the view that Heath's government changed course in mid-stream and that Major provided less clear leadership than had Thatcher, it is also true that both Heath and Major had to operate in far more threatening circumstances than she. Britain in 1970 was in a very different political 'mood' than in 1979, and some of the circumstances facing the Major government were dilemmas inherited from Thatcher's years in Downing Street. These included economic recession, the policy debacle of the Poll Tax and a party increasingly divided over the issue of Britain's integration into the European Union. Both Heath, and particularly Major, were also confronted by the rivalry of a far more effective and 'electable' Labour opposition than Thatcher ever had to confront. The seeds of the Conservative disaster of 1 May 1997 were sown as much in the 1980s as in the 1990s. That is why, following Marx's dictum, it is vital to examine the 'circumstances' in which leaders must operate, and to do otherwise is to be profoundly unhistorical.

The 1997 Labour victory cautions against making rapid political judgements. It was conventional wisdom from 1945 until 1979 that governments were normally elected by positioning themselves in the centre of the political spectrum, and that if unemployment were ever to return, no governing party could be re-elected. In the 1980s these verities were replaced by the view that since unemployment was an affliction only for the minority of the electorate it did not damage electability, and that Thatcher had managed to create a new ideological hegemony. Yet this also proved to be a transient phenomenon by the time of Thatcher's downfall, and it became apparent that she was a divisive political figure who won elections for a whole complex of reasons. When there was an increase in the numbers affected by unemployment, or at least by the threat of unemployment through the uncertainties of a changing and more flexible labour market, and at the same time, a credible centrist alternative presented itself in New Labour, then the Conservatives experienced their heaviest defeat since 1832. It also becomes clear that while the exclusion of trade unions from the centres of political power may be feasible, for the Conservatives to become careless of business interests because of a greater obsession with resisting European integration was profoundly damaging for the party.

It should also be recognised that the very term 'Thatcherism' is contentious, as it was coined by political opponents to conjure images of harshness, divisiveness and discontinuity with the past. Thatcher and her acolytes proved only too ready to adopt the title and so to underestimate the continuity between Thatcher and her predecessors. Supporters and opponents alike display evident bias. Conservative enthusiasts still maintain that the years of Conservative government from 1979 restored the ailing British economy to health, re-established political authority and raised Britain's standing in the world. They also point, and with some justification, to the emulation of Conservative policies by other countries, particularly the mix of markets, monetarism and authoritarian government; and the specific policy of privatisation. This confidence is reinforced by the knowledge of the contemporaneous collapse of state socialism in the command economies of Eastern Europe. Left-wing critics emphasise the damage inflicted by Thatcher and Major through two serious economic recessions; the destruction of much of Britain's manufacturing base; the high levels of unemployment and resulting social divisions, poverty and social exclusion; and the undermining of civil rights. Both sides of the argument rely upon selectivity in their interpretation, and even their definitions of success or failure are ideologically determined. Whether the 1980s was a golden or a gloomy age depended upon individual circumstances. The experiences of a 'yuppie' City stockbroker were very different, for example, from those of an unemployed Durham former steelworker.

Any discussion of Thatcherism must include consideration of the 'Thatcher factor' and recognise the importance of her leadership style, her dominant personality, and her exploitation of many different aspects of her femininity. Thatcherism is too eclectic a phenomenon to define except in a broad and unilluminating manner, although like the Conservative tradition in which it quite naturally resides, it is its flexibility which is most striking. It moved easily between economic freedom and social discipline, which was the secret of the skilful 'statecraft' which it embodied. Thatcherism was complex and shifting, containing ideological ingredients of both economic neo-liberalism and authoritarian neo-conservatism. While it involved the interplay both of ideas and political practice, this does not deny its status as a part of the British Conservative ideological tradition. Conservative ideology has obviously developed through interaction between fundamental political theory and the empirical reality of shaping policy in the context of 'real world' pressures. Even the term 'Thatcherism' is a misnomer, for she was no original thinker and merely articulated and implemented the ideas of others. There is even evidence that it was people rather than ideas who influenced her actions. But if the policies of the Thatcher governments from 1979 to 1990 were not as driven by a unitary ideology as is often assumed, the Major government from 1990 to 1997 was not as directionless as his own ideological uncertainty might suggest. For lack of a clear alternative strategy, the Major government resorted to the pursuit of policies which were a continuation of the general direction which had been established when Thatcher was Prime Minister.

The years from 1975 to 1997 are best described chronologically, provided such an account leads towards a more reflective theoretical conclusion. This study combines description, interpretation about the forces which produced Thatcherism and an evaluation of its impact. Chapters one to seven, therefore, critically present the events of these years, and the two concluding chapters attempt to conceptualise Thatcherism, and then to set the Thatcher and Major governments in the context both of British Conservatism and the politics of the 'New Labour' government elected in 1997.

ACKNOWLEDGEMENTS

I would very much like to thank the staffs of the Bodleian Library at the University of Oxford, the Cambridge University Library, the University of Manchester Library and the University of Huddersfield Library for all their help in my research for this book. Many leading politicians from the period 1975–94 also generously allowed me to interview them. My special thanks also to my family, Astrid, Chris and Anna, for their encouragement, and to my brother Gerard, who provided me with accommodation and academic discussions when I researched in Cambridge. My gratitude also goes to colleagues in Politics and History. It is invidious to select individuals but I am grateful to Professor Keith Laybourn for reading and helpfully commenting on the manuscript, Professor Andrew Taylor for the enjoyable and stimulating research excursions which I have undertaken with him in the past, Ms Georgina Blakeley who organised Politics research seminars, which helped to maintain my research activity when I was also Pro Vice-Chancellor of the University of Huddersfield, and Dik Esp who checked some references for me.

THE EMERGENCE OF THATCHER

The capture of the Conservative Party by Margaret Thatcher in 1975 can be understood partly as an opportunistic coup. But in political history 'events make people', and leadership is a product of circumstances. The opportunity for Thatcher to win the party's leadership, therefore, was the product of political developments in the years leading up to 1975. While the style and policy of the Conservative Party under Thatcher's leadership differed from that pursued by the party leadership since 1945, she represented a return to a purer Conservatism which had never been extirpated from the party between 1945 and 1975.

THE CONSERVATIVE PARTY: THE CHALLENGE OF DEMOCRACY

The Conservative Party has always represented order and privilege in society, although with the rise of industrialisation it moved from the defence of agriculture to the promotion of the interests of the new industrialists.[1] Much of the spirit of Conservatism can be traced back to the Whig philosopher Edmund Burke and his conservative case argued in *Reflections on the Revolution in France* (1791). He responded to the events of the revolution in France in 1789 with a reasoned case in favour of gradual, orderly and organic change, rather than a radical or revolutionary reorganisation of society. Burke's ideas date from the end of the eighteenth century and were intended to defend traditional agrarian society. They were easily reconciled with the defence of free-market industrial capitalism, however, after the triumph of industrialism in the nineteenth century. Burke was not defending the entirety of the old order in society but rather arguing for practitioners of politics to learn from experience. It was the wisdom derived from experience which taught the utility of monarchy, aristocracy and stable institutions. He was not blindly defending either traditional hierarchical Toryism or feudal society. In summary, he was a Conservative rather than a Tory and his views could readily accommodate free-market principles.[2] He was not resisting change, merely ill-conceived revolutionary political change as in the French Revolution.

Conservatism was challenged from early in the nineteenth century by the twin developments of industrialisation and democratisation. The shift from a relatively stable agricultural to a dynamic industrial society, and the emergence of a larger electorate after the passage of the Reform Act of 1832, posed a twin threat to the old order. Much of the history of British Conservatism since that time has been concerned with the process of adapting to modern mass industrial society, while simultaneously attempting to protect privilege, order and stability. This has been difficult, as industrial society became dominated by rapacious capitalists and desperate industrial workers; with each asserting their interests within an increasingly mass democratic framework with which Conservatives have never been fully at ease. The process of political adaptation has often been painful. It has also involved, although most Conservatives deny it, ideological debate within the party as to how best to respond. The desire for power has normally tempered the divisive potential of ideology, however, and minimised the splits that would imperil electoral success.[3]

The challenges to which Conservatism has had to respond altered over time, as did the extent to which the party was determined to defend the most traditional interests of the aristocracy and the Church of England. The first main threat in the nineteenth century was the rise of the new industrial middle classes, but by the twentieth century they had been absorbed into Conservatism as the party accepted the liberal and free-market economic policies which the industrial classes sought. The next challenge came from the rise of organised labour in the twentieth century. The party has adopted various responses to this new social force, ranging from resistance, through the endorsement of non-militant trade unionism, to acceptance of unions as partners in the government of the British state. The next challenge was the growth of the state itself. While continental conservatives found little to object to in the rise of state bureaucracy as an essential accompaniment to the complexity of modern industrial society, British Conservatives were alarmed. Both Burke's scepticism about the capacity of people to manage political systems, and the liberal free-market ideas generated by the demands of the industrial capitalists, led Conservatives to resist the rise of a powerful and active state. In the period from 1918 to 1939, therefore, while many foreign governments experimented with interventionist economic and social policies to tackle the economic depression, British Conservatives adhered to a minimalist, *laissez-faire* state. Thatcherism is solidly within this long tradition of Conservatism in that her governments were primarily concerned to find an effective response to the challenges of organised labour and statism. The types of response which the Thatcher government engaged in had been evident in previous eras. This is not surprising as there were many traditionalists and individualists in the party before she emerged. The claims of ardent Thatcherites that she re-educated the party are incorrect.[4]

A further challenge which occurred after the 1960s produced agonising difficulties for the Conservatives. The party has portrayed itself as the national and patriotic party, always draping itself with the Union Jack. The sanctity of the British state, united and sovereign within its borders, has been as central to the instincts of Conservatives as the values of order, stability, the Church, and liberal free-market economics. While sceptical about a welfarist state, therefore, Conservatives have always enthused over the idea of a British community. They have recognised that individuals, whose freedom they wish to protect against the encroachments of the state, are not just economic units in a market place, but people who wish to be loyal to some entity with which they can emotionally identify. This understanding led Conservatives to defend the idea of Britain, although frequently failing to discern that they are perpetuating English domination within the United Kingdom, from internal and external threat. The main internal threats arose from fragmentation within the Union, with the rise of Scottish and Welsh nationalism and republican nationalism within Ulster. An even greater threat to the integrity of the United Kingdom is posed by the increasing pattern of integration within the European Union. Yet the imperatives in favour of British participation in the EU are sufficiently strong for the party to divide on the issue. If ultimately the Conservative Party swallows the rooted objection of many within its ranks to a single European currency, with the economic and political consequences of still greater absorption into a European federal structure, it will have to undergo a substantial metamorphosis rather than merely continuing its process of adaptation.

THE CONSERVATIVE PARTY BEFORE 1945

There were major figures in the development of the party who enabled it to meet the challenges posed by democracy, and for it to become one of the most formidable electoral machines in Europe.

Sir Robert Peel was no friend of political agitation, but he inaugurated the tradition within the party of compromising with the forces which challenged it, in the interests of preserving as much of the status quo as possible. Acknowledging that the 1832 Reform Bill was unlikely to be reversed, he observed in his *Address to the Electors of the Borough of Tamworth* (1834), 'if the spirit of the Reform Bill implies merely a careful review of institutions, civil and ecclesiastical, undertaken in a friendly temper, combining, with a firm maintenance of established rights, the correction of proven abuses and the redress of real grievances, in that case I can for myself and for my colleagues, undertake to act in such a spirit and with such intentions'.[5] Peel's main impact, however, was his repeal of the Corn Laws in 1846. The Corn Laws had artificially maintained the price of corn, so protecting the landed interest, which formed the backbone of the party at the time.[6] Since their repeal passed through the Commons only with the help of the Whig Party, disaffected Conservatives led by Benjamin Disraeli combined to vote Peel out of office, and the Peelites switched over to join the Whigs. The split over the Corn Laws, while even more traumatic than the European issue for the party in the 1990s, demonstrated the facility of Conservatives to accommodate new demands and circumstances. This is not simply because of their wish to protect privilege and order in society, but also their desire to achieve and maintain power. As the committed Thatcherite Norman Tebbit expressed it, 'The Tory Party, is, above all, a party dedicated to being in office'.[7]

While for a time the Conservatives degenerated into a bucolic party defending aristocratic and agricultural interests, Disraeli was authentic enough in his commitment to the party to recognise that it is only possible to conserve such interests if the party is in power. He defined one of the main objects of the party, 'to maintain the institutions of the country'.[8] Once he assumed the party's leadership, he became flexible enough to discern that the defeat of radicalism required the

Conservative Party to adapt the cause of moderate reform. He calculated that a Conservative Reform Act extending the franchise further than that of 1832 might capture the political initiative, and his subsequent governments also passed a range of social legislation. He had the room to manoeuvre because the party was fearful of returning to the political wilderness. Disraeli encapsulated the impact which his political tactics were having on the Conservative Party in a speech in 1882, in which he added to the preservation of established institutions two other principles of Conservatism. They were, 'the elevation of the people', and 'the upholding of imperial interests'.[9] The party had now become more pragmatic, and so in addition to its traditionalist approach to British institutions, it was able to appeal to middle- and working-class voters with an ideological package combining imperialism and social reform. The consummation of the jingoist and imperialist appeal to the voters came with the formation of the Primrose League which translated Disraelian ideals into a social organisation which enjoyed a mass membership. Although formed only in 1883, by 1910 its membership had risen to 2 million.[10]

Not all nineteenth-century Conservative leaders shared Peel and Disraeli's optimistic view that, confronted with radical challenge, they merely had to keep cool and divert it. There is a profoundly pessimistic tendency in British Conservatism. Pessimism is compatible with Conservative ideas about the imperfectability of human nature and of society and of their claim to be the party of realism, but it has led some Conservatives to underestimate their capacity to control the process of political change and to exaggerate the severity of the challenges with which they have been confronted. If in the 1970s some Conservatives believed that organised labour would never allow them to govern effectively, until Thatcher demonstrated otherwise after 1979, so Lord Salisbury leading the party from 1881 to 1902 was melancholic about the impact of mass democracy. He believed that the enfranchisement of the workers would lead to disintegration, and it was possible only for Conservatives to postpone the evil day. This was because 'the danger to which in our time all legislatures are exposed is that they will make themselves the instrument of one class to the loss and peril of the rest'.[11] He was successful in achieving power, however, winning three out of the five elections he contested, and it took the 1906 landslide victory for a reforming Liberal Party to appear to vindicate Salisbury's gloom about the inevitability of disruptive radical change.[12]

The party responded to the challenges of electorally popular Liberalism, and also the rise of the Labour Party after 1900, by a reactionary Conservatism which, nevertheless, did not entirely eschew social reform. This strategy was encapsulated by Bonar Law, who became leader in 1911. The years after 1911 were marked by a disturbed social and political climate. This was exemplified by rising industrial militancy, the resistance of uncompromising Ulster Unionists to Irish Home Rule – if necessary by extra-parliamentary direct action – and the controversy over the reformist People's Budget presented by the Liberal Chancellor of the Exchequer, Lloyd George. The House of Lords rejected the budget leading to widespread demands for the reform of the Lords. Under Bonar Law the Conservatives deployed as effective a strategy as was possible. His politics was based on the assumption that 'for the Conservatives to pursue social reform was not on the whole a profitable line to pursue. If the country wanted more and better social reform it would not vote Conservative.'[13] This instinct was sound, as the main cleavage in society at that time was based on religion not class; although the 1914 Conservative Campaign Guide offered a package of social reform, demonstrating that the party was too wily to be caught resisting benefits to the burgeoning working-class electorate. Despite the extent of working-class militancy, Bonar Law resisted the neolithic demands of many in his party, and so he distinguished between being anti-trade union and anti-socialist. He accepted responsible trade unionism, but made anti-socialism the essence of his political appeal. In short, in the Edwardian era the Conservative Party adopted what was to become the thrust of its political stance throughout the rest of the century: anti-socialism and the defence of property.

The defence of property addressed the interests of all property owners, and not just large-scale industrial and landed property. Peel understood that those with only a small amount of property were often more fearful of losing it than substantial owners of wealth. The Conservative role of defending the interests of all property owners, regardless of class background, has proved a shrewd political tactic. It is often working-class or lower middle-class voters who shower most vitriol upon the welfare-dependent who fail to acquire any property of their own. The defence of property was endorsed by Disraeli, Salisbury, Law and subsequent leaders. This motif was influential in both 'the property owning democracy' of 1950s British Conservatism and Thatcher's 'popular capitalism' of the 1980s. Yet despite its mission to defend property and privilege, the party has sought for most of its history to avoid the excesses of reaction. Party leaders have generally striven to reconcile party unity, which often dictated right-wing reaction, with the impulse to remain electable by the country as a whole. The concentration of authority in the hands of the party leader, and the tendency for the membership to defer to leadership, has facilitated the party's longevity. By the outbreak of the First World War the party had survived three complex challenges: reform after 1832, democracy after 1867, and socialism after 1900.

The war hastened the rise of class politics and the demand for a better postwar order. In these circumstances it might have been expected that it would be the Liberals who would relate to the electorate as the main alternative to the emerging Labour Party. Yet as the Conservatives had assumed the mantle of the main bastion of anti-socialism, and the appeal of Labour to parts of the working class was becoming visceral in many areas, it was the Liberals, aided by the internecine squabble between the Asquithian and the Lloyd George factions, which proved vulnerable to political decline.

Stanley Baldwin succeeded in recreating the Conservative Party between 1922 and 1924 in a moderate and centrist form, in order to avoid the emergence of class-war-based party politics in Britain. Baldwin's goal of class integration was fully compatible with Law's previous commitment to preserving the social order. Lord Blake plays down the importance of Baldwin's political skills. He claimed that Baldwin failed, 'in the end . . . because the wounds on English society were not the result of malice, cruelty or spite, and could not be cured by kindness'.[14] Yet Conservative fundamentalists in the Baldwin era, and also later in the Macmillan and Heath premierships, underestimated the ingenuity required to avert social crises.[15] Baldwin managed both to resist the threat to social order displayed by the General Strike of 1926, and to be conciliatory towards the working class by avoiding the repressive response to the strikers that some Conservatives would have preferred. Baldwin considered it essential that the trade unions and the Labour Party be allowed to express their interests within the political nation rather than being forced into an anti-system posture. He stressed the 'one nation' type of politics which Disraeli had established, but added a unique rural idiom, expressly designed for a mass democracy. To avoid perpetual opposition Baldwin was right not to engage in class-war politics, although this was not a creative period for the Conservatives in the realm of policy.[16]

Baldwin's moderation was still not able to prevent the Conservatives from losing seats in the 1929 general election. While the party emerged with the largest number of seats, it was unable to form a government, as Labour formed a minority administration with tacit Liberal support. Baldwin resisted a challenge to his leadership from the right of his party. In due course the Conservatives became the dominant force in the National Government formed in 1931 in order to deal with the crisis of the economic depression. Yet much of the party was not wedded to Baldwinism and 'one nation' politics.[17] The crisis of the 1930s helped a more left-wing, and economically corporatist, type of Conservatism to emerge. A group of Tories with a social conscience, represented by Harold Macmillan and Robert Boothby, and termed 'the Next Five Years Group' after one of their publications, urged a measure of state economic planning. While most British politicians were surprisingly indifferent towards Roosevelt's New Deal, despite the favourable impact his interventionist policies were having in the United States, the progressive Conservatives argued for a similar type of experimentation in Britain.[18] Their demands were rejected by the party, however, as they involved a substantial extension of state control over private property. The type of industrial rationalisation which they proposed raised the spectre of nationalisation and was, therefore, unthinkable for Conservatives. The historical propensity of most Conservatives for free-market and neo-liberal policies is evident when the young Conservative MP David Willetts, an enthusiast for Thatcher, condemned Macmillan's book of the period, *The Middle Way*. He considered it to be hardly 'a Conservative text at all'.[19]

It became apparent in the inter-war years that Conservatives were more successful in winning power than in knowing what to do with it.[20] But by winning power the Conservatives were able to fend off the challenge of the Labour Party. They were also only compelled to depart marginally from the neo-liberal free-market policies which their members favoured, and were able to avert the activist policies to tackle unemployment that the small number of true progressives in the party were advocating. Instead, it was a combination of Baldwin's kindly image, and some limited reforms by his successor Neville Chamberlain after 1937, which softened class politics in Britain.[21] In the longer term the Conservative Party suffered at the hands of the electorate for ignoring the positive remedies which they could have adopted in order to tackle high unemployment levels in the regions. In 1945 the Labour Party's unexpected landslide victory resulted partly from the contrast between Labour's association with interventionist and reformist policies, and the Conservative image from the 1930s as the party of unemployment.

The intervention of the Second World War was also important, however, as it hastened the rise of class-based party politics. Class attitudes were particularly strong among Labour working-class voters, although middle-class Conservative voters were also increasingly affected. In short, the inter-war period witnessed a long-term electoral realignment on class lines.[22] Labour's advantage as the party of the numerically dominant working classes was enhanced in 1945 by the reformist spirit generated by war. This new spirit was evident with the Beveridge Report of 1943 urging the foundation of a welfare state, and the Education Act of 1944 which provided secondary education for all.[23] The heavy defeat of the Conservative Party in the 1945 election, despite Churchill's wartime leadership, led to a struggle for the soul of the party. Party activists never lost their enthusiasm for a traditional Conservatism of social order and free-market anti-statist policies. The leadership reacted to Labour's new found dominance by refurbishing, for the postwar world, the more benign 'one nation' politics which Peel, Disraeli and Baldwin had attempted to nurture. The party's instinct for diverting the challenges to property and privilege by accommodating some of the pressure for change and reform, only prevailed over internal opposition after 1945.

Churchill largely abnegated the process of overhauling the party to Lord Woolton, who became party chairman, and R.A. Butler, who was appointed head of the Conservative Research Department,[24] where he produced symbolic policy changes such as the Industrial Charter. The 1947 party conference endorsed the Charter, which was clearly influenced both by the ideas of 'the next five years group' in the 1930s, and by some of the collectivism which the wartime coalition government had pioneered. The impetus came, however, from the electoral imperative to present a Conservative version of the politics of the centrist consensus which had been produced by war; and which Labour had successfully pre-empted in the 1945 election. Butler was anxious to present the Industrial Charter, however, as being fully consistent with established Conservatism. He claimed that to those who are 'well-versed in Conservative principle and practice the views it expresses will not seem particularly new or startling. To those members of the public, however, who have been deluded by Socialist propaganda into believing that we have no policy, that we are opposed to the whole idea of "planning", that we are the enemies of trade unionism, that we have no answer to unemployment and that we think of nationalisation purely in terms of "unscrambling eggs", it may come as something of a surprise.'[25]

CONSERVATISM IN THE CONSENSUS ERA

There was a struggle for the soul of the Conservative Party in the postwar era. It was between those for whom the adaptation needed to reclaim power from the reforming Labour government of 1945 to 1951 could never extend to accepting such policies as the Industrial Charter, and those such as Butler himself, who wished to dispel the associations of inter-war Conservatism and to follow a 'middle way'. Lord Beaverbrook and Brendan Bracken were two Conservatives whose correspondence reveals a disgust with the Butler-influenced Conservative Party.[26] Yet the tide was with Butler and his allies until 1947, when there was something of a national 'backlash' against the planning and the postwar austerity with which the Labour government was associated. In 1949 the Conservative Party published 'The Right Road for Britain', which continued to accept the welfare state and full employment, but contained a shift in tone and emphasis away from state intervention and towards the virtues of free enterprise and competition. There was a strong emphasis upon home ownership and lower taxes, but the only proposal on cutting public expenditure was the unconvincing 'hardy perennial' of eliminating waste.[27] This reflected both the changing intellectual climate away from the planning enthusiasms of the early war years and the resistance within the party to abandoning neo-liberal perspectives.

Trade unionism was also at its strongest in this period and despite the animosity of many Conservatives to unions they could not simply write off the votes of millions of union members.[28] The concessions to the interests of organised labour which the Butler-led reforms contained left their mark on the party's hard core followers. Thatcher's contempt for the direction the party took in these years, while unhistorical in failing to recognise the electoral pressures of the time, becomes clear from the writings of some of her apologists. Roberts argues that the party was erroneously panicked into ceding 'the intellectual high ground to the collectivists for a quarter of a century', which allowed the 'ratchet effect', by which incoming Conservative governments 'preserved the shifts to the left made by the previous

Labour one'.[29] To Butler the changes in his party between 1945 and 1951 were a source of pride. He described the stance that the party adopted in the general election of 1951 in which it returned to power as 'a policy of enterprise without selfishness', regarding it as a measure of 'how far the party had come since 1945'.[30] In reality, most of the party was still resistant to 'one nation' nostrums in 1951, but they had to be realistic and so compromise with the wishes of the electorate to oust Labour. So while all Conservatives would 'have liked to denationalise both gas and electricity . . . many Conservatives of all shades of party opinion were convinced that it just could not be done'. In the same manner the party attempted, in 1951, to 'find a Conservative line of policy that would be distinctive, that would keep costs under control, but would at the same time not expose the party to charges that they would undo Labour's achievement'.[31]

Electoralism and the desire to 'conserve' existing interests loomed large in the party's reversion to Disraelian 'one nation' politics in the later 1940s, and for twenty subsequent years. There were historically specific reasons for this phenomenon: the war, the postwar economic boom, the strength of international Keynesianism to stimulate growth, the need to counter the dismal inter-war image of the party, and above all the perceived strength of the unions and the Labour Party.[32] This perception of Labour's strength resulted from the discovery that the pendulum was refusing to swing against the 1945 government, as its working-class base remained stubbornly loyal. Sir David Maxwell Fyfe remembers that it 'took us not five or six years to destroy the Labour grip over half the electorate, but nearly ten years'.[33] The 1950 and 1951 general elections are important for their ambiguity. In both elections Labour polled more votes than in 1945, and in 1951 polled nearly a quarter of a million votes more than the Conservatives, despite winning fewer seats, owing to the collapse of the Liberal vote (which largely went to Conservatives).[34]

While publicly the Conservatives were triumphant about returning to power in 1951, they were privately more circumspect. Macmillan, understanding the strength of the solidarity of the Labour vote, had gloomy forebodings about the future, and predicted a Labour majority of 200 at the following general election.[35] Woolton also observed the newly dominant class-based nature of politics, and asserted that now the Conservatives 'were back in office they must strive to create in all people a sense of belonging to one nation'.[36] This fear of Labour's electoral potential persuaded Churchill to resist his original intention of appointing Oliver Lyttleton as Chancellor of the Exchequer, opting for Butler instead because of his moderate image.[37] The right-wing radicals in the party promoted denationalisation and Operation ROBOT, a proposal to float the pound, which secured both elite and mass support in the party's ranks, and challenged the government's strategy. The 1951 Conservative government judged, however, that it had little choice but to work within the postwar settlement.[38] This anxiety about Labour's potential was dominant in the government until Butler's 1953 budget which cut taxes, ended sweet rationing, and marked the beginnings of economic expansion.[39] The process of economic recovery was assisted by a revival in world trade as much as by government macro-economic policy.

It was in this environment that the Conservatives captured Sunderland from Labour in a by-election in May 1953, by pointing to the abolition of rationing, increasing prosperity, the maintenance of full employment and the welfare state. Canvassers reported the Conservatives appealing to young voters on the new housing estates.[40] This unusual success of capturing the other party's seat when in government was interpreted by *The Times* as evidence that the Conservative Party had reverted to its function of accepting, 'the revolution which it had previously resisted and which deprived it of its power'.[41] Buoyed by this success the Conservatives began to enjoy a period in power, marred for many Conservatives only by the ideological and policy compromises which they felt compelled to make. It only became apparent in later years that once electoral success began to falter, the demand for a more traditional Conservatism would assert itself within the ranks. Thatcher was the product of this phenomenon.

It is unlikely that Thatcherism would have sprung to the forefront in 1975 if it was entirely a 'throwback' to the nineteenth century, and there were many signs, even during that period of Conservative affluence and electoral dominance from 1953 to 1961, that neo-liberal and traditional Conservatism retained its potency. Macmillan's Chancellor of the Exchequer, Peter Thorneycroft, differed from his leader in favouring a more rigorous attitude towards inflation, even if the consequence of tough anti-inflationary policies was to undermine full employment. He sought a very public commitment to controlling public sector costs.[42] Thorneycroft was convinced that the economic policies pursued since 1945 would end in catastrophe, and that consensual Conservatism was alarming the middle classes, who feared inflation and trade union power. While Macmillan made light of the resignation of Thorneycroft, together with the other Treasury ministers Nigel Birch and Enoch Powell, as 'a little local difficulty', it was an augury of what was to occur. It was shrewd of Thatcher, therefore, to resurrect the career of Peter Thorneycroft in 1975 by making him party chairman, because 'it provided her with access to the legendary resignations of 1958 as a reference point for her own desire to cut public expenditure'.[43] Macmillan reaped the electoral benefits of resisting the deflationary solutions of Thorneycroft in the general election of 1959, only for his government to be overrun by a series of crisis events from 1961 to 1963, including strikes, unemployment and spy scandals.

The main problem confronting both the party and the country in the early 1960s was that of the economy. The inadequate productivity of British industry began to produce serious problems by 1961. Treasury predictions were revealed as complacent as Britain ran up £258 million deficit on her balance of payments. This in turn led to a sterling crisis which generated a threat to the pound. The then Chancellor, Selwyn Lloyd, inaugurated a set of deflationary policies including a pay pause.[44] While this stopped the run on the pound, the trade unions were becoming angry, and a spate of books appeared at this time on the subject of British relative economic decline. This economic situation enabled Macmillan to embark upon the interventionist strategies which he had advocated during the 1930s, and civil servants who had been reared on the planning methods necessitated during the Second World War were ready to cooperate. At the same time most of the models of better economic performance in the period involved partnerships between the state and private capital; for example, French 'indicative planning'.

The first serious Conservative attempt to tackle economic decline involved the encouragement of partnership between the major producer interests of business and unions.[45] As a result, new tripartite arrangements such as the National Economic Development Council (NEDC) to facilitate indicative planning between unions, business and government; and the National Incomes Commission to restrain wages, were introduced in 1962. Yet while the Conservative Research Department (CRD) agreed with these *dirigiste* policies, it was patently only as a last resort; which explains why it was that Thatcherite solutions began to emerge soon afterwards. The CRD recognised that 'if this fails, we shall have to break the trade unions' monopoly power and/or work for a more centralised system'.[46]

Reviewing the shifts in economic policy during the Macmillan years, some commentators sympathetic to Thatcher's policies regard the resignation of Thorneycroft in 1958 as a symbolic capitulation to *dirigiste* policies of economic planning, and to inflationary policies based upon the theoretical economics of John Maynard Keynes. Particularly influential over both Conservative and Labour governments in the late 1950s and 1960s was the idea of the Phillips 'Curve'. Phillips asserted that when wage inflation rose unemployment fell, and vice versa. Given the trade-off between inflation and unemployment, it was possible for policy-makers to determine a level of unemployment and the price that they would be prepared to pay with a little more inflation.[47] This concept justified demand management of the economy, incomes policy and the array of 'Keynesian' measures designed to ensure full employment. According to this argument, the Macmillan government adopted inflationary policies to win popularity by maintaining full employment. But it was this very reflation of the economy, which caused the problems of inflation and the balance of payments deficit, which drove Macmillan into interventionist policies similar to those favoured by a Labour government.[48]

The period from 1961 to 1963 was also historically significant in that the debate about Europe, which was to become so bitter in the Major years, opened up within the party. Macmillan considered that membership of the then Common Market would both stimulate the ailing British economy and provide his government with the appearance of a modernising and outgoing party with which to confront Labour in the 1964 general election. The problem was that some Tory MPs were opposed to Britain's application to join, and many others were uncertain. Davies attributes this suspicion to the fact that Britain is an island race, 'whose security and impregnability has encouraged a strong sense of nationhood, which has in turn been buttressed by the continuity of the country's institutions'.[49] He adds that Britain has long considered itself as a partner in, 'other important non-European relationships, firstly with the Empire, then with the Commonwealth, and finally with the United States'.[50] Churchill favoured European Union, but for other European states rather than Britain, and like many other Conservative leaders including Thatcher in the 1980s, he was moved primarily by the possibility of a 'special relationship' with the United States. Macmillan's vacillations before deciding that Britain should apply for membership of the Common

Market in 1961 resulted from his fear that the party would seriously split over the issue.[51] The French veto of Britain's application in January 1963 left Macmillan bereft of a political strategy, particularly as he had striven to secure party approval of his government's negotiating position by writing a pamphlet for Conservative Central Office to win conference support.[52]

Macmillan's resignation as Prime Minister in 1963 was more the result of political exhaustion than illness – the official reason given. It is a significant event in two main ways. First, there are parallels between the political exhaustion of the Conservatives after twelve continuous years in power after 1951 and the decline of the Major government after seventeen years in office culminating in 1996 to 1997. These parallels are clear in such degenerative characteristics as sensitivity to the press, a desire to concentrate on foreign rather than on more intractable domestic issues, a high level of mutual suspicion among party members, a tendency to focus on immediate rather than strategic issues, a readiness to concede to interest groups, and a tendency for ministers to concentrate on bureaucratic and ministerial rather than party politics.[53] The second significance of Macmillan's resignation is that the outcome of the bizarre manoeuvring in 'the customary processes of consultation', which led to the succession of Sir Alec Douglas-Home as Prime Minister in 1963, persuaded two leading members of the cabinet to refuse to serve. Enoch Powell used the freedom he acquired from collective cabinet responsibility to inaugurate an alternative Conservatism, which both harked back to the past and anticipated the rise of Thatcherism. As early as October 1963, within weeks of refusing to serve under Home, Powell castigated the economic strategy of postwar Britain and urged a return to the minimal state and the free market.[54] The other leading cabinet minister who refused to serve under Home was Iain Macleod. His sense of the drift within his party was clear when he wrote even of Home's emergence as leader that 'the Tory Party for the first time since Bonar Law is now being led from the right of centre'. And he did not doubt that 'this chimes with the wishes of many good Tories who were disturbed and angered by some aspects of our policies these past twelve years'.[55] Such Tories were ready recruits for Powellism, and later Thatcherism.

While Home was more right-wing than Macmillan, the ideological differences between the two main political parties at the 1964 general election were slight, compared to those which prevailed in the early years of Thatcher's government. There was a swing of just 3.5 per cent to Labour in 1964, producing a working majority of only four, which was the smallest since 1847. It is probable that it was Harold Wilson's effective presidential-style campaign, contrasting with Home's evident lack of charisma, which enabled Labour to win narrowly. The defeat began to sow the seeds for a revival of traditional neo-liberal Conservatism, however, which the heavier defeat for the Conservatives in the general election of 1966 strongly reinforced. This time the Conservatives had reason to fear that Harold Wilson's boast that Labour had become the 'natural party of government' was valid, as Labour polled 48 per cent of the vote against 41.9 per cent for the Conservatives.[56] If emulating Labour and jettisoning core Tory values could no longer deliver electoral success, then the time had come for many activists and thinkers in the party to abandon the postwar settlement in favour of true Conservative policies.

It is a paradox that in the very year that the Conservative Party adopted a new and more democratic method of electing their leader, they began to return to a more traditional right-wing Conservatism. 1965 witnessed the election of Edward Heath to the party leadership. His family came from a humble background. He was elected through the votes of all Conservative MPs. Previously party leaders emerged from a mysterious process in which a few key figures in the party constituted a secret electorate. Contrary to the widespread assumption that it was Thatcher who led her party away from moderate and 'one nation' Conservatism, it was in 1965 that the party began to return to its earlier ideological roots. Thatcher's emergence as leader in 1975 merely consolidated the trend. A related myth is that Thatcher's impact on the party was the result of the emergence of an Anglo-American intellectual New Right. In reality, the process of ideological renewal was under way in the mid-1960s and the main influence was a reversion to liberal *laissez-faire* and 'sound money' doctrines of an earlier period. It began with individual and isolated voices, developed into a strong faction, and with the arrival of Thatcher in the leadership, once more became the authentic voice of British Conservatism. Enoch Powell noted that in 1964 'the exploration of the mechanism of the market as a method of management was still relatively fresh', but it was firmly on the political agenda by 1967/8.[57]

The changing social composition of the party's rank and file, as represented at annual conferences, reinforced the challenge to the politics of simply claiming to manage the postwar settlement more effectively than Labour.[58] The segment of society which most obviously became more visible was the small business sector, and the culmination of its politicisation became clear by the 1970s with a full-scale revolt by ratepayers, small businessmen and middle managers, all of whom felt threatened by the dominance of big business and the rise of militant trade unionism. By that time some of the revolt was accommodated by specialist protest organisations when it appeared that the Conservative Party, which some members of these groups had joined in the 1960s, failed to provide them with everything that they desired.[59]

The obstacle which impeded the return of the Conservatives to free-market concepts of the economy, after their transient dalliance with active government and collectivist policies, was Heath's own preference for pragmatic policy-making rather than the application of political principles. His emphasis upon the production of detailed policy while his party was in opposition from 1965 to 1970, was partly intended to quieten the newly vociferous critics on the right, but had the unintended consequence of providing a platform for the generation of ideas from the rising forces of neo-liberalism. Clearly many in the party had Thatcherite yearnings, but their sentiments were partially submerged for fifteen years before the mid-1960s. 'One nation' ideas were ever only popular at leadership level while a more fundamentalist approach was 'wildly popular with the Conservative rank and file'.[60] Gamble characterises the conflict between the leadership and the membership over the direction of the party from 1965 to 1970 as resulting from different objectives: respectively securing national political support and propagating Conservative ideology.[61]

There were many critics from the right. At the political level the most potent was Enoch Powell. The guru of Thatcher, Sir Keith Joseph, asserts that he and Thatcher were converted to true Conservatism through Powell's influence.[62] Powell had suppressed his views during the period when he had held office after 1959, but his own, and later the party's, ejection from office, together with the radical climate of the time generated by student protest, led him to a more aggressively right-wing posture. His response to the student radicals was that it was absurd for them to seek to manage their own institutions, and his rejoinder to their protests was that of a free marketeer: if they were unhappy with their University 'they have the same remedy as other free men . . . and that is to take themselves and their custom elsewhere'.[63]

Powell excited the party's rank and file with a heady cocktail of denationalisation, the free market, anti-Europeanism and the repatriation of new Commonwealth immigrants, as his rapturous reception at party conferences in the later 1960s demonstrated. Powell was one of the first to imbibe the ideas of the monetarist economist Milton Friedman. It was Friedman who undermined the efficacy of the Phillips Curve idea of a trade-off between inflation and unemployment. If governments had formed the view that they could regulate the relationship between inflation and unemployment by influencing the rate of economic growth by demand management, Friedman replied in 1968 that workers were not stupid. He argued that when employees 'saw governments injecting a bit more inflation into the economy through an expansion of credit or by running bigger budget deficits, the projected pick-up in prices would be factored into their wage demands'.[64] Friedman suggested that there was only one level of unemployment at which inflation would stabilise, which he termed 'the natural level of unemployment'. The natural level would itself be determined not by the manipulation of demand in the economy, but by such 'supply-side' factors as the extent of flexibility in the labour market.[65] Powell was one of a tiny number in the party to expound Friedman's monetarist theories in the 1960s.

Many of the Heathites deplored Powell's policies, and Anthony Barber, for example, described him as a 'frustrated fanatic' and 'a traitor'.[66] Yet Powell's desire to lead the Conservative Party was such that he undermined the impact of his intellectualism on intra-party policy-making in advancing monetarist ideas long before the Thatcherites by, for example, adopting crudely populist stances on immigration, as the shortest route to attaining the leadership. Yet he blazed the trail for the Thatcherites.[67] If, for example, it was premature to advocate Friedman's monetarist alternative to postwar Keynesianism and the Phillips Curve in 1968, the 'stagflation' of the 1970s, when inflation and unemployment simultaneously hit postwar record levels, converted the leadership of both parties to monetary control of the economy.

It was also in the 1960s that the Tories began to re-examine the social services. Geoffrey Howe argued against the constant bidding of politicians to raise the state pension and urged greater involvement by the private sector.[68] The Young Conservatives (YCs) challenged the principle of universal social services. Most spectacular was Nicholas Ridley's advocacy of denationalisation of such industries as electricity and coal. Even Thatcher took nearly a decade of office to reach the stage where she felt that the coal industry could be removed from public ownership. Ridley was confident that it would be easy to bring about competition between different coalfields and that the oversized coal industry had degenerated into a branch of the welfare state.[69] At the 1970 Selsdon Park conference there was an understandable concern to keep the issue under the surface, but the so-called 'wet' Robert Carr was keen that Ridley's proposals should be examined, while Keith Joseph urged a 'step by step' approach.[70] Any doubts that there was a clear move towards right-wing perspectives on Tory policy is dispelled by the pages of such intellectual Conservative journals as *Solon*, *Swinton Journal*, and the Monday Club's journal *Monday's World*. The range of arguments urging the reduction of the state, the promotion of middle-class values, and selectivity within the social services, demonstrates beyond question that the party was undergoing an apostasy against collectivist doctrines. Some right-wing Conservatives were confident that Heath was committed to introduce the more traditional policies that were becoming fashionable in the party; Arthur Seldon even asserted that Heath's approach 'causes the heart to beat faster'.[71] In reality, Heath's confidence that he had reconciled his own pragmatic and problem-solving style with the enthusiastic ideologies of the right was soon tested by the actualities of government from June 1970, and the consequent requirement of managing party and electoral tensions.

THE HEATH GOVERNMENT

The roots of the disillusionment with Heath go back further than his party's electoral defeats in 1974, although for a political party primarily driven by a lust for power, the prospect of being in opposition is sufficient to explain the demand for a change in leadership. The disquiet with Heath was partly personal, because as party leader he had shown scant regard for the feelings of his MPs. His cavalier attitude towards them, together with his authoritarian assumption that they should follow his lead unquestioningly, alienated many of his parliamentary colleagues.[72] So insensitive was Heath in attempting to compel obedience in the House that he generated the first major signs of back-bench rebellion in the postwar House of Commons.[73]

Much of the Thatcherite criticism of the Heath years fails to recognise the different and difficult circumstances under which his government had to operate. Party opinion in the Thatcher years was critical of Heath for failing to pursue a right-wing agenda, including the liberal prescriptions of lower taxes and reduced public expenditure which the 1970 general election manifesto, *A Better Tomorrow*, had promised. These Thatcherite perspectives on the record of the Heath Government were developed with the benefit of hindsight, however, as neither the country, nor to a lesser degree the limited number of postwar consensus-minded Tories, were ready for the assault upon such pillars of postwar politics as the mixed economy, low unemployment and the welfare state. Departures from these established policies were more acceptable to sections of British society in the 1980s, after the experience of continuing economic failure, the rise of simultaneous inflation and unemployment popularly described as 'stagflation', and the militancy of trades unionism culminating in the Winter of Discontent.[74] It required the failings of the Heath government from 1970 to 1974, and the unmanageable problems encountered by the 1974 to 1979 Labour government, to soften up the electorate for a dose of the traditional Conservatism, which it was not ready to consume in the early 1970s. Seldon analyses the intriguing nature of the Heath government's performance as resulting from its promotion of 'elements of both old and new worlds and [it] was trapped uneasily as one paradigm was beginning to lose its hold, but the other model had yet to secure its intellectual credibility or popular backing'.[75] In similar vein Kavanagh has written that ministers and advisers 'clung to a Keynesian paradigm which was out of date, but no credible alternative was available in the early 1970s'.[76]

Thatcherite critics are virulent in their condemnation of the Heath government, and their forcefulness explains the enthusiasm with which the shifts in Conservative policy in the Thatcher government after 1979 were accepted. Holmes describes the Heath government as the worst of either political party since the Second World War.[77] He suggests that 'Heath really did leave to his party, to the wider electorate, and ultimately to himself, only the lessons of failure'.[78] Yet the demonisation of Heath is too simple. He was a pivotal figure in modern British Conservatism, the first leader to emerge from a humble social background. He took Britain into the EEC. This was not simply a milestone for the country, but in party terms it solidified a fault-line within the party between pro and anti-Europeans, which the Macmillan application for membership had first opened up. The 1970 manifesto, and Heath's first party conference speech as Prime Minister which promised a 'quiet revolution', served to raise the expectations of Conservatives that his government would challenge the postwar consensus which party members were now rejecting as soft and socialistic. His failure to satisfy their expectations promoted the development of Thatcherism and the politics of the 1980s.

It is more difficult for Thatcherite critics to anathematise Heath's style of government at the end of the millennium, however, after the total rejection of the Thatcher/Major politics in the general election of 1997. Even in the period immediately preceding that defeat, 'the Thatcherite miracle of the 1980s dissolved into the harsh reality of renewed recession and an accelerating sense of national decay, the two themes he had sounded most strenuously – the importance of the manufacturing base and the social consequences of long-term mass unemployment – began to be acknowledged even within the government'.[79]

The Thatcherite myth of the Heath government is located, like all enduring political myths, in reality. While the Selsdon Park Hotel conference in 1969 did not commit the Conservative opposition to a more stridently right-wing course, as is often suggested, the 1970 manifesto and Heath's first speech to the party conference as Prime Minister clearly did so. The proceedings of the Selsdon Park Conference revealed a variety of views rather than an agreed movement towards more traditional right-wing Conservatism.[80] The idea that it inaugurated a return to traditional Conservative free-market and authoritarian policies is derived from two sources. First, when the press sought a statement at the end of the conference, Heath agreed to give the assembled correspondents a 'soundbite' about the primacy of 'law and order'. This led some commentators to posit the idea of a shift to the right. Second, the Labour Prime Minister Harold Wilson picked up and popularised this interpretation by referring in his speeches to the spectre of 'Selsdon Man'. In so doing he implied that the Conservative Party was more committed to a coherent strategy than the proceedings of the Selsdon conference ever warranted.[81]

The reality is that it was Heath's 'quiet revolution' speech which raised traditional Conservative hopes that the compromises of the postwar era were finally to be replaced by 'true blue' Conservatism. Heath enthused delegates with rhetoric which promised to

. . . change the course and the history of this nation, nothing else . . . Change will give us freedom and that freedom must give responsibility. The free society which we aim to create must also be a responsible society . . . Free from intervention, free from interference, but responsible. Free to make your own decisions, but responsible also for your mistakes . . .

If we are to achieve this task we shall have to bring about a change so radical, a Revolution so quiet, and yet so total, that it will go far beyond the programme for a parliament to which we are committed and on which we have already embarked.[82]

While Thatcherite Tories distorted history by setting up the Selsdon Group to promote 'true' Tory policies, it is evident that in October 1970 the 'quiet revolution' was not considered to be a transitory phenomenon.

Some of the early policies which the Heath government pursued appeared consistent with the tone of the 'quiet revolution'. Income Tax was cut in the first budget, the post office workers' strike was successfully resisted, interventionist measures such as Labour's Industrial Reconstruction Corporation and the Consumer Council were wound up and the government pressed ahead with the Industrial Relations Act, without consulting the trades unions, in order to provide a legal framework to deal with the problems of trades union militancy. These policies represented a dismantling of the institutions of economic planning so that the 'chill winds of competition' could blow more freely.[83] The rhetoric of incentives and marketisation was consummated in the 1971 budget, which moved £2 billion of taxes from companies and the better off to the bottom end of income earners.[84]

The infamous succession of U-turns soon followed. In retrospect it is apparent that years 1972 to 1974 were the high-water mark of Keynesianism and of the postwar consensus. It is an obvious corollary that the disillusionment of many Conservatives, though substantially suppressed at the time, helped to generate the enthusiasm which greeted Thatcher's election to the leadership in 1975. The origins of the U-turns can be traced back as far as July 1971, a mere year after the election, when more money was surreptitiously pumped into the economy; and in November of that year the Queen's Speech explicitly stated that the government's 'first care will be to increase employment'.[85] There were five more spectacular political somersaults, however, all of which were in areas of policy central to the credibility of the government.

Most historians lazily interpret the U-turns as beginning in 1972, by which time the change in course was unmistakable. In reality, that was merely when, from the pure Conservative standpoint, the real indignities occurred. The decisive reversal came with the special budget of July 1971. This involved 'a big departure' in macro-economic strategy with the abolition of financial targets for nationalised industries which had first been established in 1958.[86] The budget also stimulated the economy through a new £100 million public works programme for the development areas.[87] This was a clear departure from the uneasy compromise which Heath had struck with the party's right wing a year previously. The main explanation for the U-turn was that Heath was a pragmatic Conservative rather than a neo-liberal ideologue, so he was not prepared to implement neo-liberal policies when they appeared to result in high unemployment, social discontent and political unpopularity.

The bankruptcy of Britain's flagship car company, Rolls-Royce, in February 1971 may have left the government with little option but to nationalise it given its importance to the country's prestige, the dependence of the armed forces upon its engines, and the disruption which the company's disappearance would have caused Anglo-American relations. Certainly, most Conservatives regarded it as an exceptional case, although Powell asserted that the decision 'cast doubt and discredit in the belief in capitalism and free enterprise for which this party stands'.[88] If nationalising Rolls-Royce was bearable to most of the party, the saving of the Upper Clyde Shipbuilders in 1972, after a sit-in led by a Communist shop steward, Jimmy Reid, was a more difficult medicine for the party rank and file to accept. It was such interventionist breaks with the promise of the 'quiet revolution' which led to the formation of the Selsdon Group, to protest against the emerging pattern of U-turns.[89] An equally unpalatable U-turn came in the aftermath of two events which Heath and his allies found particularly traumatic. First, there was the announcement that unemployment had climbed above the psychologically significant level of one million in January 1972, which led Heath and his ministers to worry about the social and electoral consequences. Secondly, the government was humiliated by the miners' strike in February 1972, when after promising that there would be a demonstration of Conservative resolve against union militancy in order to combat inflation, the government was forced to capitulate and concede an inflationary settlement as recommended by the Wilberforce Inquiry which the government had set up to arbitrate the dispute.[90] Concerned about the decline of manufacturing industry in the regions, and by the consequent impact on employment and productivity, the government published an Industry Bill in 1972 which gave the government powers to promote and subsidise industry. As a result, the bill was more welcome to the Labour left than to the Conservatives, and the left-wing Industry minister, Tony Benn, in the 1974 Labour government correspondingly used the same Act to pour 'money into the most ill thought out cooperative schemes'.[91]

The Industry Act was but one example of the Heath government's conversion to a strategy of 'a dash for growth'. His government also accompanied a reflationary package with a prices and incomes policy. In an attempt to secure a voluntary policy Heath embarked on a long drawn out series of talks with union officials. In the middle of these protracted negotiations, in which union leaders asked for such interventionist *quid pro quo* policies as food subsidies, and the abandonment of the Industrial Relations Act, Heath told the Conservative Party Conference that his negotiations were concerned with controlling inflation and creating a fairer society.[92] This was hardly the type of rhetoric which the party faithful would be exhilarated to hear. Despite his earnest attempt to secure trades union backing there was a total failure to reach agreement, and so the Heath government resorted to a statutory policy. This was despite the fact that the Conservative Party had opposed incomes policy in the 1970 general election, and as recently as 1971 the Chancellor had reiterated his vehement opposition. Barber rejected the proposition that 'a freeze on prices and incomes is the answer. Sooner or later the dam would burst again. Nor do we believe that the answer lies in the detailed statutory control of pay settlements, with all the vast administrative paraphernalia which would be necessary. It would be crude, unworkable and unfair.'[93] Conservatives would have been justified in recalling with bitterness the opprobrium which they had thrown against Harold Wilson's comment that 'a week is a long time in politics'.

It was most certainly a detailed incomes policy which emerged in November 1972. The government announced a statutory policy on incomes, in three stages, beginning at once with a ninety-day standstill, subsequently extended to March 1973, on pay, prices, rents and dividends. A second stage took effect in April 1973 and involved a Pay Board and a Price Commission, to operate new wage and price guidelines. Stage three began in November; it set a limit on pay rises of £2.25 per week or 7 per cent, with a personal limit of £350 per annum.[94] The problem with this explicit linking of prices and wages was that it led the government into a threshold mechanism under which if the retail price index rose more than 7 per cent above the level of October 1973, an additional 40 pence for every percentage point would automatically be awarded. This was a policy more likely to maintain inflation rather than overcome it. It would have been a high-risk strategy at any time, but set against a background of an international oil crisis which quadrupled energy prices, and a 37 per cent rise in international commodity prices in the year up to October 1973, it proved disastrous. As a result, pay increases were repeatedly triggered between April and October 1974. Some of these problems should have been foreseen, and it was mainly with the unveiling of this complicated third phase of incomes policy that doubts began to emerge in the party. A year previously, John Biffen and Nicholas Ridley had rebelled against a statutory policy, and Ridley claimed later that Thatcher congratulated them while refusing to join them openly.[95]

There are a number of explanations why, despite the introduction of a detailed and bureaucratic incomes policy, most Conservatives were publicly acquiescent. First, Heath relied upon the traditional weapon of the party, that of loyalty to its leader. Secondly, there was a real fear of inflation and a desire to see it under control. Thirdly, Heath's painstaking negotiations with the trade unions won him sympathy in the party and the country. A fourth explanation is revealed by the position taken by a journal sympathetic to the Conservative Party. The Economist strongly urged an incomes policy from the outset. It criticised those ideologues who preferred to attack inflation by restraining the money supply – which merely caused bankruptcies and redundancies – and urged a statutory policy, as one agreed with the Trades Union Congress (TUC) would be non-enforceable.[96] The Economist's position demonstrates that the monetarist alternative to incomes policy as a means of restraining inflation was not yet grasped or advocated by most on the right of British politics. Incomes policy reflected the intellectual climate.[97] Academics, civil servants, commentators and politicians shared the prevailing outlook.

Heath's problem in maintaining incomes policy after the introduction of phase three in November 1973 was the militancy of the National Union of Mineworkers (NUM). Stage three of the policy proved to be 'a complicated sieve' permitting the miners to 'drive a coach and horses' through it. Heath had planned, together with Sir William Armstrong, head of the Home Civil Service, a special exemption for the miners with the provision of the 'unsocial hours' payment, and wrongly believed that they had secured the backing of the president of the NUM at a meeting in the Downing Street garden in July 1973. When the miners launched an overtime ban their bargaining position was strengthened by the rising price of oil. The government responded emphatically by imposing a state of emergency and a three-day working week, in an effort to conserve dwindling coal stocks at the power stations. At the same time, Heath wanted to avoid a further damaging miners' strike, like the one to which he had been compelled to capitulate in 1972. In January 1974 the TUC put a proposal before Heath to try to resolve the crisis. The TUC's chairman, Sid Greene, told ministers that if they were to give 'an assurance that they will make possible a settlement between miners and the National Coal Board (NCB), other unions will not use this as an argument in negotiations on their own settlements'.[98] Most ministers were sceptical about the TUC's capacity to deliver their commitment, although Heath was genuinely torn about rejecting the offer. He now regrets rejecting it and feels that it would have been a reasonable way out of the dispute and of saving the country from what came afterwards.[99] Even Thatcher later admitted that the TUC's offer should have been accepted, 'in order to have put the TUC on the spot'.[100] As it was, Heath was persuaded by ministers such as Lord Carrington, the party chairman, that the Conservatives could win a 'who governs?' election, which he called for 28 February 1974.

The tactic did not work, however, as it proved impossible to keep the political agenda on the related issues of militant trade unionism and the constitutional issue of the NUM seeking to disregard parliament's approval for incomes policy. One party official had warned that this would happen, arguing that 'a snap election because of a particularly compulsive set of circumstances . . . is not a decision that a government should take lightly, however, because . . . with a modern mass electorate . . . no general election has been confined to a single issue and . . . it would be the object of our opponents to muddy the waters and prevent one theme running throughout'.[101] In a campaign marked by the rhetoric of class confrontation, between organised labour and a government that had returned to the confrontational style from which it had departed in the 1971–2 U-turn, it was the Liberal Party which was the chief beneficiary, in securing 6 million votes on a vague programme of 'moderation'.[102] It is striking that when the two main parties were ideologically closer in the 1950s and 1960s the Liberal vote had been squeezed. The result in February 1974 was ambiguous, with Labour emerging as the largest party, and in the strongest position to form a minority government in a 'hung' parliament, although the Conservatives won more votes, 37.9 per cent to 37.1 per cent. Powell, who had thought the question of 'who governs?' silly, since the government had a mandate to rule, told his supporters to vote Labour, a stance he justified by Labour's commitment to hold a referendum on Britain's membership of the European Economic Community.[103] This effectively excluded Powell from any future role in the internal party post-mortem which followed.

Heath weakened his position with the party after this defeat, by attempting to hold on to power by forging a coalition with the Liberals. This was doomed to failure as the ranks of the Liberal Party could not accept a strategy of upholding a defeated Conservative government, and in any event, the arithmetic would still not have provided an overall majority. Heath's undignified clinging to power crystallised Thatcher's opposition to him since he apparently toyed with the idea of offering the Liberals proportional representation.[104] It is ironic that the election in which many voters deserted the main parties to vote for a continuation of a consensually based politics, set off a series of events which undermined it.

The period from February to October 1974, when the Labour government sought a further mandate, was both paradoxical and important in the development of Thatcherism. On the one hand, Heath stepped up his consensual political strategy. On the other, his return to centrist politics was confronted by the first serious ideological challenge to postwar Conservatism from within the ranks of the party's leadership – Keith Joseph's establishment of the Centre for Policy Studies. Thatcher later scorned consensus politics. She compared herself in 1979 to Old Testament prophets, who would never be heard saying, 'Brothers I want a consensus'. Again in 1981 she rejected consensus as 'abandoning all beliefs, principles, values and policies'.[105]

Heath decided to fight the next general election on the theme of national unity, promising to 'take the politics out of politics', and to form a broadly based 'Government of National Unity', embracing political opponents if elected.[106] His Thatcherite critics infer that by this electoral strategy he himself had lost confidence in his party's capacity to govern; although he managed to overcome the reputation for divisiveness which he had gained in the February election.

BETWEEN TWO ELECTIONS

Yet the period between February and October 1974 also led some senior members of the shadow cabinet to express their dissent about the drift of Heath's government. There were two main signs of this highly significant phenomenon. First, Sir Keith Joseph set up the Centre for Policy Studies (CPS) in August with Heath's permission. Heath agreed because he accepted reassurances that the purpose of this new 'think tank' was simply to learn from foreign economies, and that the CPS would not compete with the party for funds. This was wishful thinking as Joseph also intended to learn from the experience of government between 1970 and 1974, and to provide an alternative source of policy to those of the Butler-influenced Conservative Research Department.[107] Secondly, in September, Sir Keith Joseph publicly broke with Heath over economic policy in a speech at Preston. His advocacy of the free market was a repetition of the views of Powell and of radical thinkers in the long-standing right-wing 'think tank', the Institute for Economic Affairs (IEA). Joseph disarmingly admitted that he had been wrong in not urging this purer Conservatism previously.[108] His shadow cabinet colleague, Peter Walker, complained about this fomenting of internal divisions at a time when, between two elections, the Conservatives should have been concentrating their fire on Labour.[109] Instead, Joseph argued in his speech that inflation was a more pressing problem than unemployment, and monetarism was the only means of beating inflation. Monetarism was also apparently a prerequisite for being considered a Conservative.[110] Clearly, Joseph felt the time had arrived to 'go public' on the ideas gestating within the party since the mid-1960s.[111]

Thatcher's public pronouncements at this time were more subtle. They were carefully pitched between the official party position and the 'heresy' of Joseph. She condemned the rating system, a prejudice later to lead to her undoing with the Poll Tax, urged that teacher and police pay should become a responsibility of the central state, and criticised the way in which local authorities had frustrated the attempts of the Heath government to control public expenditure.[112]

Heath could draw some comfort from the result of the October 1974 general election as Labour only emerged with a small overall majority. The Conservatives secured 277 seats and Labour 319, and 35.8 per cent against 39.2 per cent of the popular vote. Had Heath adopted a more right-wing programme, he would have achieved a poorer result, and played into Labour's hands as the party best able to preserve industrial peace through its relationship with the trade unions. One portent in the results was that for the first time the Conservatives obtained a lower vote in Scotland than the Scottish Nationalist Party (SNP): 24.7 against 30.4 per cent.

The case for examining the Heath government in some depth is that a myth has developed about it within the party, which has been crucial in explaining the re-emergence of traditional Conservatism, and the rise of Margaret Thatcher. In reality, there are many defences for Heath's performance. Despite the U-turns, the existence of which Heath denies, there were solid achievements, particularly entry into the EEC. Many other achievements were short-lived, such as the introduction of the power sharing agreement in Northern Ireland, the reorganisations of health and local government and the Industrial Relations Act, which became a 'dead letter' as a result of trade union intransigence. The most convincing view is that the government failed, and that its hyperactivity in seeking to resolve too many long-standing problems too quickly was bound to lead to an unravelling. Yet this failure must be set against the context in which Heath was operating. The country had not yet been weaned away from the consensual attitudes on full employment, state intervention, the welfare state and the tripartism of business and union participation in the making of government policy. It took the events of the Heath government itself and of the succeeding Labour government up to 1979, culminating in the Winter of Discontent, for there to develop a popular constituency for undiluted Conservatism. Even after the U-turns of 1971 to 1972 Heath's policies had a great deal of support from intellectual and 'informed opinion'. Even the party in parliament and the country felt itself buffeted by events, and support for the government was based 'not upon confidence or enthusiasm, but upon the suppression of misgivings'.[113]

Heath also faced a difficult domestic and international environment. Domestically there was a collapse of deference and a rise of militancy which affected trade unions and students. This was one part of a mood of moral and cultural permissiveness which had grown up during the 1960s. Its impact on provincial Britain became obvious in the Heath years as an alternative youth culture unsettled what later became known as 'middle England'. Law and order was also becoming a serious problem. Internationally, there were three 'shocks' from the world economy which derailed his economic strategy. First, in August 1971, President Nixon, responding to American economic difficulties,

29

ended the postwar Bretton Woods agreement dating from the Second World War, which had stabilised world currencies against the dollar. Once this prop for economic stability was removed, the international level of the British pound became unstable. Secondly, there was a huge rise in world commodity prices at the very time when Heath was seeking to curb inflation. Thirdly, in Autumn 1973 the oil-producing Arab states increased the price of oil fourfold. Any account of the Heath years which neglects these problems, which the apologists for Thatcherism attempt to do, is distorted.

Holmes, Charmley and others have produced apologias for Thatcher, and 'hatchet jobs' on Heath's government. Holmes has written academic studies of the Heath and Thatcher governments which are a panegyric to Thatcher and a diatribe against Heath. In reality, it is correct to argue that this revisionist approach to history is more of a contribution to intra-party battles than to the discipline of politics.

Holmes acquits Heath of the charge of being an ideological corporatist and claims that the problems of the 1970 government resulted from Heath's lack of clear, guiding political principles. 'Rather, the moves towards tripartite solutions were ad hoc decisions.'[114] There are no more dangerous ideologies, he argues, 'than not having one'. Holmes also removes the defence of contingent disadvantages from the 1970 to 1974 government by pointing out that Heath's control of party, government and even the Treasury was total.[115] The policy about-turns were driven from above, so Heath rejected his party before it rejected him. Holmes asserts that Heath panicked when unemployment rose, which led to the U-turns of neglecting inflation and launching a 'dash for growth', legislating the interventionist Industry Act, increasing public expenditure, resorting to a statutory prices and incomes policy and suspending the Industrial Relations Act. This betrayed the 'Quiet Revolution'.[116] It was the statutory prices and incomes policy which represented the greatest apostasy for Heath's right-wing critics, as it called the authority of parliament into question when powerful groups challenged the law. It ensured that in future there would be a search for alternative methods of managing the economy which did not require the consent of trade unions.

Charmley blames Heath for losing the support of the Ulster Unionist Party by his setting up of a cross-sectarian power-sharing executive. This ensured his inability to establish a coalition to retain power after the narrow defeat in February 1974.[117] Even that most distinguished historian of the Conservative Party, Lord Blake, was attracted to the revisionist anti-Heath analysis. Observing that after unemployment passed the 1 million mark in February 1972, Heath and his colleagues 'lost their nerve . . . decided that their 1970 manifesto was impracticable. Margaret Thatcher's refusal to do the same thing in 1981 was the biggest contrast . . . Heath now embarked on a policy of humouring instead of cold-shouldering the unions.'[118] More bleakly he adds that there were no 'notable successes in other areas to offset this general sense of let-down'.[119] Blake was advancing the rather harsh judgement that it was a mere lack of political will, in contrast with Thatcher's resolution, which led to Heath's dilemmas.

Holmes confuses Heath's lack of a right-wing Conservative ideology with a dearth of principle. While Heath was flexible and pragmatic his views were in the line of Eden and Macmillan, which explains his concern about the social costs of mass unemployment. He cites Eden as his political inspiration.[120] His resort to tripartite talks with unions and business also placed him foursquare behind the informal pact dating from 1944, in which governments traded full employment in return for wage restraint.[121] Yet the disappointment expressed by Holmes and other Thatcherite historians exaggerates the disillusionment of the Conservatives with the performance of Heath's government. Ball is correct to state that while most Conservatives saw little alternative to what Heath's government did, they continued to give their loyalty as 'their enthusiasm steadily ebbed away'.[122] While the rank and file discontent was inarticulate, this 'sentiment was to legitimise Thatcher's bid for the leadership'.[123] It also served to influence the course of Thatcher's leadership after 1975.

2

PREPARING FOR GOVERNMENT

Thatcher was merely the leader of Her Majesty's opposition from February 1975, but there was still a growing confidence with each year that passed, based on political events and the changing national mood, that she was the Prime Minister in waiting. With the advantage of hindsight it is evident that 'the writing was on the wall' for the incumbent Labour government, a reality which spelt out the decline of the postwar convergence between the parties.[1] The Labour government which had been elected in February 1974 was a minority government winning power largely by default, owing to the Liberal advance at the expense of disillusioned Conservative voters. The general election of 1974 also failed to yield the result which Harold Wilson and the Labour Party had anticipated, producing an overall majority of only four. This left the Conservative Party with the awkward problem of how it could decently dispose of its unsuccessful leader. Heath had lost three out of the four general elections that he had contested as leader. This was not the record of achievement which a party with a clear lust for power was likely to continue to tolerate. It became a matter of *how* and *when*, rather than whether he should relinquish the leadership, since few thought he could lead the party into another election. Labour's performance in the October election had been less than inspiring, revealing a lack of enthusiasm for a Labour government; and as the Liberal vote also declined between February and October, the Conservative Party had every reason to aspire to an early return to government if it could produce a new leader.

THE FALL OF HEATH AND THE RISE OF THATCHER

Heath's former cabinet colleagues were best placed to challenge him for the leadership but were reluctant to do so. As chairman of the powerful 1922 backbench committee, Edward DuCann, who had long disliked Heath, began discussions in his City of London office with other critics of Heath. As his office was in Milk Street, the group became known as the Milk Street Mafia.[2] The most likely contender, if such obvious successors as Willie Whitelaw ruled themselves out in deference to Heath, was Sir Keith Joseph. Joseph's merit was that he offered a new strategy. Even during the brief interval between the two elections of 1974 he had established the Centre for Policy Studies to chart a new way forward for Conservatism. It was during this period that he had delivered the striking speech, at Preston in September 1974, assaulting the Keynesian economic orthodoxies which had guided postwar economic policy, and to which the post U-turn Heath government had enthusiastically returned. As early as September 1974 Joseph anticipated many of the directions which the Thatcher governments were to pursue. He stated, for example, that inflation is caused by governments, and that tackling it was of a higher priority than addressing the issue of unemployment. He claimed that unemployment was less of a scourge for its victims than it had been in the inter-war years, that government policies to cure it merely created inflation, and that the cure for inflation was tighter control by government of the supply of money.[3] The election defeat in February, which many Conservatives ascribed to the National Union of Mineworkers and the Trades Union Congress, led many in the party to be attracted to the sharp break with past strategies which Joseph appeared to offer.

Joseph appeared to be interested in securing the party leadership but after a speech delivered in Birmingham in October 1974, he undermined his claim. He repeated the economic arguments, which he offered as an alternative to the failed orthodoxies of the past, but went further when he complained about 'the high and rising proportion of children being born to mothers least fitted to bring children into the world'.[4] This was interpreted as flirting with eugenics as the solution to poverty and inequality, and many of his supporters deserted him for his lack of political judgement. While intellectually better equipped than Thatcher, Joseph realised his error and stood aside from the leadership contest. Thatcher saw the opportunity and stepped in, as the only member of the shadow cabinet prepared to put her head above the parapet.[5] Her succession was not inevitable, but the crucial moment came in January 1975 when Airey Neave MP switched his support to her, and became her talented campaign manager. He was a former Intelligence officer in the army who had developed a personal antipathy towards Heath. Although the various strands of discontent in the party with Heath's leadership ran deep, it took the combined determination of Neave and Thatcher to appropriate the process of change on her behalf.[6] While the party was prepared to take risks in order to recover its position, electing a female leader was a breakthrough, which even elicited the admiration of a female minister in the Labour government: the Secretary of State for Health, Barbara Castle, felt 'a thrill' at the news and predicted that Thatcher could make life difficult for Labour.[7] The deposed Heath became a bitter and resentful opponent of Thatcher, and was unable to feign a loyalty he did not feel, convincing himself that she was a stop-gap leader. This ensured he carried little weight in the party after 1975.[8]

It is common for Thatcher's victory to be dismissed as a mere rejection of Heath and a desperate search for any possible alternative. This was true for some of the electors in the electoral college of Conservative MPs, but there were already outlines of Thatcher's personal political values which served to give her strong roots in some of the main ideological tendencies in the Conservative Party. The fact that Thatcher scored 130 votes on the first ballot against 119 for Heath has been ascribed to such causes as her personality, the fact that she was not Heath, to her courage, that she was willing to challenge Heath when others would not and to the skill of Neave's campaign on her behalf. These were potent factors. Certainly, Neave persuaded some MPs who had been intending to abstain on the first round to vote for Thatcher, in order to deny Heath a victory by deliberately underplaying her strength. Thatcher's lead over Heath among MPs was obtained even though the consultation with the party's constituency associations revealed that a large majority favoured Heath's continuation as party leader. It is probable that under the 'old system of soundings by men in suits, there would have been no possibility that Thatcher could ever have been leader of the Conservative Party'.[9]

Her victory in the second stage of the contest when she obtained 146 votes at a time when her strongest rival, William Whitelaw, could only secure 79 votes is generally ascribed to the momentum she carried over from the first ballot.[10] The second ballot produced a raft of more serious candidates. Had only Whitelaw entered the race Thatcher would still have been difficult to beat, but as the 'stop-Thatcher' vote was split between a number of aspirants, she secured another advantage. It appears that even 'leftish' Conservatives voted for Thatcher in the first ballot, on the grounds that it was the only way to produce a second ballot which would permit Whitelaw to stand.[11] Yet Whitelaw appeared ideologically confused in his indecisive urging of a measure of monetarism, but not too much of it, while Thatcher radiated certainty in the policies that she offered.[12] Like many of his colleagues, Michael Heseltine had regarded Thatcher's candidacy as a joke initially, and realised too late how serious it was.[13] It was the decisions of back-benchers, who were vulnerable to the ploys of Neave, which provided Thatcher with her historic victory. This view is reiterated by Chris Patten who describes the event as 'much more a peasants' uprising than a religious war. It was seen much more as the overthrow of the tyrant king than as a great ideological shift'.[14] Even Thatcher accepted this interpretation, possibly because she was sympathetic to the notion that it was Neave's brilliant war of nerves which won her the victory. One supporter has written that her doubts about the ideological legitimacy of her victory 'vitiated her leadership'.[15]

The case for there being an ideological element in her victory is not based on the dramatic appeal of a newly created Thatcherite ideology imported into the Conservative Party from without. It is more likely that she tapped veins in her support which were already established within the party. It is also true that to the extent that she did overtly offer a programmatic shift from that of the later days of the Heath period, and of most Conservative leaders of the postwar period, some Conservative MPs were prepared to risk a change of direction in order to return to power, and to have a different governing strategy from that which had ceased to work for the party. There were few signs from her earlier life that she represented a different type of Conservatism from other postwar party leaders. She was born in Grantham in 1925, the daughter of a local grocer, who was a Conservative alderman. She was elected MP for Finchley in 1959, having graduated from Oxford University with a degree in chemistry and having worked as a chemist and a tax lawyer. As Secretary of State for Education in Heath's government she had never publicly dissented from government policy and even boasted at her success in persuading the Treasury to spend money on education. The one exception from this conventional background was a speech to the Conservative Political Centre in 1968, in which she hesitantly questioned consensus in politics as inimical to the British Constitution and advocated greater personal responsibility and independence from government. The speech has been described as lacking intellectual sweep and self-confidence, and as being 'juvenile about the future ideologue's handling of ideology . . . Like him (Heath) she was ambitious for office . . . she believed that what was good for her was good for the country as well'.[16]

It was evident as early as 1975 that she was now sympathetic to free markets and to monetarism and had an aversion to the economic interventionism which characterised the incomes policy on which the Heath government had foundered. She was known to be sympathetic to Joseph's ideas, and he was one of her open supporters. Her economic ideas may only have appealed to the committed economic liberals in the party, but her position was strengthened by her strident support for traditional authority, strong leadership and law and order. This enabled traditional Tories to vote for her. She was anathema only to the paternalist and 'one nation' Conservatives who had carried leadership positions in the party during the previous twenty-five years. In short, she had a strong appeal to both traditional Conservatives and to economic liberals. She appreciated that it was the economic liberals who spoke for the truer and more substantial elements of British Conservatism. Thatcher felt able to reject the attitudes of the more recent consensual and progressive Conservatives represented by the pre-1961 Harold Macmillan and Jim Prior. She also felt able to disregard the still smaller faction of 'whiggish' Conservatives symbolised by Heath, and by Macmillan between 1961 and 1963, who advocated the modernisation of the British economy through the method of state intervention. Both the progressive and the 'whig' Conservative tendencies in the party had established a presence during the course of the postwar era, but were only transiently in control, and even then through the preferences of the party leadership rather than the rank and file. As she was appealing to the preferences of many existing party members, including a large number of Conservative MPs, she was not changing the ideology of the party, as it contained numerous traditionalists and individualists before 1975. It is a myth that she re-educated the party.[17] Kavanagh overstates his case in arguing that Thatcher 'was something of an accidental leader, and that it is a rewriting of history to see her election as a victory for monetarism'.[18] That there were accidental elements in Thatcher's emergence is obvious, but the time was ripe to return the party to an older, brasher form of Conservatism. If some of the more patrician elements in the party did not approve, the *arriviste* journalist Andrew Neil argued that those who complained about the excessive materialism in Thatcher's ideology were beneficiaries of inherited wealth.[19]

A rather different explanation of Thatcher's election as leader is advanced by conspiracy theorists. Accepting the leaks of former employees in the security services indicating that Wilson's Labour government was being destabilised, they carry their speculations further. One such theorist argues that 'MI5 will have loved Thatcher'.[20] Another commentator points to the connections between Neave, Thatcher and Colin Wallace. Wallace was a security services employee in Ulster who was spreading damaging and false propaganda against Labour leaders. Neave was said to have spread ideas passed to him by Wallace; for example, the claim that the Soviet KGB was manipulating British Communists and Labour MPs to promote a 'troops out' campaign in Ulster. The evidence is far from conclusive but there is some indication of involvement by a group called 'Tory Action', in which Neave played a part. Tory Action had links to subversive groups such as Civil Assistance, which at this time were proposing to engineer military rule in the event of a further rash of industrial unrest.[21] Even if these stories are fanciful, the atmosphere that they reflect was one in which there was fear, and a resort to anti-democratic responses to the growing assertiveness of the left, and the election of another Labour government in 1974. In this climate Thatcher's fierce antipathy to socialism was particularly appropriate.

Thatcher's impact became apparent, in the weeks after her succession to the leadership in February 1975, owing to her style of leadership. Disavowing the 'laid back' style of earlier leaders such as Baldwin and Macmillan and recognising that the party was in political difficulties, she brought an air of bustle and activity. It was this more assertive style which led some observers to discern a distinct Thatcherite ideology, but they failed to appreciate that her approach signified a return to the traditional policies pursued by Conservative administrations before 1940, rather than a revolutionary new philosophy.[22] Her style differed from her predecessors because she lacked the inclusive instincts, as was apparent when she promoted MPs to ministerial rank, frequently asking, 'is he (sic) one of us?' By contrast, she gradually altered the party's emphasis, by appealing to the two largest factions of the party's belief-system, and in so doing satisfied the yearnings which many in the party had suppressed for decades in the interests of loyalty and unity. Iain Macleod had recognised this dissonance as early as 1963, while not sympathising with the more fundamentalist majority. He noted that the more right-wing emphasis which Sir Alec Douglas-Home was giving the party, after he assumed the leadership in 1963, 'chimes with the wishes of many good Tories who were disturbed and angered by some aspects of our policies these last twelve years'.[23] It was after Home's resignation from the leadership, however, and the impetus given to policy formulation in the parliamentary party by Heath after he became leader in 1965, which led to the resurfacing of ideas which the party's leadership had de-emphasised during the postwar period. The degree to which the Conservative Party has always been emotionally attracted to neo-liberal and free-market ideas throughout its history, and to which it increasingly reverted both intellectually and tactically from the mid-1960s, has been analysed elsewhere.[24] While such views were expounded and developed by intellectual elements in the party from the mid-1960s, the environment of the 1970s was conducive to the *entrenchment* of neo-liberal and free-market ideas as the prevailing theme within the ranks of the party.

The 1970s was a period when, exacerbated by the three external economic crises: the collapse of the Bretton Woods agreement in 1971 which destabilised the pound and other currencies against the dollar, the quadrupling of the price of oil in 1973 in the wake of the formation of the Organisation of Petroleum Exporting Countries (OPEC) and the massive rise in world commodity prices in the early 1970s, there occurred a serious inflationary crisis. The long-standing structural weaknesses of the British economy were heightened by these problems. The arrival of these economic problems and the widely canvassed idea that Britain was in a terminal economic decline, increased the readiness of commentators to support iconoclastic economic solutions. On the Labour left the ideas of extensive nationalisation, and the creation of worker cooperatives, were developing as was an 'alternative economic strategy' to that of the incumbent Labour government.[25] This 'alternative' involved the creation of a siege economy through import controls, and the compulsory planning and revitalisation of British industry under this protection. Tony Benn promoted this idea within the Labour Party, but made no impact on government policy. This may not have been a feasible strategy, but like the growing ascendancy of Thatcherism in the Conservative Party, it had the great merit of disdaining the policies which had been consistently pursued through much of the postwar era. Monetarism, which Thatcher increasingly stressed after 1975 as the basis for macro-economic management, had the additional advantage of breaking with the policies of the past.[26]

The monetarist solution to the problem of inflation, which to Thatcher's political benefit was reaching 26 per cent in the year in which she assumed the party leadership, offered an alternative for a future Conservative government. Monetarism could avoid the entanglements with organised labour which the pursuit of incomes policies in the Heath years had so damagingly produced. Many Conservatives were convinced in the years after the fall of Heath's government that the trade union movement would never permit a Conservative government to carry out its policies.[27] Monetarism facilitated a distance from detailed negotiations with the trade unions, since by rigorously controlling the amount of money in circulation, government could prevent inflationary pay settlements being agreed by the wage bargaining system, unless the trade unions were prepared to trade jobs for pay. This situation effectively passed the problem to the two sides of industry, and allowed a future Conservative government to address the problem of inflation without negotiating with trade unions. The invocation of the monetarist theorist Milton Friedman allowed the Conservatives to discover a new intellectual mentor to justify their turn from the policies of the postwar era, which had been substantially driven by the doctrines of John Maynard Keynes.

Such ideological and strategic considerations did not disturb the intellectual elements in the party. Even those Conservatives who argue that the vigour in Thatcher's style of leadership represented a break with the past, acknowledge that throughout the twentieth century Conservatives, 'had espoused the virtues of private enterprise, profit-making, wealth creation, competition, independence from the state and so on'.[28] It was also a previous Conservative Prime Minister, Neville Chamberlain, who expressed the classic Conservative position that only a growth in trade can pay for social reform, and that the state's purse is filled by the efforts of industry, because 'the state spends, it does not earn'.[29] It is true, however, that those Conservative MPs who had voted for Thatcher simply to get rid of Heath, never imagined the political earthquake they had unleashed.

THE CONSERVATIVES IN OPPOSITION: 1975–1979

Thatcher moved swiftly to establish her political authority. She began her leadership with a piece of political theatre in which she wished to appear to give her ousted predecessor Heath a shadow cabinet post, while fully aware that she did not want him to accept her offer, and that he would not do so. She then embarked upon appointing her team. Privately she had little sympathy with William Whitelaw, Jim Prior and Francis Pym, the symbols of the postwar era of 'one nation' Conservatism which she sought to extirpate, but she offered them roles in her shadow cabinet in the interests of party unity. She made some appointments, however, which signalled a change in direction, abandoning Peter Walker, Robert Carr, Geoffrey Rippon, Paul Channon and Nicholas Scott. She also rescued the political careers of Neave and Angus Maude, both bitter enemies of Heath. Maude's position was apparent as he called for policies to assist the middle classes, who were 'at bay'. He added that for ten years they had tolerated high taxation and spendthrift local councils, and now they should stop feeling guilty and realise that they were the country's wealth creators.[30] Thatcher also placed Sir Keith Joseph at the head of policy development, but most dramatically revived the career of Peter (now Lord) Thorneycroft to replace Whitelaw as party chairman. This was potent symbolism, since Thorneycroft had resigned from the post of Chancellor of the Exchequer in the Macmillan government in 1958, in protest at the profligacy of public expenditure. One Conservative intellectual welcomed the return of Thorneycroft as events had shown Thorneycroft 'stood out like a lily in the dungheap', for his attempt to resist the growth of 'the monster' that the public sector had become.[31] The appointments of Joseph and Thorneycroft were more indicative of the direction that Thatcher was to follow, therefore, than was the politically necessary retention of a number of those associated with the policies of the postwar period. She also exploited the power that Conservative leaders have over Conservative Central Office (CCO), by appointing her sympathisers to the roles previously occupied by Heath loyalists. The Conservative Research Department (CRD) led by Chris Patten was also circumvented, to allow her to draw from the ideas of right-wing 'think tanks' such as the Centre for Policy Studies.[32] She and her new advisers had no personal memory of the 1930s and had not fought in the war, but were simply reacting against the massive growth in the state sector and in industrial militancy since 1945. The letters of support which Joseph's controversial speeches had produced emboldened her to give vent to her political prejudices.

Thatcher was still, however, reined in by political realities. She had to maintain party unity, particularly within her own shadow cabinet, and to avoid moving the Conservative opposition too drastically to the right, so as not to alarm an electorate still not entirely weaned away from the policies which had prevailed throughout most of the postwar period. Thatcher was sufficiently orientated as a British Conservative Party leader, however, to place the acquisition of power on a par with the presentation of a true Conservative ideology of free markets and traditional social authority. Despite these restraints she was able to draw inspiration from 'Thatcher's People'.[33] These were a group of political outsiders who were becoming confident that the tide was turning in their direction, and that with Thatcher leading the party, Conservatism could return to its true and authentic political roots. Among the individuals who impressed her were Russell Lewis, George Gardiner, Patrick Cosgrave and Jock Bruce-Gardyne. As an instinctive rather than an intellectual politician, it was often men who pandered to her political preferences who captured her attention, rather than abstract ideas. The free-market and monetarist economic conceptions of such right-wing 'think tanks' as the Centre for Policy Studies (CPS), the Institute of Economic Affairs (IEA) and the Adam Smith Institute (ASI) appealed to her. It was often the personal influence of their leaders, however, respectively Sir Alfred Sherman, Lord Harris of High Cross and Masden Pirie, who enthused her politically. Of outstanding importance, however, were Enoch Powell and Sir Keith Joseph.[34]

Powell did not return the compliment, as he described Thatcher and her colleagues as 'the same troupe of ham actors' who had been in power from 1972 to 1974, and who were, therefore, hopelessly compromised.[35] He had been a proto-monetarist throughout most of his political career, as was demonstrated by his resignation from Macmillan's cabinet in January 1958, over the high levels of public expenditure. Thatcher could not formally bring Powell back to the front benches, as he had deserted the party in the February 1974 election campaign by urging voters to support Labour to achieve a referendum on Britain's membership of the EEC. Powell had subsequently defected to the Ulster Unionist Party. Thorneycroft's appointment as party chairman was something of a proxy appointment for her political hero. There were many facets of Powell's thought which excited Thatcher. His passionate advocacy of the free market, his endorsement of monetary control rather than incomes policy as a means of curbing inflation, and his intense nationalism evident in his hostility to 'new Commonwealth' immigration after 1968 and to Britain's membership of the EEC after 1969, all appealed to her instincts.[36]

Thatcher's caution as opposition leader led some of the declining faction of 'one nation' Conservatives to overestimate their strength. One such anti-Thatcherite argued in 1978 that 'the scene is set for a fierce struggle inside the Tory Party – one which will not be resolved simply by it winning the next election'.[37] The same commentator also inflated Heath's importance in suggesting that by being independent of Thatcher, Heath gave the Conservative left 'a strength and a power it would otherwise lack'.[38] Yet even so optimistic a voice about the future of the Tory 'one nation' enthusiasts assessed them as comprising just one third of the parliamentary party. Behrens has divided the Conservative Party in this period into two camps: 'diehards' and 'ditchers'. The diehards favoured a return to Conservative fundamentals and the ditchers argued that circumstances should determine principles, and supported government intervention in the economy and society.[39] This is simplistic since many of the MPs he defined as 'ditchers' were not highly ideologically conscious, were unthinking adherents of what had gone before, or thought it politically unfeasible to return to a diehard type of politics. Behrens is correct, however, to recognise that the Thatcherites were diehards rather than expressions of a 'new' or non-Conservative, right wing. The true extent of the 'one nation' faction's influence over the party is evident from the fact that the Tory Reform Group, which emerged in the mid-1970s, 'was no match for the combined efforts of the right-wing Selsdon Group, and the external think tanks such as the Centre for Policy Studies and the Adam Smith Institute'.[40] The party's 1976 policy document, *The Right Approach*, acknowledged the split in the party. 'The precise limits that should be placed on intervention by the state are reasonably the subject of debate within the party'.[41]

The period from 1975 to 1978 was one of 'hard slog and frustration' for the Conservative Party. In addition to being in opposition, Thatcher was uncomfortable, because she constantly had to curb her instincts on account of intra-party divisions and anxiety about how far to the right the party could move without alienating the electorate. One impatient right-wing Conservative understood the constraints within which she was forced to operate. Acknowledging that she said what she meant, he commented: 'she has, however, used her skill to avoid translating her beliefs into clear commitments until the party and the people have caught up with her'.[42] This helps to explain why there was a tension between her militant and value-laden speeches on the one hand, and her lack of detailed policy statements on the other. It was easier to demand reductions in public expenditure than to specify where the cuts would fall. The same political pressures explain the apparent paradox that she relied on right-wing advisers such as Keith Joseph, Norman Tebbitt and Alfred Sherman, while enduring a shadow cabinet which contained many former Heathites. Ultimately she was restrained by 'the collegial cannons of British politics', from sharply breaking with the immediate past, which could threaten the cohesion of the party and the chances of electoral victory.[43]

If the numbers of 'one nation' Conservatives were diminishing, and they were increasingly at odds with the growing tide of opinion in the party, they continued to make their voice heard. Ian Gilmour published *Inside Right* in 1977 to promote his version of non-dogmatic Conservatism and to warn of the dangers of the party losing its 'catholicity'. This was a thinly veiled rebuke to Thatcher. T.E. Utley reviewing Gilmour's contribution, however, asserted the wider fear in the party that she would give way to collectivism when in government.[44] The reality was that Thatcher realised the dangers in advancing too traditional a Conservative message before a general election, which would be the only chance that her party would give her as leader, until both the party and the country could be tamed. The direction which she wished the party to take was, however, becoming apparent. As she informed the Greater London Young Conservatives in 1976, for example, the Victorian era was to be lauded because of the 'burgeoning of free enterprise . . . the greatest expansions of voluntary philanthropic activity of all kinds' and because that era 'was an age of constant and constructive endeavour'.[45]

The cautious and difficult attempts at ideological definition between 1975 and 1979 were most apparent in the related issues of industrial relations, economic management and incomes policy. The industrial strife at Grunwick in 1977 over the issue of trade union claims to recognition against an employer, George Ward, who appeared to be making a symbolic issue of running a non-union company, brutally exposed the division within the party. As Conservative Industry spokesman, Joseph supported Grunwick. He claimed that it was employers who are 'wealth creators' and mass pickets who are the new oppressors. As shadow Employment spokesman, however, Prior urged the company to accept the recommendation of the Advisory Conciliation and Arbitration Service (ACAS) and recognise the trade union. The Tory Reform Group asserted that Joseph 'must be off his head' for allying the party with right-wing extremists like the National Association for Freedom.[46] The editorial in the *Daily Telegraph* represented the right of the party, when it argued that Joseph had correctly defended the company and the majority of the workers, who 'should not be frog marched against their will into the union'.[47] The issue of the 'closed shop' was thus brought into the centre of politics. At the 1977 Conference Prior rejected resolutions urging the abolition of closed shops. He told an unreceptive conference that closed shops were a 'fact of life', legislation could not prevent them from being set up and that a Conservative government seeks 'a maximum degree of industrial peace'.[48] Prior was condemned by the National Association for Freedom as being 'wholly unqualified to speak on union issues for a party that stands for individual freedom'.[49] While she remained silent on this occasion, Thatcher spoke at the 1977 National Association for Freedom conference and endorsed their belief that freedom is indivisible.[50] Norman Tebbitt was more overtly aggressive in his attack on those Conservatives who had 'the morality of Laval and Petain'.[51] As the argument continued Thatcher attempted to smooth over the dispute, commenting that both Joseph and Prior had an interest in the area, as Industry and Employment spokesmen respectively, and that each had taken 'a slightly different view'.[52]

Thatcher's caution on industrial relations was apparent in her handling of one of her keenest advisers, John Hoskyns, who advocated an assault on trade union power. In *Stepping Stones*, a document written with Norman Strauss, he urged a confrontation with the unions in the name of individualism. The document pressed for such legislative enactments as the withholding of social security payments from strikers, compulsory ballots and a requirement that unionists should have to contract in if they wished to pay the political levy. A Conservative government should openly divide trade union leaders into being either allies or opponents, and the party should make an emotional appeal to the voters on the issue. *Stepping Stones* eccentrically suggested that, in order to compensate them for their lost powers, union leaders could become members of a reformed second chamber.[53] To Prior's relief the leader's Steering Committee of the party accepted his advice that the publication of *Stepping Stones* should be withheld. Thatcher allowed Prior to encourage Conservative trade unionists to become active, in order to fight trade union militancy from within. But as the Conservative Trade Unionists (CTU) broadly supported Prior's view rather than that of Thatcher, they had lost her favour by 1979. The events of the 'Winter of Discontent' of 1978–9 weakened the CTU's case, and convinced many in the party and the country that the unions had become too powerful and disruptive. Some of Thatcher's continuing, if unenthusiastic, support for Prior was based upon her recognition that a once and for all legislative assault on the unions had been demonstrated to be unworkable by Heath's 1971 Heath Industrial Relations Act.[54]

The party's divisions over industrial relations were mirrored in its confused attitude towards monetarism. Most recognised that the Keynesian-influenced Philips Curve, with its trade-off between inflation and unemployment, had become redundant with the alarming appearance of 'stagflation'.[55] In 1975 the shadow chancellor, Geoffrey Howe, deplored the Labour government's failure to control the money supply, and urged that the Conservatives should review their former policies. They should end price controls and restrictions on profits, oppose incomes policy and support a widening of differentials in society. He accepted the economic theory that 'excessive public expenditure is helping to cause inflation and squeeze the private sector'.[56] Howe was assisted in adopting this position by the popular advocacy of its underlying economic theory by Walter Eltis, whose book *Too Few Producers* presented the 'crowding out' thesis. This maintained that there were too many wealth consumers in the public and too few wealth producers in the private sector. Sam Brittan used the pages of both *The Times* and the *Financial Times* to popularise the need for monetary restraint. There were other monetarist converts in influential positions in the party, and they were stimulated by Joseph's pleas for repentance over the party's earlier monetary incontinence. The key monetarist debates were not resolved by the party during this period in opposition. For example, did the party agree with Friedman's advocacy of targets to reduce the money supply or Hayek's call for an immediate and substantial cut? The Conservative manifesto in 1979 reflected the confusion: 'To master inflation properly monetary discipline is essential, with publicly stated targets for the growth in money supply.'[57]

The uneasy compromises between Thatcher's supporters and critics, and the intellectual evasions apparent in the manifesto on which the

Conservative Party fought the 1979 general election, were foreshadowed in its main policy statement in opposition, the ambiguous *The Right Approach to the Economy*. It was published in October 1977, and promised to control the money supply, manage government expenditure, lower taxes on earnings and savings, encourage business expansion, widen pay differences, restore collective bargaining, provide more independence for the Bank of England and – while avoiding savage public expenditure cuts – ensure that public spending consumed 'a smaller percentage of the nation's annual output and income each year'. The document significantly adopted Prior's conciliatory approach on the closed shop, however, which led the *Daily Telegraph* to condemn *The Right Approach to the Economy* for being too cautious.[58] The document did not finally resolve the question, therefore, of whether in the central policy sphere of economic management, the stances adopted for much of the postwar era were now to be abandoned in favour of a return to more fundamental Conservative principles. It reflected the diverse authorship of a monetarist in Howe, a convert to monetarism in David Howell and a sceptic in Prior. Indeed, Prior asserts that there was a 'row' during the preparation of *The Right Approach to the Economy*, leading to the compromise that 'in framing its monetary and other policies, the Government must come to some conclusions about the likely scope for pay increases if excess public expenditure or large-scale unemployment is to be avoided; and this estimate can not be concealed from the representatives of employers and unions whom it is consulting'.[59] The vagueness of this document, especially on the crucial issue of incomes policy, revealed the tensions in the shadow cabinet. As with industrial relations policy, however, opinion hardened against incomes policy during the Winter of Discontent.[60]

Other issues surfaced between 1975 and 1979. As middle-class values became fashionable, the political reaction against the postwar years which Thatcherism represented took the party into other areas. It appealed to Christian moralists who were reacting against the 'permissive society of the 1960s'. The Conservative Family Campaign grew at this time and Whitelaw informed it that the Conservatives would act against child pornography. Thatcher committed herself to a 'fight to protect the child and the family'.[61] That this was a shallow and electorally convenient stance is suggested by later charges against the Thatcher government that these statements were 'duplicitous', and 'electioneering humbug'.[62] A number of other organisations concerned with the state of the nation's morality flourished at this time, for example, the National Viewers and Listeners Association, the National Festival of Light and the British Family Life Association. These bodies perceived the Conservatives to be 'the most overtly favourable to their endeavours'.[63] There was an ideological affinity between the concerns of these 'moralistic' groups and the economic interest groups which emerged to speak for the middle classes at this time, such as organisations acting on behalf of the self-employed and the ratepayers. As one commentator expressed it, the moral campaigners opposed 'communism on the one hand and naked capitalist exploitation of the profit motive on the other', thus providing 'an interesting parallel to the economic concerns of the middle-class groups, who feel squeezed between the more powerful interests of organised labour on the one hand and large corporations on the other'.[64]

The Conservatives also dabbled with the issue of race as a part of their electioneering. Gilmour persuaded the party not to oppose the Race Relations Bill.[65] In contrast, Thatcher sought to exploit popular anxieties when she 'understood' people's fears about being 'swamped by people of a different culture', and promised to deal with such worries.[66] More surprisingly, given its central role in party affairs over a decade later, the Conservatives largely united behind Britain's membership of the EEC. The 1975 conference resolved that the party should work closely with 'our political allies in Europe' to form 'a centre–right alliance' and urged direct elections to the European Parliament.[67]

THE 1979 GENERAL ELECTION

There were two main elements that explain the 1979 general election result: the unpopularity of the Labour government and the credibility of the Conservative opposition in offering an alternative. Thatcher was not liked but she was considered competent and decisive. There had been an expectation that Labour would 'go to the country' in October 1978. Prime Minister James Callaghan's caution prevailed but he miscalculated. The Conservative Party saw benefits in the delay as they expected inflation, unemployment and the balance of payments to worsen by the spring of 1979.[68] If the party expected the government to encounter difficulties with the policy of wage restraint it could not possibly have foreseen the enormous benefit it would gain from the collapse of Labour's incomes policy during the Winter of Discontent.

The industrial militancy destroyed Labour's self-professed advantage of being able to work harmoniously with trade unions. The strikes by public sector trade unions 'really inflamed public opinion' over the plight of the most vulnerable sections of society, who were most reliant upon the public services'.[69] The Conservatives published a pamphlet on the union 'problem' and in a television broadcast in January 1979 Thatcher captured the initiative by promising to require ballots before strikes and to tax the social security benefits of strikers. Scottish and Welsh devolution had also been a challenge to the government, and the negative outcomes of the referendums in Scotland and Wales meant the Nationalist parties had no further motive in sustaining a Labour government. Labour lost a subsequent parliamentary vote of 'no confidence', which was an unpropitious way for the party to start its election campaign.

The 1970s had been a decade of partisan, electoral and class dealignment, and it was the Conservatives who were best geared up to exploit the opportunity.[70] Taking its October 1974 vote as its base the Conservatives sought to add to it by detaching 'soft' Labour and Liberal voters among the ranks of the C2s or skilled workers. Lenin's 'aristocracy of labour' was in many cases ready to desert social democracy and to respond to secular appeals based upon tax cuts, collective bargaining and wage differentials. Thatcher also appealed directly to housewives through such 'easy' political mediums as Radio Two's *Jimmy Young Show*. This marketing, together with vacuous 'photo opportunities', enabled her gradually to overcome Callaghan's initial advantage with the electors.[71] The Conservatives also crudely appealed to popular prejudices against the unions, income tax and welfare scroungers, and towards law and order, immigration controls, and nuclear defence. Thatcher was closer to the working and lower middle class sentiments of this time on such issues than the Labour and Liberal parties.[72] Such appeals were almost subliminal, however, as the Conservative manifesto was vague on specific policy. There was no suggestion that unemployment would have to increase to tackle the country's economic problems or of rises in prescription charges. The party recognised that despite recent events many electors were contented with their lot.[73]

The Conservatives secured 43.9 per cent of the vote against Labour's 37 per cent and an overall majority of 43 seats. The greatest swings were among skilled workers, younger voters and the south of England. To many Conservatives the result of the election represented a 'sea change' in British politics signalling the demise of the welfare state, the mixed economy, prices and incomes policy and state intervention. It is true that some Conservative policy, such as the sale of council houses and tax cuts had a broad appeal to all but the most deprived in society, and that the intellectual elite had turned to the right for the first time in a generation.[74] Yet it would be erroneous to conclude that May 1979 marked a popular endorsement of some new style of politics, as there was no landslide, and popular support for 'Thatcherite' policies was selective. The idea that it was the public which converted the Conservative Party to economic liberalism is incorrect.[75] Labour lost a general election through its incapacity to govern effectively during a very difficult period. It was fortunate for the Conservative Party that it could arrive in office at the time when it was able to return to its ideological fundamentals.

3

THATCHER'S FIRST TERM

An analysis of the policies and actions of three Thatcher governments is best approached by following the electoral cycle. This involves dividing the period from 1979 to 1990 into three parts: 1979 to 1983, 1983 to 1987, and 1987 to the ousting of Thatcher as Prime Minister in 1990. The main emphasis is upon ideology and policy, but the relationships between the government and the Conservative Party, and between government and the electorate are also considered.

Gamble proposes an alternative way of sub-dividing the Thatcher years for analytical purposes. This discards the electoral cycle, and breaks down the era into stages on the basis of other patterns of events. He suggests that the dividing principle should be the impact of the world economy on British politics. On this basis the first phase was characterised by economic recession and ran from 1979 to 1982, the second was based upon international economic recovery and lasted from 1982 to 1987 and the third covered the remainder of her period in office. Gamble's proposal is doubtful on at least two grounds: first, it is too deterministic in its conception of the relationship between economics and politics, and secondly, the impact of the world economy on the political process is not instantaneous.

In general, it is more appropriate to recognise that the results of general elections have a powerful effect on the personnel, style and policies of governments, and so provide natural political turning points. Each individual parliament has its own distinct character, and the electoral cycle is decisive in that government ministers are also acutely aware of the pressures of the voters when they shape their strategies.

The first term of the Thatcher government is also best divided into three sections: an analysis of her position in 1979, the period during which she established her dominance from 1979 to 1981, and the period of her dominance from 1981 to 1983.

ON ENTERING DOWNING STREET

Margaret Thatcher entered Downing Street on 3 May 1979 while still an outsider in the British political and social establishment, and in a political system which had not yet shaken off the assumptions which had guided policy-making since 1945. As a result many commentators, including a few within the ranks of her own party, expected that the programme which she was inaugurating would be a temporary aberration before normal service was resumed. While the party faithful were in the mood to support her cause, and a substantial proportion of the electorate was willing to place their trust in her to turn the country round after the economic failures of the 1970s which culminated in the Winter of Discontent, many members of her former shadow cabinet were still operating in the mould produced by the Heath and Macmillan eras. The party faithful held her in high esteem, however, as they believed that they had found a champion for many of their ideological longings; and she was fortunate in that the electorate reveals a touching desire to believe that any new government is going to be effective. Her 'honeymoon' was much briefer than that enjoyed by Tony Blair after 1997, but it was real. Thatcher's difficulty lay with the political establishment.

Some of her most senior ministers had genuinely imbibed 'one nation' policies, as had most of the senior civil servants who worked for them, so she found herself 'a Bolshevik leading a Tsarist government'. As a result, the one-time leader of the opposition who had claimed that she would not waste time in her cabinets having arguments, actually spent time as Prime Minister doing just that. This ensured that her administration was less radical than her rhetoric had promised, although it is an exaggeration to suggest that her first year in office was 'wasted'.[1] Her isolation was somewhat less bleak in reality, however, as she appointed sympathisers to the key economic departments. She took this precaution because her main priority was to revive the British economy through the application of specific remedies, particularly the liberation of the private sector, within a tight framework of monetary control. It was the ministers operating within this policy area, therefore, who were her most crucial appointments.

Sir Geoffrey Howe became Chancellor of the Exchequer. Despite a reputation for being a progressive Conservative, he had been an economic liberal throughout his career and was converted to the quantity theory of money, the idea that inflation was simply the product of an excessive amount of money in circulation, before Thatcher herself.[2] Two junior ministers whose ideas were politically compatible with his, supported Howe at the Treasury. John Biffen was an authentic monetarist who had been one of Enoch Powell's faithful adherents during the Heath years, and Nigel Lawson had been committed to the twin political goals of nationalism and the conquest of inflation since 1969. Sir Keith Joseph became Secretary of State for Industry. It had been his self-torturing public recantation in 1974 of the actions of his earlier career which provoked a fundamental challenge to Heath's policies; although Joseph was adamant that he was merely, belatedly, becoming a 'true Conservative'. John Nott became Minister of Trade. While he had served Heath as an economic minister in the early 1970s, he was rumoured to have been discontented with the drift of policy at that time, and his free-market and monetarist credentials were not in doubt by 1979. During the 1979 campaign he had stressed that it was the small business sector which was the key to Britain's economic recovery, whereas Heath from 1972 to 1974 had placed his emphasis upon negotiations with the Confederation of British Industries (CBI), which represented large business interests. Finally, David Howell became the Minister for Energy. While there is evidence that Howell was a 'weathervane' for the party, and that when he had worked with Heath he had made statements which were far from right wing, he had moved rightwards by 1965. By the later 1960s he not only advocated denationalisation, but also introduced the term privatisation to describe it.

'Packing' the economic ministries with people she considered ideologically compatible may have assisted Thatcher, but her Employment Minister, James Prior, at the time described the appointees as, 'not a very impressive bunch, with very little experience at the heart of government'.[3] They were the acolytes of the Prime Minister, however, which meant that they were both inclined to agree with her policies and to subordinate their views to hers if any differences were to appear. As the Permanent Secretary to the Treasury, Sir Douglas Wass, put it: Thatcher was 'much more the First Lord of the Treasury than any previous holder of the office'.[4]

Yet the extent to which Thatcher supplemented the intellectual baggage which she brought into office with a clearly worked out programme was limited. She had simple ideas, and had distantly read

Hayek and heard of Friedman, but she was more interested in practical politics than in theory, and many of her beliefs were acquired second-hand. The influence of people rather than ideas on her politics had already become apparent, but there is a further paradox. While she was a loyal Conservative career politician who had not opposed Heath before 1974, the people whose influence she accepted were linked to her personally rather than through the Conservative Party. She even downgraded the role of the Conservative Research Department (CRD), considering it too infected by postwar heresies, and made space to listen to the views of right-wingers, often linked to independent think-tanks.[5] The list of those who influenced her is long, and the characters slipped in and out of favour, but in the early period they included Sir Alfred Sherman of the CPS, Sir Keith Joseph and the academic economist Milton Friedman; a little later the academic economist Sir Alan Walters, Sir Terence Burns who was to become her Permanent Secretary at the Treasury, her press officer Sir Bernard Ingham, the academics Professors Brian Griffiths and Patrick Minford, and towards the end, her chief of staff in Downing Street, Sir Charles Powell.[6] Assisted by these advisers and the Policy Units such as the CPS, the Institute of Economic Affairs (IEA), the Adam Smith Institute (ASI), the London Business School and the Institute of Directors (IoD), Thatcher's policies unfolded. It is unhistorical, therefore, to impose a *post hoc* rationalisation of her entire programme in government. Her policies were actually influenced by different individuals in changing circumstances.

Thatcher was assisted by good luck. This may not always have appeared to be the case in the first couple of years with a divided cabinet, a series of challenges from the trade unions such as the strikes of steel workers and civil servants, an economy in difficulty with both inflation and unemployment rising and the so-called 'wets' anticipating the need to return to the middle ground of politics by reflating the economy. These threats were embodied with the rise of the centrist Social Democratic Party (SDP) which threatened 'to break the mould' of British politics.[7] Many commentators expected that such an *annus horribilis* would automatically lead to the type of U-turns which Thatcherites felt had disfigured Heath's government in 1971/2.

But her good fortune was also considerable. The rise of the SDP, for example, was double edged in that it divided the parliamentary and electoral opposition that she faced. The Labour Party split asunder after the 1979 defeat and the price of its achieving even a semblance of unity was the choice of the unelectable Michael Foot as its party leader. The Falklands War was also decisively important in that it rescued Thatcher from being the most unpopular Prime Minister since before such data was collected, by serving as a metaphor for 'the resolute approach' to government which she claimed. Her government also benefited from the revenues generated by the exploitation of North Sea oil, and the reaction against statist and command economies internationally would have led even a Labour government to pursue some of her policies. Thatcher was also fortunate in that her government was sustained by social changes. These 'unguided' social changes included a declining blue-collar working class. Such characteristic policies of the 1980s as the promotion of home and share ownership both reflected and reinforced this decline.[8]

THE BATTLE TO ESTABLISH THATCHERISM 1979 TO 1981

In the first two and a quarter years Thatcher had to struggle to establish the programme in the face of opposition from hostile elements in both the party and in the country. She battled through by a combination of determined persistence and some hard-headed compromises. Large pay rises were granted to the police and armed forces. Radical governments might need to defend themselves and the redemption of this election promise, she decided, would enthuse her supporters. A related set of pay increases were more difficult to swallow and were necessitated by tactical considerations. During the election campaign Callaghan had managed to extract from Thatcher the commitment to honour any recommendations which might be made by Hugh Clegg in the report of his commission to rectify pay anomalies between public and private-sector workers.[9] Thatcher's political instincts were critical of such publicly organised acts of income redistribution, but she had been concerned not to alienate large numbers of floating voters during the campaign. These pay awards contributed to the rise of inflation to an alarming 22 per cent in the new government's first year in office.[10]

The overriding aim of the Thatcher government in its first term was to defeat inflation by tight monetary control. Anxieties about inflation had been developing among Conservatives since at least 1969, when it reached 5 per cent.[11] Yet it was only among the *cognoscenti* that there was alarm about inflation. It took the oil crisis of the 1970s to make inflation a popular concern. If unemployment had been a reason for the electoral unpopularity of the Conservatives in 1945 then inflation, with Labour as the main malefactor, had replaced it by 1979. Sir Geoffrey Howe brought in an immediate budget aiming to reduce inflation by a monetary and fiscal squeeze. The new government was determined to avoid the error of the Heath government which, having come to office in June 1970, did little to alter the course of the economy until the next budget was due in April 1971, by which time other events were also overtaking it. In any event, it takes time for budgetary measures to take effect. The first Heath budget, therefore, could only begin to impact upon the economy after Heath had been in power for nearly two years.

The main attack upon inflation in May 1979 was an assault on public expenditure, starting with the year in progress. As the economy was about to turn down it was not the most auspicious time to attack the government deficit as to do so could accelerate a recession. Yet on public expenditure, and on the ideological restructuring of the taxation burden towards an emphasis upon indirect taxation, the government decided it had to act at once. This was to avoid losing momentum and, like other governments before it, to avoid being forced back into a reactive pragmatism. Thatcher later explained that a government could only act in this way without incurring a high political penalty, 'at the beginning of a parliament when our mandate is fresh'.[12]

Public expenditure was duly cut by £3.5 billion, partly through the bold decision to remove the indexation of pensions in line with wages and to re-index it against prices. While the cuts failed to reduce public expenditure as a proportion of Gross Domestic Product (GDP), they created a more austere atmosphere which made possible the goal of ultimately reducing the proportion.[13] A more immediately radical measure was the reduction of the top rate of income tax from 83 to 60 per cent, and the basic rate from 33 to 30 per cent. This was compensated for by an increase in VAT from the two rates of 8 and 12.5 per cent, to a unified rate of 15 per cent. Just as public expenditure cuts were likely to hasten recession, so the VAT increase added 4 percentage points to the Retail Price Index (RPI). Even a sympathetic commentator agreed that the reduction in standard rate to 30 per cent in the pound was an error, as it cost £1,400 million in a year and was hardly likely to have any real impact upon Britain's work ethic.[14] Yet this type of budget was an important symbol of the government's intent, and it laid the foundations for the anti-inflationary, pro-enterprise direction which the government pursued until the mid-1980s.

To prevent the thrust of the government's economic policy from being derailed, there was nil consultation on the budget, which upset some cabinet ministers. Prior favoured a shift in the burden of taxation and some expenditure reductions, but was perturbed at the scale of both.[15] Yet had the 'one nation' opponents been allowed to derail the budget and reduce the scale of the policy shift, the demonstration effect of the strategy would have been lost.[16] Thatcher confirms that this was a crucial part of her motivation, in order to 'establish the direction of our strategy from the start and to do it boldly'.[17]

To counter the short-term inflationary elements in the budget, however, the minimum lending rate was raised by two points to 14 per cent, and the monetary target for M3 (the sum of coins, banknotes and bank deposits), which was the guiding light at the time, was tightened. While revealing the government's intentions, the budget measures, particularly the interest rate rises, damaged industry. The pound, already buoyed up by its role as a petro-currency, rose to high levels, thus damaging exporters.[18] It is widely agreed that the May 1979 budget contributed to the creation of a recession, particularly in manufacturing; although Thatcherites maintained that it was the high level of sterling resulting from the effects of North Sea oil which most damaged economic prospects by impeding exports.

Thatcher's personal hatred of inflation was always clear, and it is ironic that it was the extent of inflation which led to her downfall in 1990.[19] This can be explained by the reality that ministers were not entirely in control of the economy. This was partly the result of external forces in the world economy, but there was also a lack of consistency in the making of policy in those areas well within the government's capacity to control as the 'macroeconomic strategy evolved. It did not reflect the implementation of a well-articulated design.'[20] Even among the inner circle of Thatcherites with whom Thatcher discussed economic policy there were disagreements about what constituted an appropriate monetarist strategy, and even about the direction that economic policy should take generally.[21]

It is evident that Howe's first budget had a mixed impact on inflation, for example, and the reduction in middle-class taxes was not accompanied by the removal of tax breaks and privileges to offset the reductions. Most incongruous of all was Thatcher's own passionate devotion to the cause of home ownership. While there were times when circumstances forced her to accept such extremely high interest rates as 17 per cent in the autumn of 1979, she normally viewed the problem as a political issue to assist home ownership by keeping rates lower than a monetarist perspective warranted.[22] Thatcher also refused to abandon mortgage interest tax relief, so as the 1980s progressed home owners contributed to inflation by taking out equity on their homes by borrowing on mortgages to finance other forms of consumption. When the government was forced to raise interest rates it was a paradox for Thatcher's home-owning vision that it was first-time buyers who were penalised.

During the summer of 1979 the government began to tackle the problem of cutting public expenditure. Once more, while Thatcher wished an end to them, she was conscious of the political consequences of reductions in public services, and also found it difficult to deal with the pressures from competing spending ministers. In June 1979 Howe, and his Chief Secretary Biffen, offered Thatcher a £500 million package of cuts. She was displeased and instructed him to do better. They then produced a £3,500 million package and ultimately proposed an £8,000 million reduction on existing expenditure plans for 1980/1. Yet the politician in her protested about the detail of the proposals. In particular, she was concerned at two items: an increase in parental contributions to student grants, and charges for nursery school places. Both were entirely acceptable to the self-help and individual responsibility philosophy of the government. Both were ruled out, grant contributions because 'they would hit people like us who we're supposed to be helping', and nursery charges because as education minister Thatcher had brought in these very places. As a result, by late July 1979, the package was pruned back to a mere £3,500 million.[23] By the autumn it was clear that the government felt compelled to cut back the Public Sector Borrowing Requirement (PSBR) much further, and in a White Paper asserted that public expenditure was 'at the heart' of the country's difficulties. This was no short-term exercise to achieve a better financial balance, but involved deep, permanent cuts in order to 'lay the foundations' for future prosperity. It was compatible with the government's simultaneous decision to raise the price of electricity by 10 per cent.[24] The Prime Minister advanced the old theory about the public sector 'crowding out' the private sector. Yet this argument loses its validity when a recession is developing as the 'crowding out' thesis makes sense only when there is a fully employed, rapidly growing economy.[25]

The economic decision which best represented the strategy of the government, perhaps even more than the cuts in public expenditure, was the removal of exchange controls in October 1979. This demonstrated the government's determination to open up the economy to international forces, and to underline its commitment to economic freedom, notably through the abolition of the restrictions on the import and export of capital. The political furore which ensued was based on the claim that necessary capital for investment in the British economy was being exported abroad. It was an unintended consequence that this capital outflow prevented an even sharper appreciation of the economy than actually occurred. While the Labour Party's indignation was based upon a national and statist conception of economic management which was of declining salience in most states during the 1980s, it remains unclear to this day where much of the capital flowed, and what proportion of it was ever soundly invested. Nigel Lawson was a strong proponent of this policy, which he still defends by pointing out that most other major countries had followed this course by the mid-1980s and that Britain reaped benefits by being the first country to dismantle controls.[26] Thatcher describes this decision as the one which in retrospect gives her the greatest satisfaction, because she advocates a world where markets and not governments determine the movement of capital.[27]

The next major economic reform, however, was the unveiling of the Medium Term Financial Strategy (MTFS). This was announced in the 1980 budget, by which time Thatcher was in the second year of her government, conscious that Joseph felt that the previous year had been partly wasted and ready to 'take off the gloves'.[28] Thatcher's growing confidence coincided, however, with a loss of conviction by Biffen, who found the implementation of theories which he had long subscribed to, very difficult in practice. His reluctance to make deep cuts in public expenditure in his role as Chief Secretary to the Treasury was followed by serious doubts about the efficacy of the MTFS. His argument was that it was impaling the government upon a hook which would leave it little room to manoeuvre when circumstances changed. In later years Thatcher also disavowed it as 'graph paper economics'.[29] The MTFS was the project of Lawson and Howe, both of whom were firm believers in monetary control at this stage in the government's life; even believing the more dubious parts of the theory, which postulated so simple a relationship that nine months after a 2 per cent increase in the amount of money in circulation there would be an identical rise in inflation. Buoyed by this conviction they introduced the MTFS, which set targets for the growth in money supply using the broad M3 measure which includes all notes and coins in circulation plus sterling deposits held by UK residents. It established the rate of growth for the period up to 1984, and Lawson as Financial Secretary to the Treasury was responsible for getting it accepted. The intention was to set up a framework for future economic policy and to provide a system to rein in big-spending ministers.[30] In later years Lawson admitted that 'too much hope was invested in the whole idea and . . . too much . . . claimed for it at the outset'.[31] After leaving office the classic 'one nation' Conservative cabinet minister described the MTFS as 'the uncontrollable in pursuit of the undefinable'.[32] This view was vindicated four months later when the Bank of England decided to loosen the mechanism by which it restrained the lending policy of the banks. Fearful of the economic recession which was looming and of the number of bankruptcies in the manufacturing sector of the economy, the Bank's Industrial Finance Unit, through its links with the clearing banks, was trying to help good companies stay afloat with generous advances.[33] This naturally increased M3. As a consequence, a torrent of credit was released, and M3 exceeded the growth laid down for it in the MTFS by three times. Yet inflation did not take off about a year later as committed monetarists expected.[34]

The 1980 budget contributed to a further deflation of the economy. In 1980/1 manufacturing production fell by 14 per cent, the Gross National Product fell by 3.2 per cent and unemployment crossed the 2 million threshold. Thatcher appeared genuinely surprised at the extent of unemployment, and while prepared to deflate the economy in line with her monetarist dogmas, seemed unwilling to live with the consequences.[35] If she derived benefit from high unemployment, in that as a reserve army of labour the unemployed weakened trade unions, hit their income from a loss of membership and lessened militant wage demands, this was probably a beneficial and unintended side-effect of unemployment rather than a deliberate act of policy. Yet adult unemployment increased more during 1980 than in any of the previous fifty years.[36] Despite Thatcher's apparent shock when unemployment exceeded 2 million she was determined not to change course. She informed the 1980 party conference, in a disparaging reference to the Heath government, 'you turn if you want, the lady's not for turning'. It was also the time when she pronounced, with reference to her policies, 'there is no alternative'. This led her Leader of the House, Norman St John Stevas, to describe Thatcher as Tina after the first letters of her maxim. Not renowned for her self-deprecation or her sense of humour, she dismissed Stevas in January 1981, and his dismissal was attributed to his being 'a little too outrageous and indiscreet'.[37] The defences for these damaging policies, in what an admirer calls 'the heroic phase of Thatcherism', was that the productivity of those in work was increasing sharply, which was a crucial part of the government's drive towards international competitiveness. Production was falling, but so were unit costs. So industry could be said to be becoming 'leaner and fitter'.[38] Equally, not all parts of the country were suffering severely. The 1979 to 1981 recession was most sharply experienced in the old industrial areas hardest hit by the demise of the 'smokestack' industries. Despite these points in defence of her policies, however, Thatcher's government accelerated the process of deindustrialisation, and exacerbated Britain's deficit in manufactured exports; a problem which has dogged British governments since that date whenever the prospect of economic recovery has occurred. A cabinet battle in the autumn of 1980 between spenders/investors and monetarists led to the compromise where the bank was permitted its slight loosening of monetary policy.

Industrial relations was an area where Thatcher was compelled to make concessions during 1980. The government stood firm in the steel strike to demonstrate its intentions and to clarify that it was not prepared to continue to invest in loss-making nationalised industries. At the end of the strike the government decided to add steel to the list of industries which it was going to subject to strict commercial management while retaining it within the public sector. Joseph in his role as Secretary of State for Industry hired Ian MacGregor to replace Charles Villiers as head of the British Steel Corporation (BSC). This required substantial compensation to his existing employers, and he was offered the then high salary of £48,000. A precedent was thus created for the award of other high salaries to be enjoyed by the heads of newly privatised corporations, but leading Conservatives defended it, arguing that the market should determine the level of salaries in the private and public sector alike.[39]

In the industrial relations field a strict Thatcherite approach was temporarily abandoned in 1980, when Prior's modest approach prevailed over 'the big bang' strategy which the Heath government had pursued in 1971 and which Thatcher instinctively preferred. Perhaps this was an instance where the more 'wet' members of cabinet, as Thatcher had now taken to describing her critics in the party including Prior and the trade union leaders themselves, failed to grasp the extent of the change in the public mood since the early 1970s. Prior's goal was to increase the responsibility and accountability of trade unions and he was able to resist Thatcher's preference for weakening them legislatively. As a result, the 1980 Act was confined to restricting lawful picketing in order to limit secondary action, making public funds available for trade union ballots, compensating people who suffered as a result of the closed shop and requiring a four-fifths ballot before a closed shop could be set up.[40] Yet Thatcher undermined Prior's cautious approach by making it clear that further reform was on its way and by encouraging the ultras to maintain pressure on him from within the party. Certainly, the Thatcher government had longer-term changes in mind, but accepted that the problem should be tackled in stages. The longer-term philosophy, according to one leading Conservative of the time, was driven by Thatcher's own visceral dislike of trade unions. The principles which the harder elements of the party had in mind were to encourage employers and employees to move from a collectivist to an individualist model of industrial relations, to shift from workplace to postal ballots on industrial action, to outlaw closed shops, to strengthen 'the right to manage', to reduce the capacity of trade unions, to reduce union power and to remove legal immunities from certain kinds of industrial action.[41]

The year 1981 was a crucially pivotal year in the history of Thatcherism. At the start of the year, the polls recorded Thatcher as the most unpopular Prime Minister since polling began, and she was widely opposed even in her own cabinet; but by the end of the year she had imposed her will on her 'wet' critics, and begun to believe that she could, with the assistance of the incipient economic recovery, aspire to win the next general election. She was massively assisted by the fragmentation of the Labour opposition. Just as the Conservative fear about the strength of the Labour electoral challenge began to decline after 1952 with the rise of the Bevanite split, the events of 1979 to 1981 were devastating for Labour, and correspondingly encouraging for Thatcher. During this period Labour embarked upon a civil war, elected an unconvincing candidate for Prime Ministerial office in Michael Foot, and lost four of its leading members to form a new political party, the Social Democratic Party.

The so-called 'wets' or 'one nation' Conservatives in the cabinet also failed to cabal and unite, and despite their criticisms of Thatcher, they offered little by way of a coherent alternative, except traditional Keynesian reflation. The failure of the 'wets' to challenge Thatcher is less a comment on their courage or party loyalty, and more a reflection of their political weakness, lack of support in the party and their philosophical vacuity. It was becoming apparent that the course set by Thatcher was increasingly hard to reverse. Thatcher was now playing for high stakes which the 'wets' could not challenge: 'to remain the dominant party of government in a country where 'business' could once again flourish, and where the public had returned to pre-social democratic – if not pre-democratic values.[42] The manufacturing recession was sufficiently deep, however, to ensure that the anti-Thatcherites in cabinet had allies in their call for reflation. The president of the CBI, Terence Becket, rashly promised Thatcher, 'a bare knuckled fight'.[43] A cabinet meeting in July 1981 saw the Prime Minister and chancellor almost alone in advocating continuing deflation of the economy, and some ministers began to talk darkly of 'monetary madness' and 'political suicide'. Finally, 364 of the country's leading economists in a 'round robin' to *The Times* argued against the government's budgetary strategy. Their letter claimed that there was no basis in economic theory or supporting evidence that by deflating demand inflation woud be brought permanently under control and thereby induce an automatic recovery in output and employment.[44] This intervention led to intense debate in later years as to whether it was the government or the economists who had got it right. In the short term it was patently the economists who were vindicated, as by the spring of 1992 there had been a 5.5 per cent fall in output over two years, and unemployment had climbed to 2.2 million. By 1987, and after five continuous years of economic growth and a mounting 'feel good' factor in the country, it appeared that the economists had been mistakenly trapped in an outdated Keynesian paradigm of the economy. The recovery by 1987 was in part a reflection of how far the economy had fallen before bottoming out at the end of 1981, however, and the improvement also reflected a worldwide economic upturn.[45]

Any doubts about Thatcher's determination to adhere to the economic course that she had set were dispelled by the March 1981 budget. It is true that there had been a weakening of monetary controls, but since this was not widely appreciated, at the public level the budget appeared to continue the linear path on which Thatcher had set out two years previously. Not all the party's left wing opposed her. Sir Anthony Meyer, for example, who was later so disgruntled that he contested the party leadership with Thatcher in 1989, supported the general strategy of the budget because he considered that British industry did not require to be bailed out by artificially low interest rates, and that it should become leaner and fitter.[46] At that stage in the Thatcher government Meyer even thought that Macmillan had allowed inefficiency to take hold of British industry, and that harsh medicine was required.

The budget of 1981 demonstrated that the government was not subordinating economic to political strategies, since it was designed neither to end the recession nor to capture votes. It can be variously interpreted as a triumph of ideology, the appropriate remedy to set Britain on the road to permanent non-inflationary economic recovery or as a policy to assist the City and those sectors of capital which the Conservative Party was most anxious to support. In any event, there is agreement that it was a 'courageous' budget. Sympathisers confidently assert that the 1981 budget 'enabled recovery from recession to take place without the re-emergence of inflation'.[47] As has been pointed out, this interpretation is resisted by those who suggest that it was a revival in world trade and the international economy, fuelled by American trade deficits, which re-established economic growth.[48] Gamble recognises that the economic improvement which began slowly in 1981 was partly caused by 'a one-off improvement related to the huge shedding of labour in the recession', and 'the more flexible economic management made possible through the crutch provided for the domestic budget by the oil revenue and the asset sales'. Yet he places greater stress upon the 'global recovery stimulated by the reflation of the American economy through deficit financing'.[49] In reality, there were both domestic and international forces at work, but any explanation that neglects international forces is incomplete; and it is noticeable that when the economy was in recession, as at the time of the 1992 general election, Conservative leaders always pointed to international forces.

Nigel Lawson argues that the Public Sector Borrowing Requirement (PSBR) had to be cut in the 1981 budget because there was a continuing 'crowding out' of the private sector through the growth in public expenditure. The expected PSBR before the budget measures was £14.5 billion, but by ceasing to index income tax allowances and thresholds, together with increasing excise duties beyond the rate of inflation, the expected PSBR out-turn could be reduced to £10.5 billion. The actual out-turn proved to be still lower, however, at £8.6 billion.

A budget which actually reduces public expenditure at a time of recession is unorthodox, but folklore within the Conservative Party later established that it was the cause of the subsequent eight years of economic growth. Howe was adamant in rejecting the advice of those who urged that he should 'abandon the battle against inflation as our top priority and look instead for ways of expanding the economy . . . . But to change course now would be fatal to the whole counter-inflation strategy.'[50] The budget increased taxes, cut university funding and further raised prescription charges. Sir Alan Walters is usually credited with having produced the intellectual structure of the budget, which Howe merely legitimised by formally presenting it. If that is the case, Lawson points out that much of the intellectual input was unjustified, because the benefits which Walters and Thatcher expected to flow from it, suggested by the simultaneous reduction of interest rates by 2 per cent to 14 per cent, proved to be mistaken. Six months later the rates had to be raised once more to 16 per cent.[51] This was required because the situation of the economy overall was threatening a run on the pound.

The budget almost led to the resignation of Peter Walker, Jim Prior and Ian Gilmour from the cabinet because of its deflationary character when they were urging economic reflation, to generate growth and employment. They decided not to resign, however, because such gestures would not change the budget and would merely damage sterling and the economy.[52] These ministers, who were by now widely described as 'wets', were haunted by the fear that in the future people would look back and question why they assented in cutting public expenditure at a time when there were nearly two and a half million unemployed and the country's industrial infrastructure 'was crying out for modernisation'.[53] It was apparent that the 'one nation' cabinet ministers had underestimated Thatcher's determination, and that their expectations, or even hope, that the consequences of her monetary policies for employment and social stability would lead to her replacement by a more traditionally paternalist Conservative leader were misplaced. Lord Hailsham, the then Lord Chancellor, describes their mood at the time as one of total unpreparedness for 'the extent and duration of Margaret Thatcher's hegemony of British politics in the ten years which followed'.[54] In any event, with their decision to remain in government, the final opportunity for the 'wets' to force Thatcher to change course evaporated.

Thatcher was alert to the need to carry the party in the country with her as she pursued difficult policies, although she was aware that her support would increase if she was able to stifle dissent in the cabinet.

She addressed the Central Council of the party, in which key members and officials from across the country were represented, and repeated her message of courage and resolution.[55] Yet there were signs of the party's nerve beginning to crack by the summer of 1981. It is significant, however, that this tendency was more marked in the cabinet and the parliamentary party than in the National Union. The party in the country was loyal, and not simply because of traditional rank and file support for incumbent leaders, but because she was offering policies in harmony with the membership's long-standing preferences.

The summer crisis was generated by an outbreak of rioting in the streets of certain British cities, such as London, Liverpool, Leeds and Manchester, and over a thousand riot police were injured. Ian Gilmour has no doubt that the riots were stimulated by unemployment and poverty.[56] While Thatcher is reputed to have sympathised only with the shopkeepers whose property was looted, the riots added significance to the cabinet's deliberations at a famous meeting on 23 July 1981, by giving the 'wets' ammunition. Some ministers such as Biffen 'jumped ship for the first time', saying that the heroic holding down of public expenditure had gone far enough. Certain policy modifications did flow from this dispute, for example the postponement of the abolition of the tripartite Manpower Services Commission (MSC), and the idea of the Youth Training Scheme (YTS) to mop up and conceal youth unemployment which the MSC would deliver.[57] The adoption of the YTS, which was implemented in 1982 after protracted and skilful negotiations with the TUC, has been described as marking 'a new beginning for the Thatcher administration', presumably because it allowed the government to point to its social concern for the young unemployed without having to alter macro-economic policy.[58]

Among the more 'ideologically unacceptable' policies rejected at the July cabinet meeting were Heseltine's proposal for a statutory pay freeze and Walker's call for more state planning of production and investment. Yet the forcefulness of the more progressive Tories on this occasion, coupled with the apostasy of Biffen and Nott, alarmed Thatcher, as did Hailsham's identification of Howe with President Hoover, whose failure to intervene in the American economy had greatly exacerbated the depression of 1929.[59] Whether to avoid a repetition of previous policy errors, or as a convenient alibi, Thatcher reiterated her determination to avoid another Heath-type boom as had occurred after the 1971/2 U-turns. She added that an inflationary strategy would damage millions of people who saved in building societies. While this anti-inflationary comment was consistent with the government's overall strategy, it also revealed Thatcher's sense of her own constituency, and of the part of the nation that she was most anxious to protect. The overall result of the crisis cabinet meeting was not, however, new ideas and policies, but new faces. Her main lesson from the cabinet meeting was that it was necessary to have a purge to assert her control over the government.

The ensuing reshuffle on 14 September 1981 gave Thatcher the domination over her cabinet which she had desired since May 1979. The 'wets' were either purged from the government or moved to less influential positions.[60] Prior had hoped to be appointed to the post of Industry Secretary, at the productive end of the economy, but he was dispatched to Ulster, to be as far away from her as possible.[61] This was the most spectacular part of the reshuffle as Prior had let it be known that he would not go to Ulster, but after hours of agonising he accepted the post. One Thatcherite summed up the situation by saying that Prior 'had been caught out bluffing publicly, and his bluff had publicly been called'.[62] Joseph was moved from the post of Industry Secretary, where contrary to his non-interventionist principles he had felt compelled to support ailing state industries with subsidies, to the Department of Education and Science. Lawson replaced David Howell at Energy with the clear brief to prepare for a future coal strike. Howell clearly 'carried the can' for Thatcher's enforced capitulation to the miners earlier in 1981. Norman Tebbit replaced Prior at Employment, and while it augured badly for the trade unions, it did not actually alter the legislative 'salami slicing' tactics towards union power which Prior had inaugurated, although it ensured that the reforms would continue.[63] Tebbit's appointment was regarded as an insult to the unemployed, particularly after he informed them at the party conference that, like his out-of-work father in the 1930s, they should not riot, but rather 'get on their bike' to look for work.[64] Tebbit symbolised the 'new right' Tories attracted to the party by Thatcher's style. Significantly for the later conception of 'Essex man' as the archetypal Thatcher supporter, he represented the Essex constituency of Chingford. This distinction earned him the sobriquet of 'the Chingford skinhead'. Lord Thorneycroft was removed from party chairman, partly because he had lost the stomach for monetarism, to be replaced by Cecil Parkinson. Parkinson was politically sympathetic to Thatcher, but also appealed to another aspect of her complicated make-up, as she liked to have tall and attractive men around her, and to be fussed by 'chaps' she admired.[65] She also dismissed Lord Soames from the cabinet, whom she blamed for the 21-week long civil service strike earlier in 1981, even though she had then settled for a pay rise which he had been urging on her for seven weeks previously. Ian Gilmour lost his ministerial post at the Foreign Office, and unprophetically responded by predicting that 'the government is heading straight for the rocks'. While the reshuffle placed her in full control of her own cabinet for the first time since the election it did contain one irony. Nine years later when she fell from power the cabinet was less sympathetic to her position than it was in the autumn of 1981, and her promotion of Lawson planted a seed that contributed to her later downfall. It was at the time of this move from being a Treasury minister to his new post at Energy that he lost his faith in domestic monetary targets, and became convinced that Britain becoming a member of the European Monetary System (EMS) was the best available mechanism to constrain inflation. This policy was the core of his increasingly open disagreement with Thatcher in the second half of the 1980s.[66]

After the reshuffle, Thatcher was at her most formidable, while still facing political adversity. If many professional and career-orientated MPs still feared the party's electoral prospects, the rank and file support for Thatcher was apparent from the reception which the grass roots gave to Heath's speech to the autumn 1981 party conference, in which he demanded a change in economic direction. Despite the party's poor position in the opinion polls, and the electoral threat being posed by the recently formed Social Democratic Party as a breakaway from Labour, the delegates gave Heath a rough reception.[67] It was evident that those elements in the party's leadership left over from the heyday of the Keynesian welfare state were now isolated. Some argue that the majority of MPs were not committed Thatcherites, and that the isolation of the 'wets' reflected the fact that Thatcher's supporters were simply better organised and intellectually dominant.[68] This is only a marginally different perspective from the view that the anti-Thatcherites were now isolated. Even if some Conservative MPs did demur from particular aspects of Thatcher's programme, her leadership, and her control over the party's direction was secure. She described the 1981 conference as 'the last assault of the wets', and claims that Lawson devastated them with his remark that they offered 'cold feet dressed up as high principle'.[69] Her domination was unaffected by the cryptic contributions of Biffen at a fringe meeting where he sought to portray the government almost in 'one nation' mode. Claiming that the government was much misunderstood, he pointed out that state expenditure had risen in the previous two years by 2 per cent, which was far from the prescriptions of Milton Friedman's monetarist school. He added 'we are all social democrats now'.[70] This was a doubtful argument as the rise in public expenditure, both then and throughout the 1980s, reflected a shift in priorities away from social democracy and towards such traditional Conservative preferences as law and order and defence. Public expenditure was also on an upward trajectory because of the pressures on the social security budget as a result of mass unemployment and the impact of an ageing population.[71] Biffen's attempt to reunite the party fell on deaf ears at the conference, where the leadership had no desire to portray itself as a friend of the policies of the previous three and a half decades.

At conference fringe meetings the dismissed ministers attacked the rigidity of Treasury policy, while those left behind in government like Walker and Heseltine resorted to opaque messages. There was speculation that a former Heathite minister, Geoffrey Rippon, would challenge Thatcher for the leadership. While he was not expected to perform well, it could lead to a more effective challenge from Heath or DuCann.[72] It was never seriously in doubt that she would be able to prevail, and while there were still serious by-election defeats in store – particularly the dramatic SDP victory at Crosby in the autumn of 1981 – the slowly developing economic recovery bolstered Thatcher's confidence as the new year approached.

Yet Thatcher's dominance over the entire government machine was still incomplete. In the first year of her government she had visited the major departments of state in order to make her presence felt. If the view that the Heath government had allowed itself to be in thrall to senior civil servants is justified, then Thatcher was determined that the same problem would not bedevil her government. The head of the civil service, Sir Ian Bancroft, had collaborated with some of her government's initial attempts to improve civil service practice, for example the cost-cutting initiatives of Sir Derek Rayner, who had been imported from Marks & Spencer to join the Efficiency Unit. In the spring of 1980, on the other hand, he had arranged a dinner to allow civil servants to express their dissatisfaction with the drift of government policy and to express their misgivings about the early signs that the Thatcher government wished to deprivilege the civil service. Thatcher was unimpressed by the comments made at the dinner, as she was by Bancroft's attempts at mediation during the protracted civil servants' strike of 1981. Her displeasure was conveyed to Bancroft, who resigned his post in November 1981. Thatcher took the opportunity which this presented to wind up the Civil Service Department (CSD) and to transfer its personnel functions to the Treasury. This, coupled with her newly achieved domination of the cabinet, marked Thatcher's unusual degree of control over the entire governmental machine. Naturally, one individual cannot be entirely dominant over a vast complex machine spread over the whole country, but at least she took all the main levers of power in her own hands.[73] She took a similar level of control over the entire party organisation with the appointment of Cecil Parkinson as party chairman. While the relationship between party leader and chairman is necessarily asymmetrical, because the chairmanship is within the leader's patronage, the harmony between Thatcher and Parkinson was especially evident and was a factor in the party's electoral success in 1983. Parkinson proved to be a success as chairman, and he imported new marketing techniques such as direct mailing, as well as patiently and effectively making the government's case on television.[74]

THATCHERISM TRIUMPHANT

While 1981 saw an improvement in the fortunes of the Thatcher government, 1982 produced a spectacular transformation, as a result of the Falklands War. Yet it is an error to attribute the Conservative victory in 1983 solely to the fallout from the war, despite Thatcher's skilful exploitation of it by 'unfurling the patriotic flag'.[75] The war made the SDP appear irrelevant. The Labour Party, led by an ageing Michael Foot, fought the 1983 general election on a left-wing manifesto, later referred to as 'the longest suicide note in history'.[76] The other explanation for the Conservative electoral revival during 1982 is that while unemployment continued to rise, and did so until 1986, the economy revived on the back of a supply-side and tax-cutting economic strategy by the new American President, Ronald Reagan. Inflation fell, despite the considerable monetary incontinence after the autumn of 1980, which undermined the mechanistic monetarist claim about a simple one-to-one link between monetary expansion and consequent inflation. There was also a slow recovery in output. As a result, Thatcher rarely talked about M3, the PSBR became less prominent in her statements and the 1982 budget marked a less rigorous approach. This limited economic recovery was of great electoral significance. The Essex University school of political analysis tends to link, in a deterministic fashion, a party's electoral fortunes to the general state of the economy, and particularly to the level of interest rates.[77] In reality, mono-causal explanations of Thatcher's political recovery during 1992 are misplaced, but the sharp swing in the opinion polls suggest the Falklands factor was the biggest single issue.

The Argentinian invasion of the Falkland Islands could have led to the fall of the Thatcher government. It was one of her Foreign Office ministers, Nicholas Ridley, who presented to the Commons a proposed lease-back arrangement, under which sovereignty would pass to the Argentinians. This implied that the government was uninterested in retaining the islands in the South Atlantic, of which many British people had not even heard.[78] This government proposal emboldened the Argentinian military junta to attempt to capture the islands. The Foreign Secretary, Lord Carrington, took responsibility for the debacle and resigned; but Thatcher was determined to go to war, to win it, and to retrieve the political setback which the loss of the islands represented. The war was fought as much for domestic reasons as for issues of high principle of international morality about resisting aggression. Once the war was won Thatcher immediately invoked the Falklands spirit. In July 1982 she informed the voters, 'we have ceased to be a nation in retreat. We have instead found a new confidence . . . born in the economic battles at home and tested and found true 8,000 miles away . . . we rejoice that Britain has rekindled that spirit which has fired her for generations past and which today has begun to burn as brightly as before.'[79]

There is a paradox about this triumph. The Falklands War created an opponent in her party. Sir Anthony Meyer was troubled by the bellicose mood which the war aroused and voiced his concerns in the Commons and on television. As a result, Parkinson as party chairman clumsily sought Meyer's ejection by his local party association, but he failed.[80] Meyer's developing anxiety about Thatcher's style was ultimately expressed in his decision to challenge her as a 'stalking horse' for the leadership in 1989. This undermined her position for future contests.

While the Conservatives could be confident that the next general election could be won as a result of the Falklands factor, incipient economic recovery and the divided and ineffective nature of the opposition, there were still potential threats. First, unemployment remained high and threatened to cross the 3 million threshold before an election, in comparison to the figure of 1.2 million inherited in 1979.[81] Second, there was a fear that the Labour Party would abandon Foot as leader and replace him with the more belligerent and effective Denis Healey, who was the sole remaining figure in the Labour Party that Thatcher still feared. Third, opinion polls revealed that Thatcher was still thought to be out of touch with the feelings of ordinary people. Finally, a Central Policy Review Staff (CPRS) pamphlet urged that the government should replace the National Health Service with a private insurance-based system for health care, cease state funding for higher education and stop linking benefits to inflation. These were highly controversial ideas, and because the CPRS was inside the cabinet machine it could reinforce popular views that Thatcher was out of touch with the lives led by ordinary people.

In reality these Conservative fears were misplaced. The lesson of the period after 1979 was to explode the myth that governments cannot survive extended periods of high unemployment. Labour was also far too sentimental to replace its leader. The main threat came from the linking in the public mind of Thatcher's reputation for failing to understand the problems of ordinary people with the CPRS proposal to remove large tracts of the welfare state. Thatcher hesitated, but after the CPRS report was leaked to *The Economist* she was persuaded to disown it.[82] She was also persuaded to pledge that 'the health service was safe in her hands'. For good measure she abolished the CPRS. This pleased her, as the CPRS had been set up by Heath, and it personified a technocratic approach to policy-making while she was more enthused by ideological imperatives.

As the election approached, the chancellor decided that a give-away budget would undermine the central appeal of the party, that it was fearlessly attacking Britain's problems. Unemployment continued to rise inexorably, reaching the 3 million mark in May 1983, just one month before the general election. And even the country's tax burden had increased in violation of a central thrust in Thatcher's 1979 appeal. On unemployment, the introduction in 1982 of both the Youth Training Scheme (YTS) and the Community Programme (CP) for adults, massaged the unemployment figures downwards by taking individuals off the dole for either training or a period of work-experience. Thatcher even acquiesced in the retention of the tripartite MSC, even though, uncharacteristically for her government, it gave the trade unions a voice in policy-making. She lessened the difficulty, however, by agreeing with her new Employment Secretary, Tebbit, not to renew the contract of Sir Richard O'Brien as chairman of the Commission. Before Tebbit's appointment the chairman enjoyed some autonomy, but after 1981 O'Brien's bifurcated view of his role as both the MSC's executive manager, and as a semi-independent expert offering advice on labour market policy, was at odds with Tebbit's position. Tebbit had no sympathy with O'Brien's self-image as an impartial chairman, neutral between government, industry and trade unions. Tebbit did not consult the CBI or the TUC before appointing David Young, who was then special adviser to the Industry Secretary, Patrick Jenkin, to the post of chairman. One commentator concluded that under Young's chairmanship the MSC would degenerate and its functions would be transferred to private job agencies.[83] This was a misperception which failed to understand that the MSC was a useful tool to reshape the labour process, change attitudes to training and manage the long-term and youth unemployment crises.[84] Despite the more direct control which the government was now taking over the MSC's activities, it 'remained the Corporate State personified', although 'few other bodies could have dealt with the emergencies'.[85]

Conservative Central Office set up nine policy committees which produced papers for inclusion in the 1983 manifesto. The work of these policy groups was ignored, however, and the party produced a shapeless manifesto which emphasised continuity in the battle against inflation and public expenditure. There was only a limited reference to privatisation, and the forward proposals were largely confined to a further assault on trade union immunities and on the independence of local government with the promise to abolish the Metropolitan County Authorities. Yet Thatcher lacked complete confidence, and despite a mass of advice suggesting that she call an early summer election in 1983, she insisted on waiting for the May local election results before deciding. The planning groups that she set up reveal a lot about Thatcher's style and demonstrate that Conservative leaders need only use the party's Central Office as much as they wish, since external advisers are often more valued. The groups she chose to consult included only a small number of ministers, for example Lawson and Joseph. The party machine was represented by Gordon Reece, Cecil Parkinson and Ian Gow, but other trusted advisers included Tim Bell and Michael Dobbs from the advertising agency Saatchi and Saatchi, which held the Conservative party's account for ten years until 1987, and a junior minister who was a passionate Thatcherite, Nicholas Ridley.[86]

While the rhetorical appeal in the election campaign was one of reaffirming toughness and resolution, as if the government had behaved with total consistency since 1979, it is evident that there had been tactical flexibility. The Department of Industry had continued to subsidise 'lame ducks' such as British Leyland, because it was calculated that to allow it to collapse would jeopardise ten parliamentary seats.[87] Howe has since asserted that it was the continuing need to write cheques to support ailing nationalised industries which convinced him of the need to accelerate privatisation by 1983.[88] There had also been the loosening of monetary control in the autumn of 1980. Above all, there was Thatcher's retreat when confronted by the National Union of Mineworkers in 1981. She strongly believed, along with the Coal Board president Sir Derek Ezra, whom Lawson describes as having 'in practice delegated the running of the industry to the NUM', that uneconomic pits had to be closed.[89] She reversed her proposal to do so, however, and it is difficult to contradict Gilmour's account that this was because 'stocks of coal were low, the miners clearly backed the moderate Joe Gormley (NUM president) and were ready to strike and the government was both acutely unpopular and ill prepared to take on the union which had brought down the previous Conservative government. Accordingly, Mrs Thatcher and the cabinet very sensibly executed a smart U-turn and surrendered to the miners.'[90]

The general election outcome was a foregone conclusion with the only speculation surrounding the size of the Conservative majority. This majority rose to 144, although there was a slight drop in the party's vote to 42.4 per cent, and the total popular vote of just over 13 million was 100,000 less than that secured in 1979. It is not valid to interpret the result, therefore, as a victory for Thatcherite ideological hegemony. While the government had some clear goals such as privatisation, it was Thatcher's style which dominated the election, and her style helped define the party's ideology rather than the reverse. The tendency for the government to drift for a period after the 1983 election suggests there remained a lack of policy clarity at this stage. On the other hand, the collapse of the Labour vote, the change in the party system that it implied and the lack of any major challenge on the political front, created the potential for the Conservative government to begin a process of sharper policy preparation for the future, based on fundamental Conservative principles.

4

THE LOST OPPORTUNITY? THATCHERISM IN POWER 1983–7

The second term of the Thatcher government from 1983 to 1987 is sometimes regarded as a lost opportunity. Given the size of the majority obtained by the party in 1983, the circumstances were certainly in place for a concerted drive to secure the consummation of the goals and values which Thatcher and her allies sought to achieve. It is suggested that because so little was achieved during her term of office there was a vast amount of 'catching up' to be done in the years after 1987.[1] While there may have been a lack of strategic coherence to the second term of the Thatcher government it is unconvincing to suggest that the years from 1983 to 1987 were wasted. Apart from the first few months when the government appeared to fall over a number of 'banana skins', the government used its majority to good effect. The suggestion that opportunities were lost after 1983 is based on the assumption that the Thatcherites had a clear blueprint of where they wished to go, when in reality her government was similar to most: policies emerged through an annual ad hoc process of determining programmes.

The view that the years from 1983 to 1987 were lost opportunities also disregards some of the circumstances which confronted the government. Michael Heseltine's ambitions were becoming more obvious and the difficulties which he created climaxed with his dramatic resignation in 1986. All governments find that their popularity is fragile, particularly if they neglect to avoid pitfalls which constantly lie in wait for them. The Thatcher government still had to address the 'unfinished business' of the challenge posed to it by the militancy of the NUM, and to recognise that a reforming Labour Party under the leadership of Neil Kinnock posed a more potent electoral threat than a left-wing Labour Party under Michael Foot.

The main error in the suggestion that the 1983 Thatcher government frittered away its chance to make a real impact on the country, however, is the degree to which it managed to promote its own positive agenda. The most enduring 'jewel in the crown' of Thatcherism is privatisation. It was during the second term that Thatcher triumphantly moved privatisation from being a mere experiment into a policy carrying great momentum. In any event, the party's main *raison d'être* remained that of retaining power, and the government managed the economy to ensure propitious circumstances by the 1987 general election.

APPOINTMENTS, DISMISSALS AND CONFLICT

It is evident that the diminishing band of non-Thatcherite or 'wet' Conservatives recognised the danger from their standpoint of a big election victory, which would be interpreted as a vindication of the government's strategy. During the 1983 election campaign, Pym had expressed concern about the dangers of the Conservatives securing too large a majority.[2] When in the aftermath of victory Thatcher dismissed him as Foreign Secretary, there remained no political interest, faction or group to save him. Pym had offended Thatcher by glorifying the term 'wet', which she had intended to be highly pejorative. After his dismissal he was singularly ineffective, however, and resorted to forming a factional group called Centre Forward which made little impact, producing a superficial book on his political ideology, *The Politics of Consent*, and opposing the abolition of the Greater London Council in the Commons in the autumn of 1983.

The senior posts in government were now reallocated according to Thatcher's personal taste. The loyal support of Willie Whitelaw was an important element in the government's durability. Thatcher appointed him as deputy Prime Minister in 1983, and he chaired cabinet committees and most crucially the so-called Star Chamber which she set up to arbitrate difficult-to-resolve disputes over the allocations of public expenditure between spending ministers, and between ministers and the Chief Secretary to the Treasury. Whitelaw's firm support for Thatcher, coupled with occasional checks upon her intermittent rashness, was crucial. As a former Heathite, and one-time sceptic about monetarism, he played a central role in Thatcher's capacity to defeat the 'one nation' remnants in the party's leadership. Thatcher once famously commented that 'every Prime Minister needs a Willie'. Many cabinet ministers of the time are now convinced that his role was vital and that when his restraining hand was removed after he was compelled to resign because of illness at the end of 1987, her political judgement went awry.

Thatcher replaced Pym at the Foreign Office with Howe, Lawson became Chancellor of the Exchequer and Leon Brittan was appointed Home Secretary. Pym's dismissal symbolised both the exhaustion of the 'one nation' tradition at leadership level and the social revolution that was taking hold of the party. One writer only slightly overstates the case when he describes the relationship between Pym and Thatcher with an anecdote. Pym once was alleged to have murmured to a receptive back bencher, 'we've got a corporal at the top not a cavalry officer'. This line was fed back to Downing Street. It did not enrage Thatcher, but merely confirmed her natural suspicions. 'Francis is just a snob', she said to her informant. For her, Pym epitomised 'in manner and class and . . . squireish paternalism . . . everything she wished to defenestrate from Conservative politics'.[3]

Pym's removal led to the demise of many of Thatcher's critics. Prior resigned in 1984, Heseltine in 1986, Biffen was sacked in 1987, and she even alienated former fans such as Tebbitt, who left the cabinet in 1987.[4] Some of these differences were personal and others had their roots in disagreements about policy. Prior made clear his differences with Thatcher when he urged greater social harmony, support for industry and sympathy for the European project, including membership of the European Monetary System (EMS).

Heseltine's disputes were the most profound. After his resignation in January 1986 his ambition to capture the party's leadership was barely concealed. He also published his own alternative Tory strategy, which while mainly focusing upon the need for an active and interventionist Department of Industry to revive manufacturing, demonstrated that there was still an alternative to the Thatcher government's economic strategy. He argued that Britain's industrial decline could be halted if the government formulated a national strategy to enable workers, managers and owners to respect each others' roles. He described *laissez faire* as 'romantic', 'impractical' and of little relevance to the Conservative Party.[5] Heseltine urged a 'caring capitalism' based upon partnership. Yet he was not a traditional 'one nation' Conservative. Not for him Lord Stockton's bewailing 'the sale of the family silver'.[6] On the contrary, he praised the privatisation that had taken place. He also advocated the sale of council houses and had been instrumental in promoting the policy when he had been at the Environment Department in the early 1980s. His main difference with the Thatcher government, other than the short-term crisis over the Westland affair and his dislike of Thatcher's style in cabinet, was over industrial intervention. He urged the British government to cease being a referee and onlooker and to become a partner of industry. He even claimed that the Thatcher government engaged in planning, but in all the wrong areas. The Department of Trade and Industry was 'up to its neck in business life' and was making commercial judgements by the hour. The MTFS also involved 'regimenting public expenditure programmes in precise quantifications for three years ahead'.[7] Heseltine also dissented from the government's view that the free market would be able to achieve full employment. In short, 'most modern governments play a bewildering role in the life of those that they serve. Even in the most open of societies, free peoples look for leadership, and expect their governments to make full use of the powers entrusted to them.[8]

Biffen's demise resulted from a television comment in May 1986 when he urged a 'balanced ticket' at the next election. This implied a shift away from radicalism to consolidation, at a time when Thatcher was losing support for her radical rhetoric. It also implied that Thatcher's successor should be a more balanced, moderate Conservative. She never forgave him for this effrontery.[9] Tebbitt's case is more complicated. The son of a jobbing builder, not remotely intellectual in his political approach, his political style was that of a street-fighter, which made him a politician after Thatcher's heart. Yet after she appointed him party chairman in 1986, to increase the forensic content of the party's propaganda, he emerged as her coequal, made little attempt to conceal his ambition to succeed her as Prime Minister and used the party organisation as an alternative power base to Downing Street.

EARLY SETBACKS

After its impressive election victory, the government surprisingly sank temporarily into a period when its political errors came to the forefront and there was much press speculation about 'banana skins'. First, the Commons disregarded the government's advice and voted for a pay increase for MPs.[10] Secondly, even Thatcher's own renowned energy and durability were temporarily thrown into question when she had to undergo laser surgery for an eye problem, and after the treatment failed she had to undergo a serious operation to deal with a detached retina. For a few days it appeared that Whitelaw might have to assume the duties of Prime Minister.[11] Thirdly, shortly after the election, the ennoblement of Willie Whitelaw led to a by-election in Penrith and the Borders in which there was a swing away from the Conservatives with their vote falling by 3 per cent.[12] Fourthly, there was an outbreak of strikes in the newspaper industry.

By the time of the so-called victory conference in October 1983 the party was in considerable disarray with new problems developing. Biffen, who was still a leading cabinet member, expressed strong doubts about the stated policy of Chancellor Lawson. While the chancellor was proposing tax cuts to be financed by swingeing cuts in public expenditure on such areas as housing, social security, agriculture and defence, Biffen claimed that savage cuts would prove politically and electorally impossible.[13] The Bow Group of Tory intellectuals also published a pamphlet criticising the government's 'patchwork' social policy which, it argued, avoided radical decisions about the future of the welfare state. Pym launched an attack on the government's economic policies arguing that even with an economic recovery the established policies would not make a substantial impact on the levels of unemployment. There was also political embarrassment about the infiltration of right-wing 'moles' within the party. The party chairman, John Selwyn Gummer, reacted to a report from the national advisory committee of the Young Conservatives which asserted that some of the party's candidates had close links with 'right-wing and fascist' organisations. Among those named was a candidate in a winnable seat in the 1983 election and two sitting MPs, Gerald Howarth and Neil Hamilton. Howarth's defence was embarrassing for the Prime Minister in that he quoted his support for her position that people were frightened about being 'swamped' by immigrants.

The most serious problem confronting the party was the Parkinson affair. He had been the successful party chairman before the 1983 election and a Thatcher favourite who had become Secretary of State for Trade and Industry after the election. It emerged that he had had a long-standing relationship with his secretary, who was expecting his baby. While only one MP had demanded that Parkinson step down there were growing whispers in the party. The affair dominated the newspaper headlines throughout the conference and he ultimately did step down after some political damage had been inflicted. All of these problems coincided with the election of Kinnock as the new young Labour Party leader and a marked revival of Labour's standing in the opinion polls as a result.[14] Even after the conference the government's claims about Britain's world standing and influence over the Americans were undermined when President Reagan ordered US forces to invade Grenada in October without consulting Britain. There were also mass riots in November to mark the arrival of the first American Cruise missiles on Greenham Common.[15] By the autumn the clarity of apparent Conservative dominance had become rather clouded.

THE PARTY AND THE STATE

It was less clear whether the nature of the party in parliament had changed after the 1983 election. Some new members were recruited from new right 'think tanks', but the main shift was the demise of the Tory knights of the shire and their replacement by professional career politicians interested in office, electoral success and security. Clearly, this implied a greater enthusiasm for political ideology than their predecessors had ever displayed. For example, Sir William Anstruther Gray as chair of the powerful backbench 1922 Committee had defined Conservatism in the early 1960s as 'merely a strong pound, strong defences and a healthy agriculture'.[16] Yet a senior Conservative in the 1983 parliament asserts that the newer breed of Conservative MP was still quite prepared to adopt any 'ideology thrown at them' by the leadership.[17] The party in the country had, however, long nurtured Thatcherite yearnings, and from the evidence of the delegates and speech makers at their annual conference, its social composition had been changing in a petit bourgeois direction since the 1960s.

There were changes in the machinery of government to facilitate an increased momentum behind the government's strategy after 1983. The fruits of the changes were not immediate, but the actual abolition of the CPRS and its replacement by the Number 10 Policy Unit, enhanced Thatcher's capacity to dictate the strategic direction of government policy. David Willetts, later to become an MP, was a member of the Policy Unit during this period, and the increase in ideological purpose which flowed from its establishment is suggested by his comment that two questions were asked about every policy paper which came before it. First, was there a less interventionist solution which has not been fully considered; and second, was there a less expensive option?[18]

Thatcher's direct control over Whitehall was not extended substantially in the second term, although more sympathetic permanent secretaries were appointed to run major departments. For example, Sir Peter Middleton replaced Douglas Wass at the Treasury. Thatcher was also accused of interfering in the selection of senior officials. An enquiry by the Royal Institute of Public Administration partly exonerated her. While conceding that she did not impose an ideological test (is he one of us?) of which she was accused, when senior civil service posts became vacant, it did suggest that she intervened unduly and sought the appointment of energetic individuals.[19] Yet she disappointed two of 'her people' in not pursuing a major structural change in Whitehall. Sir John Hoskyns and Norman Strauss favoured the appointment of senior civil servants from outside Whitehall on short contracts and with precise objectives. They argued that it was impossible to achieve the values of an enterprise culture with a traditional civil service.[20] Hoskyns had already predicted that there would be a lack of strategic clarity in Thatcher's second term if the government merely continued to respond to specific problems or symptoms, when what was required was a new system of decision-making and inter-departmental coordination.[21] Hoskyns viewed the problem from a managerial perspective and failed to understand the party political instincts and constraints which informed Thatcher's judgements. Yet if the cautious politician prevailed over the radical reformer in the early years of her government, Thatcher was to launch a radical restructuring of the state in her last term after 1987.

The government continued to alter the role of the local state after 1983. The party had included in its manifesto in 1983 a pledge to abolish the six metropolitan councils set up by the Heath government and the Greater London Council (GLC). The official reason was that these councils had few functions and had become redundant, but by 1981 all seven had fallen under Labour control and the GLC leader, Ken Livingstone, had become a popular focus of opposition to the government, with his headquarters at County Hall directly across the Thames from Westminster.[22] In the October 1983 White Paper, rational justifications were advanced for removing the upper tier of local authorities, such as reducing bureaucracy and waste and ending policy conflicts between the two levels. The functions previously carried out by the metropolitan authorities and the GLC were taken over by quasi-government authorities (quangos) or by joint committees. The precise pattern for the delivery of these functions varied from area to area, but the common feature was the removal of the principle of direct election.[23] Thatcher's government also attacked local government as part of its broader economic strategy to reduce public expenditure and to slim down the public sector. Yet it was only in the third term that a clearer vision of the direction that Thatcher wished local government to take became apparent, with the concept of 'the enabling council'.[24] While the detailed pursuit of the idea of the enabling rather than the directly providing council may only have appeared after 1987, the approach towards tightly controlling intergovernmental financial relations which culminated in the Poll Tax, began in the mid-1980s. Government decided that the control of local spending could only be achieved by a statutory limitation of rates. This led in the 1984 Rates Act to the introduction of general rate and expenditure capping.[25] Government also began its legislative process of forcing local authorities to open themselves up to competition and collaboration with the private sector during its second term. This began with the Transport Act of 1985, which provided for the deregulation of the buses.[26]

There are many instances of the complexity and lack of ideological clarity in Thatcher's second term in her attitude towards the role of the state. She claimed to have been influenced by Hayek's diatribes against the growth of the modern state. Yet it was evident that she was not a Hayekian neo-liberal anxious to construct a minimal state, since she also had a Burkean commitment to authority and order, and a moralistic preference for the family as the bedrock of capitalist society. Thatcher invoked the idea of working for the good of one's family as a justification for seeking personal gain and greater wealth. This desire for social order and for the preservation of those institutions which can promote it explains Hayek's reservations about British Conservatism, and of the limits to Thatcher's support for radical rather than traditional Conservative policy. Hayek feared that British Conservatives placed greater emphasis upon governing according to circumstance, even where it involved the exercise of arbitrary power, rather than on principle.[27] Some British Conservatives, particularly of the minority 'one nation' variety, are unmoved by Hayek's comments defining him as a Liberal, and his ideas as 'Conservatism dogmatised'.[28]

Thatcher's commitment to order and authority was evident in her second term in a number of policies. She rejected the libertarianism advanced by some vociferous elements in the party after 1983, particularly in the legalisation of drugs; and in Burkean terms she rejected such social rights as full employment.[29] She also enhanced state power in a range of areas. Some cabinet members sought in vain to try to soften her stance on the removal of trade union rights from employees of the Government Communications Headquarters (GCHQ) in 1984.[30] The abolition of the metropolitan authorities and their replacement by nominated bodies more easily controlled from the centre, together with centrally determined rate-capping, exemplified her enhancement of the power of the state. The security services also became more vigilant after 1983 with the surveillance of members of the Campaign for Nuclear Disarmament (CND), the Zircon affair which involved a raid on BBC Scotland to prevent a programme from being transmitted and the attempts to stop the memoirs of a former MI5 officer, Peter Wright, from being published in Australia.[31] There is little doubt that the tentacles of the Secret Service expanded in the 1980s as part of an official strategy.[32] Even that school of political analysis which claims that the British state is now so diverse and fragmented that the will of the centre cannot prevail, accepts that Thatcher's governments sought to centralise, even if its attempts are seen as being 'riddled with failure'.[33]

INDUSTRIAL RELATIONS

A further spate of industrial relations reform emerged in the second term of the Thatcher government and reflected a greater increase in state authority. The Trade Union Act of 1984 prescribed that the only lawful strikes were those which were endorsed by a majority of the workforce voting in a secret ballot. Trade unions were also required to elect their senior officials by secret ballot if their members requested it. The 1984 Act also addressed the political activities of trade unions by requiring them to hold ballots every ten years in order to determine whether members wished to continue with a political fund, generally used to finance the Labour Party.[34] There is evidence that although the greater use of ballots did transfer power to the rank and file from the leadership and reduced the incidence of strikes, the union members substantially voted to continue with political funds. A source of finance for Labour was not terminated, therefore, despite the Conservative government's best efforts.

The most dramatic episode in industrial relations during the second term was, however, the miners' strike. Thatcher was determined to avoid a repetition both of the early 1970s when she considered that the Heath government, of which she had been a member, had been humiliated, and of her own climbdown over pit closures in 1981. The Ridley Report of 1978 was an early aggressive Conservative response to the issue of how to react to challenges from the NUM.[35] Its leakage produced a furore. There is a telling anecdote that when Ridley went to apologise to Thatcher, she merely commented, 'never apologise, never explain'.[36] The real preparation for the strike, however, was undertaken by Lawson as Energy Secretary after 1981. He proudly describes the detailed actions which he undertook at that time to ensure that nothing was left to chance.[37] Coal stocks were built up at the power stations, alternative sources of energy were identified, the security services were prepared to become involved, a pseudo-national police force was mooted and a tough chairman, Ian Macgregor, was transferred from British Steel to manage the National Coal Board (NCB).

Lawson considers that it was the political challenge to the state which was the main reason for the government's fierce response to the NUM. It was the countering of this political challenge, rather than the need to insist upon a more commercial approach to coal production, the nationalised industries and the entire public sector, which was the main motive of the government. While the Conservative Party clearly wished to exact its revenge on the NUM, and defeat the one remaining industrial threat from organised labour, there are signs that the NUM General Secretary Arthur Scargill's motives differed from those of the miners. While the miners wished to preserve jobs and communities, even NUM sympathisers asserted that, for many union leaders, the 1984/5 dispute was 'a political strike with industrial arguments laced with syndicalist rhetoric'.[38]

While the government maintained the fiction that the dispute was between the NCB and the miners, the direct intervention by government was obvious. The Energy Minister at this time was Peter Walker, who admits that 'every day I phoned the Prime Minister at No. 10 and told her what was happening throughout the dispute. I had a close relationship with her . . . she backed me totally.'[39] It is apparent that Walker's relations with Macgregor were anything but smooth. The outcome of the dispute was never in doubt. Lawson's thorough preparations, together with Arthur Scargill's failure to hold a ballot to legitimise the strike through all regions of the country and with public opinion, ensured that the government would win. This outcome was made the more certain by the emergence of a conciliatory breakaway union, the Union of Democratic Mineworkers (UDM) representing the more profitable mining region around Nottinghamshire, and by a mild winter in 1984/5. Despite the courage and sacrifice of the striking miners they underestimated the power of the state under the will of a determined Prime Minister. The mineworkers' union lost 72 per cent of its members between 1979 and 1986, and the total number of trade unionists also fell from 13.5 million in 1979 to 10.5 million in 1986, shrinking to less than 10 million by the time Thatcher left office in 1990. 'Margaret Thatcher appeared to have slain another of her dragons.' The defeat of the NUM was a crucial symbol of her continuing triumph.[40]

The victory was traumatic for the left and the TUC, and seriously set back the Labour Party's recovery under its new leader. Kinnock could not support the government, but neither could he wholeheartedly support the NUM, both because it had failed to hold a ballot and because the dispute became violent on the picket lines. It was equally ironic, however, that the outcome of the strike did not provide any electoral gain for the Conservatives. Thatcher had crudely attempted to exploit the Falklands factor in her struggle with the NUM by describing it as 'the enemy within' in August 1984, but her ultimate victory against the miners after a year-long dispute was ambiguous. The miners continued to attract sentimental support from the British people, so her victory did not provide the dividends which might have been expected. The opinion polls turned against the government in 1985 and the Conservatives were heavily defeated at the Brecon and Radnor by-election in July 1985. The seat was won by the SDP/Liberal Alliance on a 16 per cent swing with the Conservative candidate beaten into third place. The result was described as the worst by-election defeat since 1962. Since the then Prime Minister, Harold Macmillan, had responded in 1962 with a cabinet reshuffle, it is ironic that Thatcher, who had prided herself on her departure from the behaviour of her 'wet' Conservative predecessors, resorted to the same stratagem. Convincing herself that the government's problems were to do with presentation rather than policy, she replaced Leon Brittan at the Home Office with Douglas Hurd and Tebbit replaced Selwyn Gummer as party chairman. Thatcher described Gummer as lacking 'political clout'. She supported Tebbit's role as party chairman with the appointment of Jeffrey Archer as deputy chairman. Archer's mission was to rally the rank and file because she perceived him to be 'the extrovert's extrovert'.[41]

There were other significant industrial disputes during Thatcher's second term. There were two years of intermittent industrial action by the teachers. MPs were thus able to blame government for neglecting children.[42] Joseph's position in government as the minister responsible for education was undermined by these disputes, despite his earlier role as Thatcher's mentor. The government also profited in terms of its own ideological agenda, however, by removing the capacity of the teachers to negotiate separately.[43] There were also strikes in the newspaper industry, but the combination of legislative muscle, heavy policing of pickets and the introduction of new technologies was sufficient to achieve the defeat of these strikers. The weakening of trade union power led to multinational, particularly Japanese, companies imposing single-union or no-strike agreements on workers. In any event the rise of unemployment, which was peaking in 1985, and the readiness of government to exploit it to undermine wage bargaining, intensified the weakening of the unions which the spontaneous changes in the labour market had begun. The overall result was the development of a very different pattern of industrial relations, with the rise of the unskilled service sector which offered part-time and mainly female employment.[44] It was estimated by the end of the Thatcher era in 1990 that the part-time and self-employed sectors of the economy had risen to 40 per cent of the workforce. The unions now had to reshape themselves by offering a new type of workplace support to a different clientele, and to communicate directly with workers in order to recruit members rather than rely upon the closed shop to deliver recruits.

PRIVATISATION

The control of inflation had been the central objective of Thatcher's first term in office, but the 'jewel in the crown' of her second term was undoubtedly privatisation. It was the momentum and success of this initiative, much emulated abroad, which belies the view that Thatcher wasted her second term in government. While the common belief that the government merely stumbled upon privatisation by accident is erroneous, only during the second term did privatisation become dominant. It was not until the mid-1980s that the government propagated the policy in the context of an ideology of 'popular capitalism', and refined the innovative methods of regulation with which the creation of private sector monopolies had to be accompanied in order to be credible.[45] There had been privatisations in the first term, of which the enforced competition between local government and the private sector is an example. The compulsory offer of the sale of council houses to sitting tenants is an early example of a form of privatisation in action. Fifty-five thousand council houses had been sold in 1979/80, and the figure increased to 204,000 in 1982/3.[46] Even during the years in opposition there had been enthusiastic proponents of denationalisation such as Lawson, Joseph, Howe, Nott and Howell. Privatisation had thus been a central plank in the Thatcherite programme from the beginning and the caution in the 1979 manifesto was the result of Thatcher's fear of frightening the voters.[47] Lawson takes the issue of privatisation as demonstrating that waiting for the approval of the electorate before launching a policy is a recipe for inaction.

There were two main aspects to the policy of privatisation: denationalisation and deregulation. Denationalisation involved the sale of assets owned by the state. It involved shifting private utilities into the public sector. By the 1992 general election about two-thirds of formerly state-owned industries in the United Kingdom had been transferred into private ownership. Yet the Thatcher government's motivation was only partly to increase efficiency and to reduce the extent of public subsidy. There were also financial, political and moral reasons.

Financially, the sale of assets raised money to sustain tax cuts, and it has been estimated that asset sales secured £19 billion between 1979 and 1987.[48] One junior minister in the government underlined this by likening the buying of shares to betting on horse racing and 'putting a few bob on a sure winner'.[49] His confidence was based upon the government's capacity to set the price of the shares at a level which people could both afford and which could guarantee them a profit whether or not the shares were retained or immediately sold to large City institutions. Politically, Thatcher hoped that the sale of shares would increase share ownership in society, entrench capitalist values more extensively and 'dish' Labour with those electors who wished to retain their shares and who would eschew voting for a party which threatened to re-nationalise newly privatised industries. Lawson argued in 1985, for example, that those who feared mass democracy in the nineteenth century were afraid of the behaviour of voters who had no stake in the country. 'But the remedy is not to restrict the franchise to those who have property; it is to extend the ownership of property to the largest possible majority who have the vote.'[50] This would presumably entrench 'popular capitalism'. Privatisation was also a policy which served to unite all elements in the party. The moral dimension of privatisation was encapsulated in the idea that it would increase individual enterprise and personal vigour, or in Thatcher's words 'reverse the corrosive effects of socialism'.[51] Privatisation also fitted Thatcher's simple moral idea that business should be run by businessmen not government.

The first major privatisation to be announced was that of British Telecom in 1982. Even here the process had begun in 1981 when Joseph, who was then still at the Department of Industry, split BT from the Post Office, removing its monopoly over telephone sales and licensing Mercury to compete with it.[52] The employees disregarded the advice of their union leaders and bought shares in large numbers. Complicated systems of regulation were instituted alongside privatisation, however, and the formula calculated for BT was subsequently refined and developed after 1983, and extended to other firms. The various regulatory bodies established, for example, the Office of Telecommunications (OFTEL) for BT, and OFGAS for the gas industry, were required to apply the formula of the Retail Price Index (RPI) minus x, in proposing annual price increases.[53] This was to ensure that price rises were below the level of the cost of living. The state remained highly active in the management of the privatised industries, therefore, and some even contest that state control was more intrusive after privatisation than it had been before.[54]

The most audacious privatisation was that of British Gas, sustained by the media success of the 'tell Sid' campaign. 'Sid' was presumably a streetwise working man. Walker at the Energy ministry actively persuaded the advertising agents to avoid the type of middle-class campaign of which the City might approve, 'but would be meaningless to the ordinary bloke in a three bedroom semi-detached house'.[55] It is evident that with the issue of privatisation, Lawson and other ministers were convinced that they had discovered the counter to the traditional Tory fear of mass democracy, and that 'people's' or 'popular capitalism' was the best way of making the world safe for both property and Conservatism. The mass sale of assets, often under-priced to ensure the success of the flotation, certainly did the Conservatives no electoral damage in the second term, but the theory was ultimately proved to be fanciful, because privatisation did not result in the spread of share ownership that had been anticipated. In 1991 over 80 per cent of the shares in British firms were owned by institutional investors, a proportion that had grown in the Thatcher years.[56] The rapid sale of shares by individuals had implications for Thatcher's stated objective of extending share ownership and establishing a truly popular capitalism. By 1990 'the number of shareholders in British Airways which was privatised in 1986/7, had fallen from over 1,000,000 to less than 350,000 while share ownership in British Gas reduced from 4,407,079 to 2,780,813. Share ownership in Rolls-Royce also declined, falling from 2,000,000 to 924,970.'[57] For the rest of the Conservative government's period in office it remained unclear whether it wanted the new private companies to be highly commercial in their operations, milch cows for the Treasury or experiments in the restructuring of industry.

Privatisation in the form of deregulating the public sector was aimed at increasing consumer choice, opening up local government and the public services to the market and increasing efficiency by compulsory competitive tendering. This required public organisations to test the provision of their services against the challenges of the market and the private sector. This ending of monopoly provision in the public sector was compatible with public choice theory, but as with many policies, it produced unintended consequences at the implementation stage. The majority of the contracts were won by the public sector, and the process of winning contracts for particular bundles of work often increased the solidarity and autonomy of specific units at the expense of highly paid managers.[58] The ultimate conclusion of the policy was to transform local government into being merely an 'enabling' mechanism, although this concept was only advanced explicitly by the government after 1987.[59]

ECONOMIC POLICY

The second term of the Thatcher government was interesting as it led to the abandonment, if not of monetarism *per se*, then of the rigorous quantity theory of money through the setting of targets. Thatcher astonished the public with her comment in January 1985 that she had never been a monetarist believing in the setting and achievement of targets.[60] Lawson clarified matters in his Mansion House speech. He proclaimed the end of the M3 target and argued that the behaviour of the narrowest measure of money, MO, the exchange rate and the actual inflation rate itself were more important. Clearly this reflected an internecine battle within the monetarist school, rather than the total abandonment of monetarism. In fact, it was in order to provide a framework of monetarist discipline that Lawson attempted, unsuccessfully, to persuade Thatcher that Britain should enter the Exchange Rate Mechanism (ERM) of the European Monetary System.[61] However, a doctrinaire monetarist faction sought to portray Lawson as having abandoned monetarism, instead of merely the £M3 measure after his Mansion House speech. Clearly, if monetarism was meant to depoliticise the battle against inflation, it failed. It not only required an interest rate strategy which was economically rather than politically determined, much to Thatcher's chagrin, but it also led to serious disagreement within the monetarist camp. This was at the root of the clash between Alan Walters and Lawson in 1988 which contributed towards the destabilisation of Thatcher's leadership. Since the tight monetarist targets were now regularly loosened, the case for monetarist theory had been tested and found wanting.

Lawson's definition of supply-side economics was more acceptable, however, which is why it influenced the government's thrust towards greater labour market flexibility in the second term. Supply-side economics involved lowering taxes in order to increase incentives and increasing deregulation of the labour market to ease restraints upon employer flexibility. It was in his important Mais lecture in 1984 that Lawson defined his new economic orthodoxy, which had the effect of inverting the Keynesian strategy which had been unpopular in Tory ranks for decades. Basically Lawson reassigned the two arms of macro- and micro-economic policy. 'It is the conquest of inflation and not the pursuit of growth and employment, which is or should be the objective of macro-economic policy.'[62]

Lawson did instigate one policy which, while compatible with his Mais pronouncement in seeking to improve economic performance by creating more employment through enhancing competitiveness, actually made the attainment of monetary control more difficult. The Financial Services Act of 1986 introduced self-regulation in the Stock Exchange, but also facilitated greater competition between banks and building societies, leading to a credit explosion in personal finance. This expansion of credit further contradicted the government's previous desire to limit the growth in money. While at one level this was merely a theoretical problem, in practice it helped undermine the government's strategy against inflation. It is little wonder that Lawson had so little faith in his own government's stewardship of the nation's finances that he thought it necessary to enter the ERM. If his lack of confidence was warranted, however, 'membership of the ERM would not be a substitute. Indeed, the belief that it could be a substitute could actually lessen the determination to follow appropriate domestic macro-economic policies.'[63]

It was also in the second term that some of the consequences of the removal of capital controls came home to roost. While British business may have expanded abroad by 1986, two popular British businesses, British Leyland (which manufactured Land Rovers), and Rowntrees, were bought up by foreign companies. Many have suggested that this is a serious contradiction at the heart of Thatcherism: a commitment to nationalism alongside the free flow of international capital. Gamble argues that the Thatcher government's economic policies 'ended the prospects of any restructuring based on the traditional manufacturing sectors and regions. By reasserting the traditional international orientation of British economic policy the government gave priority to the maintenance of the openness of the British economy over the protection of domestic industry . . . This policy favoured those sectors which were already dominated by transnational companies . . . Despite the efforts of a few ministers the government gave little support to developing manufacturing and research capability.'[64] The contradiction is not a real one to Conservatives, however, and Gamble appears to neglect the fact that the interventionist and statist strategy which the maintenance of traditional British manufacturing companies would have involved was alien to the Conservative ethos. Churchill, for example, had combined free-market economics with intense patriotism, and a leading Conservative claims that the imperialist and nationalist writer, Rudyard Kipling, deplored wartime economic controls.[65] Yet Gamble, in suggesting a contradiction between economic internationalism and political nationalism, is correct to detect a dissonance between Thatcher's later enthusiasm for the free movement of capital in Europe and her intense desire to retain national political sovereignty. In short, if there is a contradiction it is not confined to Thatcherism, but lacerates the history of the British Conservative Party. It is likely that patriotism takes precedence for the ordinary member, but a commitment to neo-liberal economics has priority for most of the leadership.

One possible contradiction in economic policy in the course of the second term was the emphasis upon reducing public expenditure on the one hand, in parallel with an enthusiasm to preside over increases in spending during the public expenditure round in November 1986. The policy departure in 1986 can be explained by the imminence of the general election and the party's desire to reassure those who accused it of undue severity towards public services. Seven and a half billion pounds was added to the expenditure plans for the next fiscal year, and there were to be spending increases in politically sensitive areas such as health and education and more generous pay settlements for teachers and nurses. The contraction in higher education which Joseph had planned was reversed by the new Secretary of State Kenneth Baker.[66] This added a note of compassion to the more general government message of toughness and resolution. The economy was now beginning to 'boom' with little sign of the inflationary overheating which was to come later. This promised well for the forthcoming election, after the difficult period of 'mid-term blues' from which the party suffered.

MID-TERM BLUES

One symptom of the party's problems was its financial deficit. By June 1986 there was a party overdraft of £1.5 million and problems at the grass roots were evident in the failure of constituency associations to meet their financial quotas. Some constituency parties, notably Edward Heath's in Bexley, paid nothing in 1985/6, and nationally only £892,000 materialised out of an expected £1.8 million from constituency associations.[67] There was also a growing concern that the party was becoming too dependent upon company donations which were being raised by the Conservative Board of Finance under Sir Brian Wildbore Smith, because of the possible conflict of interest which they might create. While the board did not actually sell honours directly to tycoons it was noted that honours frequently followed munificence towards the party's funds. The replacement of Lord Sanderson as chair of the National Union of Conservative Associations provided an opportunity for a new chair who would place fund-raising at the top of the agenda. Yet in other respects the party was seeking to broaden its appeal to demonstrate that it was not simply the party of business, and was making overtures to new groups such as the ethnic minorities.[68]

Norman Tebbit improved the party's campaigning when he assumed the party chairmanship and there were attempts to link themes in direct mailing initiatives, party political broadcasts and major speeches.[69] Yet a series of problems assailed the government in 1985 and 1986. There was, for example, the resignation of Ian Gow as a Treasury minister in protest against the Anglo-Irish Agreement of 1985. He considered the involvement of the government of the Republic of Ireland in tripartite arrangements together with the British government and politicians from Ulster to be a concession too far towards nationalist opinion. This deprived Thatcher of her best and most honest conduit of opinion from the Conservative back benches. There was also the defeat of the government over the proposed reform of Sunday trading in April 1986 which was caused by nervousness on the back benches in the face of a campaign by Christian activists in the constituencies; the American raid on Libya using British bases in the same month; the capture of the Federation of Conservative Students by extreme libertarians who advocated such measures as the legalisation of heroin; and the loss of the Fulham by-election in April 1986 to Labour's Nick Raynsford. Raynsford's style foreshadowed the type of New Labour candidates who appeared in the 1990s.[70] Many of these episodes simply excited the 'chattering classes' rather than the masses, particularly the arcane Westland affair, but they suggested a measure of governmental ineptitude.

The Westland affair warrants a longer analysis despite its secretive nature. While it can be interpreted as a curious and untypical event, it both reflected and intensified divisions in Thatcher's government and led indirectly to her ultimate downfall. Even during the event itself, in January 1986 it threatened her very survival.

Westland was a firm which manufactured military helicopters. It ran into financial difficulties in 1985. As it was the last British firm operating in this area there was political capital to be gained by keeping the firm alive with a measure of British ownership. Thatcher and Leon Brittan, her minister at the Department of Trade, were happy with the only offer of a partnership to rescue the Westland company, which came from the American firm Sikorsky. It was part of the United Technologies conglomerate, which was seeking a European base. Thatcher and Brittan were content both because of Thatcher's belief in the Anglo-American relationship and because the Sikorsky bid resulted from the operation of market forces. The Defence Secretary, Heseltine, was both pro-European and an economic interventionist, and he favoured the construction of a rival European consortium to rescue the company. He repeatedly tried to raise the issue at cabinet meetings in December 1985, but was prevented from doing so, and the cabinet's agreed position was one of neutrality between the rival bids. Over the Christmas and New Year break in 1985 Heseltine continued to canvass business and political support for a European deal which many thought violated cabinet policy and so breached the constitutional doctrine of collective cabinet responsibility. As Heseltine continued to campaign publicly against her policy, Thatcher got the Solicitor General, Sir Patrick Mayhew, to write a letter complaining about the 'material inaccuracies' in Heseltine's campaign. This phrase was a real benefit to the anti-Heseltine camp and Brittan discussed with his private secretary the possibility of leaking the letter to discredit Heseltine. Brittan was enthusiastic but wanted Downing Street to leak it.[71] Within hours selective passages were leaked to the Press Association. This was done by the Department of Trade and Industry's chief press officer Colette Bowe, but the action was later explained as having received 'cover' from Downing Street, from Thatcher's own press secretary, Bernard Ingham. The next day the *Sun*'s front page featured Heseltine with the headline: 'You Liar.' Mayhew was outraged at the leaking of what he had understood to be an internal and confidential letter and demanded an immediate enquiry into the source of the leak, even threatening Thatcher with the police if she refused.[72] It was days later, however, before she acceded to an enquiry. On 9 January Thatcher informed the cabinet that all future statements about the Westland issue had to be cleared with her office. Heseltine was not prepared to accept this restraint so he literally walked out of the cabinet. Thatcher remained cool during this moment of drama and immediately announced that George Younger would take over the post of Defence Secretary.[73] It is unclear whether either or both Thatcher and Heseltine had sought the resignation.

Immediately after his resignation Heseltine summoned a press conference. He complained about the way the affair had been handled, rejected the outcome and declared that Thatcher's methods of government and cabinet control were 'not a proper way to carry on government and ultimately not an approach for which I can share responsibility'.[74] Brittan subsequently misled the House of Commons on important details of the affair and had to apologise. He later resigned on 24 January 1986, admitting that his continued role in the government would weaken its effectiveness.[75]

Matters came to a head on 27 January when there was a full-scale Commons debate on the issue. There are anecdotes suggesting that Thatcher was afraid that she would be forced to resign. She was saved by a long and ineffective speech by Kinnock. Tory MPs sought to disrupt his speech and succeeded in doing so, leading him to complain, 'once again, Conservative back benchers have decided that, because they cannot take the truth, they will try to bury it'.[76] The SDP leader, David Owen, posed more searching questions about the affair stressing that, 'the question that the Prime Minister has not answered is what conversations took place in her private office between her and Mr Ingham and her principal private secretary, Mr Powell', as 'the decision to leak a document written by law officers is a very serious decision'.[77] Owen also quoted a damaging comment of Mayhew in which the Solicitor General expressed 'dismay that a letter containing confidential legal advice from a law officer to one of his colleagues should have been leaked in a highly selective way'.[78] If Heseltine had any intention of joining a parliamentary attempt to oust Thatcher, then Kinnock's disappointing speech dissuaded him. Instead Heseltine appeared ready to mend fences, saying that 'I heard the Prime Minister clearly say that she deeply regretted the fact the letter had been leaked. She went on to say that a number of other matters could have been better handled, and she regretted that, too.' He also confessed that 'I have no doubt that the things that I did are open to criticism.' He drew the curtain on the affair by asserting that Thatcher's speech had brought 'the politics of this matter to an end'. He rubbed Labour's nose in it by adding that in the previous decade the House had never listened 'to a worse parliamentary performance than we heard today' from the opposition leader.[79] Labour's former leader Foot scathingly contrasted Heseltine's condemnation of Thatcher when he resigned to the speech that he had just made, asserting that 'It's all right to rat, but you can't re-rat.'[80]

The problem with the debate from the opposition's perspective was that it could not prove the central charge, that Thatcher had directly leaked Mayhew's letter. The Labour MP Tony Benn came closest by pointing out that, 'Bernard Ingham was my press officer for some time and I know a little bit about him. He is a very tough customer but he would never dare to agree to betray a cabinet minister without the authority of the Prime Minister . . . I do not believe for one moment the account that has been given. What happened was that the Prime Minister used some powerful words – "who will rid me of this turbulent priest?" – and the rest was done by civil servants to rid her of the Secretary of State for Defence.' He went on to claim that 'Thatcherism, which the Rt Hon. Lady created and believed in, is a myth. People are asking whether that myth is capable of leading the Conservative Party to victory at the next election. The Conservative Party is looking for a new leader.'[81] Yet Thatcher did not fall at this stage. 'Her survival owed much to a combination of the poor performance by Labour, the lack of a challenger and economic recovery . . . As with the challenge of 1981, the threat to her leadership had remained purely speculative.'[82]

If Thatcher held on to office the immediate political effects were serious. Coming during what was already a difficult period, the Westland affair seriously dented the popularity both of her government and of her personally.[83] Her personal position was damaged in a number of respects. Heseltine's attack on the way she ran her cabinet hit home. It became widely appreciated that she was much given to 'handbagging' her ministers to the detriment of cabinet government. The Westland episode also demonstrated mismanagement at the heart of government. When the cabinet secretary Sir Robert Armstrong appeared before the Defence Select Committee of the Commons in February 1986, he agreed that it was 'strange' that Thatcher appeared ignorant of the leaked letter, admitted that the leak should not have happened and spoke of a 'direct disagreement between one government department and another'.[84] Thatcher also lost two able cabinet ministers. Brittan was a loss because he was a loyal supporter. It is interesting that the post-Westland reshuffle gave the cabinet a less Thatcherite appearance. Brittan's departure was accompanied by the retirement of Joseph and his replacement by Kenneth Baker at Education, in addition to the promotion of Kenneth Clark to Employment, Malcolm Rifkind to Scotland and the higher profile assumed by Hurd as Home Secretary. It was Heseltine's departure, however, which was the most serious loss because it unleashed on to the back benches not simply a potential critic but an obvious, and newly unconstrained, rival for the party leadership. Finally, the dispute over Westland was significant because it rehearsed the bitter arguments which were later to break out over Britain's role in Europe. These arguments were central to the events which led to Thatcher's downfall in 1990, and to the disastrous defeat for the entire party in May 1997.

While it can certainly be argued that the intricacies of the Westland affair were closely followed only by the political *cognoscenti*, many sections of the intelligentsia had never been reconciled to Thatcher's leadership. Two events reveal that there was endemic conflict between her government and some sections of the social establishment traditionally associated with the Conservative Party. This does not support the common misconception that Thatcherism marked a departure from Conservatism, but indicates that it was now much more in alignment with Conservative rank-and-file activists, rather than the party's traditional allies in 'the establishment'.

Opposition to Thatcher patently emerged from Oxford University when its dons refused her an Honorary Doctorate. The subsequent election of Lord (Roy) Jenkins as Chancellor of the University demonstrated that the Oxford elite remained more comfortable with the intellectually tired 'better yesterday' offered by the SDP than with the intellectual cutting thrust of pure right-wing Conservatism.[85] The Church of England, often regarded as the Conservative Party at prayer, also expressed a growing discomfort with the social consequences of government policy and the divided nation which it feared was the result. Its report 'Faith in the City' asserted that 'it is arguable that rich and poor, suburb and inner city, privileged and deprived, have been becoming more sharply separate from each other for many years, and that the impoverished minority has become increasingly cut off from the mainstream of our national life'.[86] Government ministers felt that the Church had committed *lèse-majesté*, that it should confine itself to the issues of the 'next world' and one cabinet minister even described the Church's document as 'Marxist'.[87] While Thatcher affected scorn at her intellectual critics she was more troubled by her conflict with the churches. As a childhood Methodist and professed Anglican, she was concerned about the opinions of the churches, and as a Conservative was aware of the historic role of religion as a source of social stability. It was to answer these anxieties that in her third term she delivered her 'sermon on the mound' to the General Assembly of the Church of Scotland. Her vision of Christianity was evidently individualised, solitary and other-worldly.[88] Ultimately, Thatcher was more interested in the views of the voters and, to a lesser extent, the Conservative activists, than the ideas of the intellectual and social elite.

PREPARATIONS FOR THE 1987 GENERAL ELECTION

The claim that the Westland affair was of little enduring political importance is best supported by the Conservative Party's remarkable recovery during 1986, which culminated in a successful party conference in October, and the public expenditure increases in November. 1986 was, like 1981, a pivotal year in the history of Thatcherism. In each of the two years the party and its leader were unpopular and vulnerable in the early part of the year, but in a position of dominance as the year closed. The specific theme of the 1986 party conference was 'The Next Move Forward', which aimed to demonstrate that the Conservatives remained the party with ideas, momentum and future-orientation. This positive re-launch resulted largely from Thatcher's post-Westland establishment of a strategy group to 'review political developments and consider new initiatives'.[89]

The appointment of Tebbit as party chairman in place of Gummer should have given Thatcher more direct control over the party's preparations for the 1987 election. The relationship between the party chairman and the party leader is always crucial. Leaders normally seek to appoint sympathetic figures to the chairmanship particularly in the period leading to a general election. No sooner had Tebbit inherited this key position, however, than relationships were soured by Thatcher's fear that Tebbit was using his position in Conservative Central Office to advance his claims to the succession. 'This was the background to Mrs Thatcher's decision to put Lord Young into Central Office to assist Mr Tebbit . . . and to the tensions and "wobbles" over strategy during the election.'[90]

There was even confusion over which advertising agency was acting for the party. After the triumphant cooperation between the party and the Saatchi and Saatchi agency in the 1979 general election, relations deteriorated in succeeding election campaigns, a phenomenon which continued up to the 1997 debacle.[91] The problem in 1987 was that Saatchi and Saatchi offered unwelcome advice to Thatcher about her own and the party's failings in public relations and so she arranged for an alternative firm, Young and Rubicam, to undertake research on her behalf. She also consulted Tim Bell, who had worked for her before when he had been at Saatchi's. The rivalries between these three alternative elements working on the same campaign leaked to the press. It was a curious situation in which the party's advertising agents had become the expression of the intra-party structural splits, and the phenomenon is a clear demonstration of the way in which a determined Conservative leader can sideline the party's central bureaucracy at will.

Thatcher took the lead in the preparation of the party's manifesto, but delegated the precise writing of it to a small sub-group under John Macgregor, the Chief Secretary to the Treasury. The other members were Professor Brian Griffiths from her own Policy Unit, together with some sympathetic journalists.[92] The manifesto appeared to get to the kernel of Thatcher's convictions about the empowerment of the people, and included proposals to reform education, housing, local government finance and trade unions in support of this central radical theme. *The Next Move Forward* was a lengthy document and reflected the shift from the bland manifesto of the previous general election. If Thatcher suffered from hubris in office after 1987, most of the policies which led to it were described in the 1987 election manifesto. Local government was to be shorn of its powers in housing, education and planning. The Community Charge was described as the replacement for domestic rates. There were to be further privatisations, such as electricity and water, more share ownership, tax cuts and trade union legislation. Council tenants were to be given the right to change their landlords and to replace council ownership with Housing Action Trusts, and parents and teachers the opportunity to opt out of local authority control of their schools. Finally, both public expenditure and borrowing were to be heavily reduced.[93]

The rivalries which characterised the campaign were damaging. Lawson is convinced, for example, that there was an attempt to exclude him from the campaign, but he got involved independently and was responsible for the effective challenging of Labour's taxation and expenditure policies, and undermining their credibility.[94] Labour fought a good media campaign, however, which was televisually very attractive. An opinion poll one week before polling day suggested that the gap between the two parties was closing.[95] This fed Thatcher's anxiety about the slickness of Labour's campaign and her fear that the Conservative campaign was unfocused, and produced 'wobbly Thursday'. Thatcher describes this as a bitter row culminating in a 'ding-dong' with Tebbit. He attributes the row to the advisers of Lord Young, arguing that they were unduly pessimistic about the true state of the party's campaign and were excessively protective towards Thatcher's concerns, which led Young to panic. Young himself admits to losing his temper with Tebbit.[96]

The outcome of the 1987 election was never in doubt. Some commentators were puzzled at the anomaly of voters informing pollsters that they preferred better social welfare and higher taxes while voting for a party proclaiming the opposite goals. The data compiled for the Conservatives by Young and Rubicam suggests that electors distinguish between what is good for the country and what is good for themselves. They focus on the national interest in responding to pollsters, but act on personal or 'pocket book' factors in the privacy of the polling booth.[97] Certainly, many of the radical proposals in the manifesto were a minority taste, and it is because elections are a blunt instrument for determining popular preferences on specific issues that the Conservatives could both win the election, and become unpopular for subsequently implementing their manifesto proposals. Voters paid little attention to manifesto proposals anyway, since a sunny mood of affluent optimism, almost a re-run of the 1959 campaign, accounted for some of the Conservative vote. The economy was flourishing, and even satirical attempts to suggest that Tory materialism and the 'yuppie' culture which it spawned were vulgar, misfired. When one comedian introduced an affluent but offensive and foul-mouthed plasterer called 'loadsamoney', who constantly waved his wad of bank notes at the audience, he captured the optimistic mood of the times rather than damaged the Conservatives. City wine bars and the construction of Canary Wharf in the old London docklands symbolised the new wealth. Yet this prosperity was regional and focused particularly on the south and Midlands of Britain. The Conservatives made fewer electoral inroads in Wales, Scotland and the north of England. This explains why Thatcher appealed to sections of the skilled working classes, the C2s according to the Census Office, by connecting with their aspirations for self-improvement. This gave her an 18 per cent lead over Labour among manual workers in the south-east. In fact, in 1987 '40 per cent of council house owners voted Conservative, virtually the same as the Tories' global share of the vote; only 25 per cent of council house tenants did'.[98] While many middle-class voters who worked in the public sector defected from the Conservatives as never before, as they now felt beleaguered, Thatcher was aware that their votes were split between Labour and the SDP and Liberal Alliance. In any event, a coalition of private sector middle-class voters and significant elements of the working classes, even if it only comprised 43 per cent of the electorate, was sufficient for her to win power. Throughout the 1980s Thatcher's Conservative Party was a clear beneficiary of the traditional 'first-past-the-post in single member constituencies' system of voting.

The radicalism of the Conservative manifesto would have alienated some of the support that the Conservatives achieved in 1987, but the contents were only evident to 'political junkies'. For example, few were affected by the press conference in which Thatcher appeared to support the re-introduction of fee-paying in opted-out schools. Thatcher admits to using 'public statements to advance the government and push reluctant colleagues further than they would otherwise have gone. In an election campaign this was certainly a high-risk strategy.'[99] Baker believes that she inserted the issue of fee-paying into the campaign because she was seeking to return to a 'battle that she had already lost and wanted to keep the question open'.[100]

As with the general election result in 1959 this was a third consecutive victory for the Conservative Party with a 100-seat majority, and even though in 1987 the majority fell rather than increased, it was from a far higher base line. The 1987 result was also a personal triumph for Thatcher since in 1959 there had been three different leaders in each of the successful elections. The only disappointment for the Conservatives in 1987 was their continuing failure to make inroads into the deprived areas of the country. Thatcher recognised the position in the cities, and at the central office victory party said, 'we have a big job to do in some of those inner cities . . . to help the people get more choice and politically we must get back in there'.[101] Her remark was more an expression of political regret that her ideology had not captured the total dominance that she sought, rather than any intention of diluting her policies to apply new public spending to regenerate the inner cities.

The 1987 victory appeared to justify those journalists given to using the term Thatcherism and to proclaiming its triumph. While many of her government's policies had been long in gestation, held greatest appeal to the party's activists, were about style as much as content, were often expressed in the most reductionist terms by Thatcher for a television audience and were only endorsed by 43 per cent of those voting, the future appeared to be hers. The idea that Thatcher had wasted the period from 1983 to 1987 has no foundation in the evidence.

CHAPTER

5

THATCHER'S FINAL TERM: 1987–90

Thatcher's final term began in triumph with a third successive electoral victory, and ended in disaster with her enforced ousting by her own cabinet. She patently contributed to her own political downfall, and it was her own hubris which led to her tearful removal from Downing Street, complaining that 'it's a funny old world'. Given her three successive victories she could be forgiven for believing that her ideological hegemony had been established. In the immediate aftermath of her victory, while she deplored the loss of a few inner city seats and pledged to do something to remedy the economic and social problems in these areas, there was a calm period in which none of the hyperactivity which came to characterise her third term in office was apparent. A Stock Exchange collapse in October 1987 also threatened to put the brake on her reforming ardour. For reasons not fully explained, but related to the curious psychology and infection-prone behaviour of international speculators, shares lost much of their value in the course of one day. Lawson's response was to raise interest rates by 1 per cent. As inflation was beginning to 'take off' at this point more substantial increases could have been justified, but the government was afraid of a recession undermining the 'boom' that it had helped create before the 1987 general election, and refused any further interest rate rises. This was the start of a series of economic errors, which let to a major recession, substantially created by the policies pursued in numbers 10 and 11 Downing Street.

The Stock Exchange crisis passed, however, and Thatcher launched upon a series of policy decisions which were more ideologically determined than some of her more cautious tactics before that date. It was not merely the shift towards a more radical Conservative agenda, the plethora of legislation which resulted from it, or even the speed with which this agenda was implemented after 1987 which signified the over-confidence which was now affecting government. What was significant was that while before 1987 most of the reforms had addressed broadly economic areas of British life, after 1987 Thatcher blithely turned her attention to transforming civil society and experimenting with some of her prejudices about the welfare state.

THE IMPACT OF EVENTS

The triumphalist mood within the party was understandable, but it sometimes led activists to encourage Thatcher to move further and faster on policy innovations than her instincts told her she should. There was the boost to the confidence of party activists of a third election victory, even against a 'slicker' Labour Party under a new young leader. To add to this domestic political success, there was the growing evidence during Thatcher's third term that her message was spreading, as delegations visited Britain to consider the possibility of transferring the policy of privatisation to their own countries. The same encouragement could be derived from Eastern Europe with the weakening and ultimate collapse of Communist regimes.

It was with the case of the Community Charge, which became universally described as the Poll Tax, that party activists became particularly assertive. The original proposal had been for a dual-running tax in which rates would be phased out and the Poll Tax introduced. Dual-running was completely abandoned as a result of pressure from the delegates at the 1987 party conference. With vast but unjustified political confidence, the delegates convinced themselves that the Poll Tax would be popular, and as a result of their noisy demands and their loud cheers for speakers who urged the immediate introduction of the tax, party leaders decided to introduce it in one step. This was the wrong decision. As one cabinet minister put it, 'the conference had not the slightest idea of the consequences of what it had done. They had the illusion that the Community Charge was so perfect that the nation was just thirsting to take it down in one gulp.'[1] He added that the only other time the conference had changed government policy was when it made the commitment in 1952 to build 300,000 houses a year. In the case of the Poll Tax, however, the government disregarded the advice of the opposition, many of their own back benchers, members of the cabinet including the Chancellor of the Exchequer, Whitehall and even its own previous analyses of the proposal which had been assisted by expert opinion. Thatcher had the enthusiastic backing of her Environment Secretary, Nicholas Ridley, in abandoning dual-running, and he has been described as regarding the unpopularity of a policy as proof of its correctness, and believing that 'sticking to your guns is a virtue regardless of the issue'.[2] Even sections of the Conservative press issued warnings about the tax's unpopularity. *The Economist* argued that it was curious that a measure completely unrelated to economic management should be regarded by Thatcher as 'the flagship of her administration'.[3] It added that the unease felt by her back benchers was a warning that the voters would exact their revenge upon her government.

In general, however, it was Thatcher who pursued radical instincts in the period after 1987 without prompting from her party. The passion for a fundamental reform of the National Health Service (NHS) was driven through despite the doubts of her once favoured successor, John Moore, at the Department of Health and Social Security. More significantly, she disregarded the advice of both the Treasury and professional opinion in insisting upon the introduction of tax relief for private medical insurance for the over-sixties. Lawson opposed the concession on fiscal grounds. He also understood that it would help those who were already disposed to invest in private health care and so would not expand the size of the sector. Yet despite overwhelming opposition from the public, the professionals and the Treasury, Thatcher was determined to reduce the demands placed on the health service by the vulnerable older end of the population.[4] Despite repeated reassurances from ministers that the NHS would remain free at the point of delivery, the reforms were unpopular with the voters. Thatcher knew that she was never going to defeat Labour on the issue of the best party to provide health care and so there were fewer votes to be lost specifically on this area of policy than in most others.

These two examples of a radical challenge to two of the pillars of the previously assumed consensus in society: that there should be a link between taxation and the ability to pay, and that the NHS was a sacrosanct institution, helped to undermine Thatcher's popular appeal. Yet far more damaging was what was happening in the economy. The country's economic performance after 1987 was also undermined by Thatcher's style. This was because of her tendency to have favourites, which led to dissension in the economic policy-making process, which in turn damaged international confidence in the British economy. If prosperity had been the key to Tory electoral success, the appearance of a second economic recession in a little over a decade, threatened Thatcher's standing in both party and country.

This chapter reviews some central areas of policy after 1987, such as education, training, health, privatisation, the changing boundaries of the state, the Poll Tax, Europe and the economy. This does not exhaust the hyperactivity of Thatcher's third term, but covers the most significant areas. There were many other legislative concerns in the final term and it can be argued that the scale of legislative intervention, which was uncharacteristic of Conservative governments, also alienated swathes of voters. Examples of this last category of policy-making 'on the hoof' are the Dangerous Dogs Bill which predictably led to tabloid headlines about 'dogs on death row'; the Football Supporters Bill, ultimately modified under pressure, which required all casual football supporters to join a football club and to possess an identity card, and the legislative clause which banned local authorities from engaging in activities which could be construed as encouraging homosexuality.[5] The vendetta against local government continued, while the Conservatives suffered politically from rising crime during this period as well as from an outbreak of prison rioting. The rioting was embarrassing because of the acknowledged overcrowding in British gaols and the official policy of sending offenders to prison for offences which, in most other European countries, would receive a non-custodial sentence. A whole series of prison riots broke out after 1987, but the most spectacular was that at Strangeways, Manchester. On 1 April 1990 prisoners took over the gaol and held it for three and a half weeks. The Home Secretary, Kenneth Baker, promised better sanitary conditions and less overcrowding as well as a new serious offence of prison mutiny.[6] There were also bizarre security events, such as the attempt to publish a book by a former secret service officer, Peter Wright, which had already appeared in many parts of the world. After long and fruitless litigation both in Britain and Australia, the case went to the European Court which found against the government's attempt to prevent publication. Thatcher embarrassed the cabinet secretary, Robert Armstrong, by sending him to argue the case in the courts. He admitted in court to being 'economical with the truth'.[7] While Thatcher could indulge herself in this incident to defend the principle of secrecy in government and to relish upsetting the secret service and the mandarinate, the affair ultimately rebounded to the discredit of her government, with Armstrong perceived simply to be doing her bidding.

EDUCATION AND TRAINING

In 1986 the government was ready to turn its attention to education reform and Thatcher had begun to listen to the Hillgate Group which was concerned to protect traditional schools and elitist standards. This had the effect of reducing the influence of Lord Young, with his desire to enhance vocationalism and technical skills. Thatcher acknowledges that the detail of education policy was far from being worked out when she surprised those present at an election press conference on 22 May 1987 by suggesting that an incoming Conservative government was prepared to consider encouraging schools to leave local authority control, and even to charge fees within the state system of education. This led Tebbit to stress that opted-out schools would continue to be state schools, and while Thatcher endorsed this position she did so in the context of praising grammar schools.[8] In fact, some aspects of the measure to reform education were being amended as the bill proceeded through the House of Commons. The idea of reforming education had been emerging on to the political agenda even before Baker was moved to the Department for Education and Science (DES) in May 1986. Ideas were already gestating within government, for example, Joseph's concern with improving quality and standards and Tebbit's advocacy of a credit system at local level to enhance the satisfaction of parental 'customers'.[9] Many of the main ideas in the Education Bill, which was introduced into parliament at the end of 1987, emerged through discussions between Thatcher and Baker. The City Technology Colleges which were industry-sponsored and free from local education authority (LEA) control had already prepared the way before 1987, but other ideas – the national curriculum, opted-out direct grant schools, the *ersatz* voucher scheme where schools would be entirely funded by the number of children whom they attracted through a system of open enrolment, the national system to test all children as a check both on their individual progress as well as on the comparative performance of the schools themselves, the incorporation of the polytechnics and their consequent removal from local authority control – all emerged over a period of time and were incorporated in the one major bill. The extent to which the measure was motivated by the animus against central government rather than the desire to reform the education system is debatable. A leading minister in the government has since suggested that one of the problems with the final stage of Thatcher's last government was an obsessive preoccupation with local government.[10]

Baker was convinced by the new Conservative orthodoxy on the declining standards of state education and he also accepted the theoretical analyses of many New Right thinkers about the undesirable motives and consequences of having large numbers of employees in public sector organisations. He approached the reform with the view that comprehensive schools had lost their way, and that only testing could retrieve standards. Thatcher and Baker were both convinced that the DES was in thrall to the professional educational interests. Baker thought that the department accepted the comprehensivisation of schools as it had been captured by the producer interests of the trade unions and the LEAs, with the inspectorate, itself recruited from the same background, acting as the high priesthood of the system.[11] Thatcher regarded education as one of the fields in which the interests of publicly funded professionals were too powerful, resulting in 'a secret garden of cosy consensuality'. The Education Act, which involved the largest recasting of the British education system since the portmanteau Act of 1944, reached the statute book in July 1988. Its main consequence was to change the control of British education, with a diminished influence for LEAs, teachers and 'informed' educational opinion. The gainers were theoretically school governing bodies which acquired more direct control over their own affairs through the Local Management of Schools (LMS) or by direct opting out.[12] In reality, the government's wish that school governors should reflect local community interests, particularly business, and that they should check out complacent teachers, failed. This was because few governors understood or wished to discharge their new functions. In practice, head teachers 'managed' governors.

The upshot of the 1988 Education Act was a characteristically Thatcherite 'mixture of free-market ideology and state control'.[13] Further reforms followed in the aftermath of this legislation. To aid the consumer to make the right choice in the market place, the DES required schools to publish league tables, in which GCSE and A-level results became the main feature. Obviously schools in favourable and more middle-class catchment areas were advantaged, and the consequence was that parents simply chose to send their children to already oversubscribed schools in smart residential areas.

Other reforms emerged after 1988 including the expansion of numbers in higher education, but this was without a commensurate increase in resources, and was accompanied by the freezing of student grants and their replacement by student loans and the setting up of two funding councils to finance higher education. Thatcher was ambivalent towards this last development, however, as she feared that the funding councils would degenerate into lobbies for more money.[14]

Training policy had been dominated by the tripartite Manpower Services Commission which continued to operate even after the 1987 election, with Norman Fowler the new Employment Secretary giving it responsibility for a new mass training scheme to mop up the high numbers of long-term adult unemployed. This was Employment Training (ET). The TUC concluded that ET was inferior to previous adult training schemes, such as the Community Programme in 1982. This was because ET was based on the receipt of benefit plus a small top-up rather than a proper wage, and because it delivered an uncertain quality of training. As a result the TUC was reluctant to support the scheme, and after the 1988 TUC conference the trade union members of the Commission were unable to sign up to ET. This marked the end of even a toehold for the trade unions in the policy-making process, and also of the MSC serving a useful purpose of legitimising government labour market policy. Fowler was now convinced of the need to abolish the MSC and to investigate new mechanisms to provide training schemes. This marked the demise of the last substantial tripartite and pseudo-corporatist body in British government.

The MSC was replaced in due course by eighty-two Training and Enterprise Councils (TECs), across England and Wales, which were locally based and employer-led. TEC boards were able to circumvent local authority and trade union representation. As a new experiment in policy implementation, they have developed as rather bizarre hybrid organisations. They are private companies, but depend upon public funding through their main customer, the Employment Department (ED). While they are encouraged to seek autonomy in the preparation of training and enterprise policies locally, they are largely reliant on the government for their income, and are closely audited for the way in which their money is spent and for the achievement of targets set by government. They have had varying degrees of success, and have mainly continued to deliver mass training schemes rather than launch exciting new initiatives, but some have been condemned for a loose control over public money.[15]

HEALTH AND SOCIAL SECURITY

The health service reforms have many similarities with the reform of education with money following patients in a more market-sensitive system than previously. General Practitioner (GP) fund-holding and opted-out National Health Service (NHS) hospital trusts bear some resemblance to opted-out grant maintained schools. Owing to the popularity of the NHS, Thatcher proceeded cautiously. In 1982 she had responded to the CPRS report by declaring the safety of the NHS with her government, and in her memoirs recognised that, 'the NHS was a huge organisation which inspired at least as much as it exasperated . . . and whose basic structure was felt by most people to be sound'.[16] Left-wing critics of the government were fearful that the intention was to privatise the health service when in 1988 Thatcher ordered the establishment of a major review. The fact that the review consumed a year, that it saw off one minister and required direct intervention by the Prime Minister, indicates the difficulty the government faced in trying to reconcile its declared goals of equity, efficiency and cost-cutting.

Organisations such as the Institute of Economic Affairs (IEA), the Conservative Political Centre (CPC), the Centre for Policy Studies (CPS) and the Adam Smith Institute (ASI) urged a far greater involvement by the private sector in health care. Yet Thatcher was cautious about privatising initiatives, since free health care for all at the point of access was a principle which was politically difficult for the government to breach. The alternative was to simulate the market mechanism as far as possible by introducing a system of internal markets involving local health authorities buying and selling services from each other. Most significantly, this would involve separating the purchaser from the provider: the purchaser being the health authorities or GP fund-holders and the providers the trust hospitals. The internal governmental NHS Review was published in January 1989 and was patently influenced by the ideas emanating from the radical right-wing organisations.[17] Underpinning the policy was both an emphasis on consumer choice and the operation of the market, but there was also an implicit attack on the medical profession.[18]

If the educational reforms proved an uneasy blending of market and statist elements, the NHS reforms produced less of an incentive and market-driven programme and much more a bureaucratic and audit-led process. Labour was able to thrive on the argument that it would shift

NHS employees towards bureaucracy and management and away from front-line health care during the 1997 general election campaign. There was also a decline in equity in health care provision after the reforms were implemented, as GP fund-holders and more financially sound hospital trusts were best placed to provide high-quality care. One former Thatcherite who switched his allegiance to Labour early in the 1990s condemned the reforms as 'a bureaucratic apparatus of internal markets that is both costly and inefficient, diverts scarce resources from patient care and threatens the autonomy of the medical profession . . . this experiment in imposing market forces on the NHS through the agency of a managerial revolution from above has been a ruinous failure'.[19]

The reforms in the social security system related closely to those in the area of health. The government's goals were to use the welfare system to target those in greatest need, to encourage self-reliance, to end the so-called dependency culture and to cut expenditure on social security. These were to be achieved by instituting a system of loans rather than grants for hardship payments, denying young people support unless they participated in approved training schemes and requiring the unemployed, later euphemistically redefined as jobseekers, to prove that they are looking for work in order to be entitled to claim benefit.[20] This anxiety about dependency was particularly characteristic of new-right thinkers who feared that it created an 'underclass'. While the desire to avoid dependency is eminently sensible, it neglects those vast sections of the population who are unable to cope: children, pensioners, the sick and disabled and the involuntarily unemployed. Lawson does not conceal the fact that the Thatcher government was united in the view that families with large numbers of children, or unmarried mothers, were the authors of their own misfortunes.[21] Ridley expressed the sentiment with the claim that for single mothers to put themselves 'in that position as a way of living, deliberately eschewing the husband's role in the family by not having one is clearly undesirable'.[22] The desire to abolish the dependency culture also mistakenly assumes that there are no barriers to opportunity in society on the basis of race, gender or other established forms of discrimination. The reforms in health and social security are evidence of the Conservative Party's distaste for much of the postwar welfare state, and of a desire intensified by the new right-wing theories of the period, to seek to change civil society as well as the economy.

PRIVATISATION

Privatisation was the breakthrough of the second term of the Thatcher government. The policy was continued after 1987, but as with the reforms to the welfare state, it took the government into new and more dangerous territory, as more difficult privatisations were attempted. The response to the proposal to privatise water after 1987 was muted in contrast to the storm of protest which this proposal had evoked in 1986 when it had led to an outcry on the part of customers, regional water authorities, anglers and environmental interests. While a majority remained opposed in 1990, in 1987/88 the opposition was modest compared to 1986.[23] This change in the political mood must have further encouraged the government to believe that its ideological hegemony had been established. Yet some in the Conservative Party continued to believe that because it was a natural monopoly, water privatisation was undesirable.[24]

The privatisation of electricity was complicated by the determination of the minister, the redeemed Cecil Parkinson, to institute competition in the industry. While the lack of competition in earlier privatisations had been a flaw, it was difficult to establish competitive arrangements in an industry, such as the generation of electricity, which relied on a single national grid. Lawson convincingly argues that it was only through the process of privatisation that the unprofitability of the nuclear power industry was made apparent. The process revealed the unsaleability of assets which would involve enormous costs through the need to decommission old plants. This is only partly true, because Thatcher's own personal prejudices in favour of nuclear energy, and the proselytising role of Sir Walter Marshall at the Central Electricity Generating Board (CEGB) also served to conceal the true costs of nuclear power generation. The former Energy Secretary from 1983 to 1987, Peter Walker, had also strongly entrenched nuclear power as a central feature of policy. He had formed the policy of the Energy Department as one in which nuclear power was thought to be the safest option and a necessity to 'solve the energy problems of the next century'.[25] Lawson argues that it was this very element of state ownership, protected by Whitehall policy interests, which caused the lack of enlightenment about nuclear power.[26]

Parkinson was determined not to take electricity to the market as a highly regulated monopoly.[27] He discovered that his pledge to the 1987 party conference that the industry would not be sold off as 'one vast monopolistic corporation' was well received.[28] He took the precaution of discussing the issue in detail with Brian Griffiths in the Policy Unit to ensure Thatcher's continuing support, and introduced competition by subdividing the CEGB into two generating companies, PowerGen and the larger National Power. The privatisation of water and electricity demonstrated a readiness to tackle the hardest privatisations and not just the soft targets. More ambiguously, however, it was becoming apparent that there was a contraction in post-privatisation share ownership. Contrary to the aspirations for a 'popular capitalism', in reality a 'process of concentration of privatised shares in the key City institutions has taken place'.[29]

THE CHANGING BOUNDARIES OF THE STATE

Thatcher was unusual among British politicians in conceptualising the role of the state. She even disliked the term 'public policy', as she claimed that she wished to confine the 'public' arena to as narrow an area of life as possible. It is also evident, however, that it was the local state which in practice she most deplored, and she was happy to increase the power of the central government to restrain the activities of the local authorities. Thatcher was also critical of the welfare state because of its costs, its tendency to crowd out the private sector and its removal of individual responsibility by its generation of a dependency culture. She was also an economic free marketeer, although she would sometimes breach this principle if it produced outcomes which she deplored. In place of an interventionist state she proposed 'an enterprise culture'. Her frequent invocations of the need to 'roll back the state' should be 'unpacked', however, to appreciate her true intentions.

In her early years in Downing Street she placed little emphasis upon restructuring the British state. In her first two terms she had supported the introduction of new managerial devices in Whitehall ministries to ensure that ministers could better control their departments, and to encourage efficiency, economy and effectiveness. She had imported Sir Derek Rayner to carry out a cost-cutting programme through an Efficiency Unit. While she never engaged in improprieties she took a greater interest in senior civil service appointments to bring Whitehall more under the control of the elected government. This principle was made clear in 1985 following the Ponting affair, in which a senior civil servant leaked documents showing that a minister was lying. In its aftermath the cabinet secretary stated unequivocally that civil servants did not have a 'constitutional personality' in which they can place a duty to some entity of the public good over their responsibility to their minister and the government of the day. Thatcher also presided over a reduction in the number of civil servants, and in 1990 the civil service was 23 per cent smaller than it had been in 1979. But despite such interventions, the 'old civil service was still recognisably in place' in 1987.[30]

It was during the third term that Thatcher began to address fundamental philosophical questions about the exact role, boundaries and functions of the state. Even then it took the promptings of Sir Robin Ibbs, who had taken over the running of the Efficiency Unit from Rayner in 1983, to galvanise Thatcher into action. The unit had gone as far as it was possible to go with tinkering on the margins and by 1986 it had either to wind up its work or produce something more substantial. It was Kate Jenkins, who was the assistant to Ibbs, who came up with the *Next Steps* report. Ibbs endorsed it and sent it to Thatcher in 1986, but owing to its scale and its sensitivity she shelved it until after the election. It was in February 1988 that she announced to the Commons her intention of implementing the *Improving Management in Government: The Next Steps. Report to the Prime Minister* by the introduction of the principle of agencies in government.[31] This did constitute a serious change in the structure and organisation of the civil service. One commentator remarked that 'Next Steps is more like a report from a management consultancy firm than a civil service review. It is bold, glossy, evangelical. The traditional mandarin style . . . has been replaced by a fresh passion for revitalisation and change . . . It is predicated on the belief that there is an important discipline of management which has been mistakenly overlooked by the civil service in favour of traditional policy skills.'[32]

The basic principle of the report was that management and the delivery of services to the public should be differentiated from the central function of providing policy advice to government. To that end agencies would be set up to work on a contractual basis with its sponsoring department of state, and to provide outputs and services within the resources envelope with which it would be provided. The contract was to take the form of a framework agreement. Chief executives were to be remunerated according to their ability to produce quality services and employed on short-term contracts the renewal of which would be dependent upon their performance. A two-tier civil service was thus being established. A core civil service would continue enjoying job security and career development alongside 'a peripheral staff employed on a wide range of employment conditions'.[33]

Sir Peter Kemp was transferred from the Treasury to carry out the process of creating the new Executive Agencies. He was a true believer and later fell foul of the minister appointed to oversee him. His vision was to reduce the state to Victorian proportions, and he regarded the new Executive Agencies as transitional, since many of their functions could be transferred to the private sector. He thought it appropriate to free up ministerial and senior civil service time to develop policies, and to introduce competitive efficiency and managerialism into the implementation of policies to the public at street level.[34] Whether Thatcher understood the full potentiality of the Next Steps initiative was not clear, but Kemp's vision would have been ideologically attractive to her. In short, a managerial initiative to address the problem that 'the civil service is too big and too diverse to manage as a single entity, is being turned into an ideological assault upon the expanded state and in a manner fully consistent with traditional British Conservative scepticism about the state'.[35] As with her attack on the professional ethic in education and health, this reform undermined the established government ethic of public service.

Thatcher's government, assisted by Kemp's enthusiasm, set about the task of the agencification with gusto, and in five years ninety-seven agencies had been set up employing over two-thirds of the civil service. Many agencies were small, but some such as the Benefits Agency, the Employment Service and the Prison Service employ tens of thousands.[36] These agencies have been given discretion on issues of recruitment and pay levels, and although agency employees remain as Crown Servants, each agency is encouraged to develop its own character.

In practice the distinction between policy-making and policy implementation has broken down. There is little point in the sponsoring department setting targets without consulting the chief executive of the agency in order to agree on attainable outcomes before precise targets are finalised. Nor in practice has it been possible for ministers and sponsoring departments simply to opt out of events for a full year when a framework agreement and a quantity of resources has been negotiated. In sensitive areas such as unemployment, for example, there has been a good deal of central intervention in the performance of the Employment Service. It has not been realistic for government simply to opt out.[37]

There has also been controversy on the issue of the collapse of accountability. If 'policy' and 'operations' are separated then responsibility for maladministration is blurred. There have been several cases which cause concern. In 1995, for example, after a series of break-outs from prisons it was the chief executive who was forced to resign. The Home Secretary, Michael Howard, considered that it was entirely an operational issue even though there was evidence of his intervention. At other times accountability has been entirely evaded by both ministers and chief executives.[38] The multiplicity of complaints about the work of the Child Support Agency was such that ministers could not hide entirely behind their chief executives. Some slight enhancement of accountability has been added through the appearance of chief executives before the relevant parliamentary select committee.[39] This has been dismissed by Mike Fogden of the Employment Service, however, as merely a 'spectator sport'.[40] There is a conflict between departments and agencies, with departments anxious to maintain their established monitoring role. But with agencies now given the responsibility to make their own financial bids in the public expenditure round, there is a further questioning of the purpose of traditional departments. The rise of inter-departmentalism, and of special task forces to address specific policy problems in the interests of obtaining 'joined-up' government under the Blair administration, may further challenge existing departmental arrangements.[41] It is apparent that the civil service at the start of the millennium is a very different entity from what it was in the mid-1980s, and bears the stamp of the Thatcher style and ethos. It is consistent with Thatcherism that the constitutional ground rules of ministerial responsibility were not re-thought to address the problem of the democratic deficit created by the reduction of ministerial responsibility for the work of agencies.

Thatcher's final term also witnessed the extension of quangos, but most innovatively the introduction of a new hybrid in the form of the TECs. Their function has already been discussed but their impact on the changing character of the British state is also significant. They involved the circumvention of local authorities and trade unions and were entirely new instruments in the British system for policy implementation. They are hybrids because they are private companies, but they survive through public money and act on behalf of the newly merged Department for Education and Employment (DfEE). They are also, like the Executive Agencies, heavily audited for the way in which they spend their money and for the achievement of the targets that government sets them. They emerged as partnerships between government which continues to sponsor them and the business community which dominates all their boards. If tripartism, involving trade unions, died under Thatcher, then a form of bipartism relating business and government took its place. The TECs are engaged in 'the private government of public money'.[42] Despite a public accountability problem, TECs were patently conceived to align with the enterprise culture which Thatcher wished to nurture.

THE POLL TAX

The most contentious piece of legislation in Thatcher's final term in office was the Community Charge. This description never captured the imagination, and the less flattering title of Poll Tax proved ubiquitous. The tax provoked strenuous opposition even in such unlikely places as the streets of Tunbridge Wells. The riots in Trafalgar Square and elsewhere suggested a breakdown in public order, and as a result some militant Marxist groups claim to this day that they brought Thatcher down.[43]

The proponents of the tax were quite clear about their motives. Thatcher had long opposed the rating system and remained determined to replace it even though investigations in government departments during her time in government had pointed to the impracticality of a Poll Tax. Paradoxically it was the political situation in Scotland which precipitated the Poll Tax. Middle-class Tories in Scotland had been badly hit by the rating revaluation and rebelled at their conference in May 1985. The Poll Tax was invented by Madsen Pirie of the Adam Smith Institute and himself a Scot, and Thatcher thought it a good solution to the clamour which Scottish Conservatives were raising. As a result, the Poll Tax was introduced a year early in Scotland. The charge that Scotland was being used as a 'testing ground' because of Thatcher's antipathy to the country is not valid, and while the tax was unpopular in Scotland, it generated more hostility south of the border.[44] The myth that Thatcher was uninterested in Scottish sensitivities may have derived from the low support which this quintessentially English politician received there, and from her own admission that there was 'no Thatcherite revolution in Scotland'.[45] She did not make a practice of 'piloting' policy there, however, because of any antipathy to Scotland.

Thatcher disliked the rating system because she thought it a non-Conservative practice as it redistributed wealth away from those who used local services on a limited basis, such as old people living alone, to substantial users who, if they were on benefit, did not pay any rates at all. Accountability was lacking, therefore, and the best check on high-spending local authorities was to spread the process of controlling local councils to the entire electorate. Thatcher is convinced that had the Poll Tax been persevered with, it would have become, 'one of the most far-reaching and beneficial changes in local government ever made'.[46] While there is a self-deluding failure to recognise that in the circumstances of 1990 it was politically impossible to maintain the tax, it is likely that had the tax been introduced in the phased manner, based upon the dual-running of Poll Tax and rates for the transitional period that had originally been envisaged before the excitements of the 1987 conference, it would have become embedded. Introduced in one decisive step, however, the Poll Tax was evidently revealed as regressive and unpopular. While it may be an exaggeration to argue that the Poll Tax evoked altruistic and socialistic impulses in the electorate, as the fiercest opposition came from those whose bills increased, there was a mood of injustice in the country over the tax. Thatcher had hoped that it would play badly for the Labour Party as it was likely to be their councils which would wish to levy a high charge. In reality, because the tax was being introduced by a Conservative government it became known as a 'Tory tax'. Thatcher seemed to believe that 'by appealing over the heads of the political establishment to her people – the ordinary house owners of suburban and rural England – she would be vindicated. She was wrong.'[47]

Many ministers and MPs in marginal constituencies soon tried to distance themselves. This had been anticipated by Whitelaw who once emphasised his view that the tax was 'TROUBLE'.[48] Lawson regarded the entire proposal as 'unworkable and a political catastrophe'.[49] While Lawson can legitimately claim always to have opposed it, others now argue that if the tax had been introduced in the form in which they wished, it would have been successful. Even Thatcherite MPs were compelled to recognise the political reality. Alan Clark noted 'the Community Charge has got on everyone's nerves of course, and generated the most oppressive volume of correspondence'.[50] Baker later claimed that 'the tax would have survived if the system of dual-running had continued, exemptions made for all young people under twenty-one and a large rate support grant provided to the local authorities to allow them to cushion the bills in the first year'.[51] Even a right-wing Thatcherite minister posited his support for the tax on the assumption that the rate should not be too high.[52] He asserted, 'I never saw it as a revenue raiser; indeed, I believe I suggested at the time that another source of revenue might be necessary in addition to the Poll Tax.'[53] He acknowledged that a tax with flat-rate payments was unfair without an appropriate system of rebates.

The White Paper, *Paying for Local Government*, was introduced in 1986 and prescribed the Poll Tax. The initial reception was not very hostile, which again suggests that had it been introduced more circumspectly it could have endured. At the 1987 conference, however, every delegate who spoke on the subject urged that dual-running should be removed, and Thatcher was picked up on camera mouthing to Ridley, 'We shall have to look at this again'.[54] Lawson remains unapologetic about his refusal to increase the rate support grant more substantially in 1989. By this stage he was convinced that, despite Thatcher's caution on many matters in which she rejected his more radical ideas, for example, removing the dock labour scheme, which remained in place as a flagrant piece of outdated trade union privilege; and her reluctance to increase interest rates when the monetarist case for doing so was overwhelming, on the Poll Tax she was reckless and domineering. He offers three reasons for his refusal to facilitate the tax with a larger grant to local government. First, his macro-economic policy was to reduce central government expenditure. Secondly, there was no good reason for throwing public money at a tax that was fundamentally flawed. Thirdly, the theoretical justification for the tax had been that it was through the constraints of accountability to the local electorate that the extravagance of local councils would be prevented.

As the Poll Tax was viewed as a Conservative imposition, and local government did not receive criticism on the subject, it impacted upon the government's standing. Thatcher accepts that the mid-Staffordshire by-election result in March 1989, in which Labour won despite a 19,000 majority for the Conservatives two years earlier, was directly attributable to the Poll Tax.[55] While some earlier Thatcherite policies, which had at first seemed impractical, were carefully designed in order that they could be fully implemented, the Poll Tax was riddled with practical and operational difficulties. It 'embodied every known feature of a bad tax. It was wholly unfair . . . it was expensive; it was difficult to collect.'[56] One obvious administrative consequence of the tax appears to have been entirely neglected by government. While the rates were paid by 14 million people, the Poll Tax had to be collected from

38 million people. But as many people moved, removed themselves from the electoral register, and went into hiding, much remained uncollected. If local authorities pursued the non-payers it would be a very costly legal process, and if they raised the costs of non-payment to those who were paying then the problem was worsened for the majority. In short, the tax was impractical, unfair, unpopular and inefficient.[57] It had the one logical advantage of accountability, as it removed the principle of representation without taxation because of the millions who used services but did not pay taxes. This was the very characteristic of the tax which was removed, however, as, mistrustful of local government, the government retained the power to cap the tax.[58] One detailed study of the episode considers the tax to be the single most disastrous decision taken by a postwar British government.[59]

Revolutionary Marxist groups, such as Militant and the Socialist Workers Party, who claim that the public demonstrations and civil disobedience campaigns involving non-payment of the tax brought Thatcher down from office, take too mono-causal a view of both the fall of Thatcher in 1990, and the replacement of the tax in 1993. Thatcher's downfall was brought about by the cumulative effect of the actions of the 1987 parliament, and the Poll Tax was removed because it was a thoroughly flawed and unworkable piece of legislation. If much of Thatcher's legislation was compatible with traditional Conservatism, the Poll Tax added some uniquely Thatcherite perspectives.

THE EUROPEAN ISSUE

The European issue was catapulted to the top of the political agenda in 1988 by Thatcher's remarkable Bruges speech in which she re-established Euroscepticism in the party. It is now apparent that although Thatcher presided over the parliamentary endorsement of the Single European Act in 1986, to remove barriers to the movement of capital and to create a single market, she regarded it as the apogee of European integration. She misunderstood the conception of the other major European leaders, however, which was that the process of integration would go still further. Thatcher either stands accused, therefore, of changing her mind dramatically between 1986 and 1988, or of insensitively failing to understand precisely what other European leaders were seeking to achieve. It was also likely that a single market would inexorably lead in time to a single currency, if not to a single political entity, so Thatcher again displayed signs of naivety. One of the leading Eurosceptical MPs in the 1980s, Bill Cash, was somewhat more aware of the implications of the Single European Act. After initially welcoming it unreservedly in the early stages, he switched before the final reading of the bill in the Commons to table an amendment, which insisted that 'nothing should derogate from the sovereignty of the British parliament'.[60] The Bruges speech contained some extreme statements, although it is now apparent that the Foreign Office greatly softened the first draft of the speech which Thatcher's aide in Downing Street, Sir Charles Powell, had written with her cooperation.

Many contemporary commentators had assumed that she was expressing a widely held view, but others consider her speech to be recidivist, by re-legitimising arguments which had long since been disposed of within the party. The impact of the Bruges speech demonstrates the capacity of leaders to move issues to the top of the political agenda by highlighting them. In reality, the issue was largely dormant in the party in 1988, but was certainly one of underlying concern to some MPs and activists. The problem was that the case for the surrender of some British sovereignty in the interest of a more effective Europe had never been properly made in an easily digestible form; although Macmillan, Home and Heath may have addressed it in rather intellectual language.[61] The suspicions of a united Europe had a long lineage in the party, 'entering the bloodstream in the 1950s'.[62] Since it was a Conservative government which actually took Britain into the European Community in 1973, the protests in the party were quite limited until Bruges. Nor were all Conservatives consistent in their reaction to the Bruges speech. Thatcher considered that for Britain to join the ERM would involve a further drastic step in the direction of national surrender. Yet Lawson both favoured Britain's early membership of the ERM for purposes of economic management, and sympathised with the nationalist suspicions towards the European Community (EC) which Thatcher expressed. For this reason, if Thatcher was awakening dormant anti-European instincts in the party then Lawson considers that she was at least being sensitive to the feelings in the party at the time, and suggests that there were similar reservations in continental Europe which their Christian Democratic leaders were ignoring. In summary, there were viscerally held objections within British Conservatism, as well as populist instincts in the country, against the loss of British sovereignty to a European super state; but it is also true that the Bruges speech re-ignited the intra-party controversy. It certainly caused serious problems for John Major over the Maastricht Treaty in the early 1990s.

The charge that Thatcher was inconsistent in supporting the Single European Act and then delivering the Bruges speech is partly valid, but some events did intervene which partly explain her apparent *volte face*. Two of the justifications which she advances are questionable as they should have been as apparent before 1986 as in the following years. First, there was the unattractiveness of the 'un-British combination of high-flown rhetoric and pork-barrel politics which passed for European statesmanship'. Secondly, there was the growing domination of the Franco-German axis, the exclusive focus upon Western Europe at a time when the East was gradually becoming liberated, together with a commitment to a mega-state at a time when the Soviet Union's collapse demonstrated the futility of such organisations.[63] The certain catalyst for her speech was, however, the remarks of the president of the European Commission, Jacques Delors. His comments constituted 'a full-frontal challenge to the British leader's opinion, not merely of Europe but of the liberal *zeitgeist* she was bent on infusing into the new age'.[64] Delors even predicted that within a decade 80 per cent of the laws affecting the economy and social policy would be passed at a European and not a national level. The offence was exacerbated for Thatcher by the appearance of Delors at the TUC conference in 1988, in which he held out the prospect of his working with the trade unions to undermine the Thatcherite achievements of economic, social and labour market deregulation, through European institutions. This almost converted the TUC from a sceptical to a pro-European stance overnight.

The Bruges speech depicted Europe as a threat to all that Thatcher believed that she had accomplished for Britain: 'We have not successfully rolled back the frontiers of the state in Britain only to see them re-imposed at a European level, with a European super state exercising a new dominance from Brussels.'[65] She also presented a very different vision for Europe's future development from that advanced by Delors. She advocated a family of nations in which there would be 'willing and active cooperation between independent sovereign states' rather than a single endeavour. Recent research has revealed that the first draft of her speech was far more contentious than the final version, but Howe, who was by this time the Foreign Secretary, managed with the assistance of the Whitehall civil service network to have the inflammatory sections removed. There had been attacks upon the inferior colonial record of other European countries and suggestions that they were less attached to liberty than the British.[66] In any event the Bruges speech caused, in her own words, an atmosphere of 'stunned outrage' throughout Europe. What it did not do was impact upon the course of European developments.

The main impact of the speech was upon the fate of the 1987 Conservative government. Her speech led Howe and some others in the cabinet to lose respect for her political judgement and to perceive that she was allowing her heart to rule her head. It also inflamed divisions in the cabinet which contributed to Thatcher's nemesis in 1990. Gilmour is convincing in arguing that Thatcher's confidence that the party had an endless vista of power before it led her to the illusion that it could now do exactly as it wished, which is why the EC became a prime target for Thatcher's dislike of pluralism. As a brake on Thatcherite power the EC had become 'the international equivalent of a British intermediate institution . . . Once again as in 1979/80 she was fuelling anti-European prejudices in Britain.'[67] Gilmour discerns a relationship between the two issues of the Poll Tax and the EC, which, as well as bringing her down from power, similarly 'prevented the untrammelled exercise of plebiscitary democracy'.

Yet Gilmour himself underestimated the degree of support which Thatcher's stance on the EC evoked among Conservative MPs. Riddell refers to her approach as 'striking nationalist chords among many Conservative MPs and voters'.[68] There were gradations of opposition to the European project. Even ministers such as Hurd, who was then Home Secretary, and Major at Social Security had sympathy with the substance of Thatcher's position, but were alienated by the tactics and style. They wanted a phased approach towards economic union, but still hoped to prevail by cooperation. Thatcher's unwillingness to compromise with colleagues on her spiralling hostility towards European institutions created difficulties. This process culminated in her behaviour after the Rome summit of European leaders in November 1990, when she portrayed that meeting to the Commons in an entirely negative light, and adamantly refused to consider any further European integration. This led to Howe's resignation and to a series of events which brought her down from office.

ECONOMIC POLICY

The decision as to whether Britain should attach itself to the Exchange Rate Mechanism of the European Monetary System was an issue which straddled the fields of European and economic policy. It is more appropriate to consider it in the context of economic policy, however, as it is at the heart of the debate within the party as to how inflation can best be countered and the principle of sound money upheld. The dispute about whether the monetarist means of controlling inflation was best implemented by the MTFS and tight financial targets, or by shadowing a strong and non-inflationary currency such as the Deutschmark, is an arcane dispute among the ideologically committed. The growing and damaging conflict between Thatcher and Lawson was essentially about this decision, however, although both revealed inconsistencies. Lawson sought a free market, yet resisted market forces determining the relationship between the pound and the DM on the international exchanges; while Thatcher preferred the market principle of allowing the pound to float, while being reluctant to use the instrument of high interest rates to maintain the pound at a suitably high and non-inflationary level.

Two major observations should be made. First, either the approach of the managed currency through the method of shadowing the DM, or a floating pound within a strict monetary framework, might have been successful. The development of a major conflict between Prime Minister and chancellor, however, over a central aspect of economic policy was disastrous. There is also validity in the comment of a leading Conservative in the 1987 government that British economic policy has long been undermined by a tendency to test to destruction. His examples are incomes policy and the control of monetary aggregates, whether through shadowing the DM or formally belonging to the ERM at too high an exchange rate. Failures inevitably followed, because economics is an inexact science, and the economy does not work predictably in response to economic stimuli. External, psychological and inexplicable factors often occur within an economy.

In any event, the Conservative government can be accused of 'taking its eye off the ball' in its anti-inflation strategy after 1987. If concern with inflation increased gradually in the party after 1956, and became a major guide to policy-making after 1979, a more permissive regime occurred after 1987, perhaps caused by a tendency to believe the government's own propaganda about Lawson's economic miracle, and its success about having defeated the cyclical business cycle. Yet many commentators shared this complacency. *The Economist* observed in July 1987 that the economy 'was hotting up but not overheating'.[69] Yet it was aware of the views of 'the few surviving monetarists', who feared that 'a surge in credit and house prices' represented 'an early warning of higher inflation'. It concluded that the economy was buoyant, but that higher taxes and reduced state spending were necessary to prevent the economic boom from getting out of control. Even though Thatcher left office in November 1990 never acknowledging that the economy had fallen into recession, by then the technical definition of two consecutive quarters of negative growth had been met. There were signs of the problem as early as the summer of 1989. Baker argues that at that point the economic indices were pointing unmistakably towards recession, although Chancellor Lawson was still claiming that the inflationary pressures were a mere 'blip', and that Britain could experience 'a soft landing' rather than a recession.[70]

The first sign that the economy was vulnerable was when Black Monday occurred in October 1987 with a crash in the Stock Exchange. This seriously reduced the value of shares, and many converts to Thatcherism who had acquired shares in the mid-1980s became disillusioned with popular capitalism. One commented that she had foolishly 'believed Maggie that it was possible to have it all'. The alarm generated by the sudden fall in share prices led Thatcher to accept Lawson's proposal to increase interest rates by 1 per cent. Within a few weeks, however, the effect of the fall in the Stock Exchange was to persuade the government that it should act to prevent recession and two half percentage-point cuts in interest rates occurred. Yet Lawson was also quite consciously following German interest rates as part of his strategy of shadowing the DM. Thatcher claims not to have noticed that this was what he was engaged in.[71] It is surprising that even after commentators began to comment on Lawson's policy she claimed to be unaware of it. This was not the behaviour of the omniscient leader that she sometimes wished to portray.

Once she became aware of Lawson's actions, however, although she objected to his strategy, she felt constrained from altering the policy because the financial markets had become accustomed to the idea that such a strategy was the guarantee of financial reliability. The markets also assumed that policy was being artificially manipulated to prepare for the inevitability of ERM membership. Lawson recognises Thatcher's commitment to a floating pound and describes a series of meetings with her, in which she objected to the amount of financial intervention required to hold the pound below the value of 3 DM which he had taken as the guide.[72] This was a grave situation for the economy. When a Prime Minister and chancellor disagree on policy to such an extent that

> they must either sort out their differences or the chancellor must go. On the other hand she did not feel strong enough to sack him. She may have been asking herself what she should do with a chancellor with whom she disagreed so violently but whom she could not move, first because of his standing in the party and the government, and then because there really was no other post, except perhaps her own, to which he would wish to move . . . The logic of the situation was that he should resign. But . . . he brought to his convictions a certainty equal to hers, and he thought he might prevail.[73]

It is evident that the economic policy pursued after 1987 was inflationary, and led directly to the severe recession which began in 1990. Yet Lawson was unapologetic about his exchange rate policy. He argues that it was the longer-term totality of economic policy which caused the damage, and that had Britain joined the ERM when he first advocated it in 1985, the results would have been beneficial. The government would then have been able to pursue the inflationary strategy it adopted in 1986, which he considers to have been more harmful than what happened after 1987. He cites in his defence the Treasury review of the exchange rate policy which was undertaken in late 1986, which argued that because of lags in the effects of economic policy, the roots of the recession can be traced back to the decisions taken in mid-1986.

The same Treasury review argued that it was the failure to understand the decline in the savings ratio and the effect of the investment boom which caused the problem, and that the policy of shadowing the DM had 'no bearing on our underestimation of the strength of the boom'.[74] There was no evidence that intervention in the markets to sustain a particular rate of exchange had been inflationary. With hindsight, 'the problem was simply that the overall stance of the policy . . . taking both exchange rates and interest rates into account . . . was not tight enough.'[75] Lawson admits that the government's policy of financial deregulation made any anti-inflationary strategy more difficult.

The debate over whether Lawson or Thatcher were correct in their ascription of blame for economic policy failures is difficult to resolve. It is abundantly clear, however, that the Conservative government was responsible for effecting the transition from boom to bust between 1987 and 1990. It is also evident that the conflict over economic policy was substantially rooted in politics and personalities. Lawson himself asserted that

> the very close relationship between me and Margaret Thatcher lasted for a long, long time. . . . We are very close. It was only after the 1987 election that the drift apart began. Howe had been a candidate for the leadership in 1975 and she continued to see him as a potential rival. That's the way she is. After the 1987 election, I was written up in a number of places as being the man who had really won the election, and she suddenly started to see me as a rival and her attitude changed . . . she began to see me in a different light altogether, and began to distrust me politically for that reason.[76]

The recession produced a spectacular political fallout. Despite the effects of Europe, the Poll Tax and welfare state reforms; without the problems of inflation, and the emergence of recession, the challenge to Thatcher's leadership would have been unlikely. Lawson was evidently guilty of a policy error in his 1988 budget which, at a time when fiscal tightening was required, reduced the top rate of tax to 40 per cent and the standard rate to 25 per cent. These were the most badly timed taxation changes in postwar history and fuelled inflation. Yet the situation was made worse in the same budget when, even though the housing market was already overheating, Lawson decided to make the morally determined gesture of limiting tax relief on mortgages to one per household, in order to encourage stable relationships, but deferred the implementation until August. During the four months which followed there was a singularly dangerous boom in house prices as people rushed to beat the deadline.

The method which Lawson used to curb the boom was interest rate rises which increased progressively to a peak of 15 per cent, which had the effect of devastating consumer spending by the end of the decade. The balance of payments also collapsed into deficit. This was the inevitable outcome of the devastation of manufacturing industry in the 1981 recession. Lawson's use of the interest rate method alone to slow down the boom and to counter burgeoning inflation, earned him the criticism that he was 'a one club man'. Yet he had previously allowed the boom to continue for too long. In the middle of the runaway inflation Lawson tried to persuade Thatcher to grant independence to the Bank of England, giving it control over interest rates. She declined and argued that it looked like a shuffling off of responsibility at a time when prices were rising fast. Certainly, Lawson's timing for this suggestion was inappropriate.[77]

The return of Sir Alan Walters to the position of close adviser to Thatcher in May 1989 began a period in which Lawson's resignation became inevitable. It brought back to the political agenda Britain's membership of the ERM. In the summer of 1989, shortly before his resignation from the government, Lawson and Howe had effectively ambushed Thatcher and manoeuvred her into the position where she conceded that Britain would ultimately join the ERM when the circumstances were propitious. That the two senior ministers with responsibility in this area were able to force Thatcher into a position she would have preferred not to be in was a sign of her failing political control. Thatcher is derogatory about their behaviour and Lawson is anxious to point out that the meeting was predictably tense, and that it was the only time that they had ever caballed against her.[78] In any event, she had every intention of stalling about when the conditions for membership would be right. The momentum was building, none the less, and there was no prospect of her avoiding entry in October 1990, when another chancellor, John Major, might have resigned had she not agreed.

The return of Walters, and Thatcher's transparent preference for his advice over that of her chancellor, led to Lawson's resignation. Walters had not intended to provoke the resignation. Unfortunately, the press picked up on writings in a learned American journal from several months previously, in which he repeated the case against British membership of the ERM, which highlighted his fundamental disagreement with Lawson on a central aspect of policy. Lawson resigned the chancellorship as a result in October 1989 when Thatcher refused his demand that Walters should go. In a resignation speech to the Commons, he argued that the article represented 'the tip of an ill-concealed iceberg'. He echoed the message which the Westland affair should have made apparent, that 'the Prime Minister must appoint members he or she trusts and then leave them to carry out the policy'.[79] The publicity surrounding the Walters article gave Lawson the opportunity to retrieve the moral high ground, at a time when he was personally ready to return to the private sector, and when the economy was on the verge of recession. The episode has a deeper significance, however, and demonstrated both Thatcher's preference for advisers from outside the leadership of her party and her increasing isolation. The personnel surrounding her changed frequently, as she became disillusioned with successive individuals or they lost their enthusiasm in working for her. After Lawson's resignation the position of Walters became so invidious that he felt compelled to resign, with the result that Thatcher was down to two fully trusted advisers: Sir Bernard Ingham, her press secretary, and Sir Charles Powell, who was on secondment from the Foreign Office. They were guilty of confusing their total loyalty to her in the autumn of 1990 for the mood of the majority of Conservative MPs, and led her to stay in the leadership contest, when it had become clear that she could either not win, or that it would be a pyrrhic victory.

THATCHER'S FALL

The events leading to Thatcher's fall from office can be traced back at least a year, to the challenge to her leadership from the 'stalking horse' candidacy of Sir Anthony Meyer. He had supported her up to the Falklands War, despite being a Europhile and 'one nation' Conservative. By 1989 he had concluded that her proclaimed infallibility had become unacceptable as a style of leadership. He thought her lack of generosity and understanding was turning the party into an 'intolerant, small minded image of herself'. He was also appalled by the role of her new acolyte as party chairman, Kenneth Baker, whom he described as 'the grinning face of Thatcherism'.[80] There were vigorous attempts within the party to prevent Meyer from standing, and he was widely pilloried in the Conservative press as 'Sir Nobody', but he scored a total of sixty MPs either voting for him or deliberately abstaining. He was subsequently deselected by his local constituency party, the first case of this happening in the Conservative Party since that of Nigel Nicholson a quarter of a century earlier over the Suez affair. Thatcher attributes the discontent and instability which Meyer's embarrassing challenge reflected, to the worsening state of the economy.[81]

The economic and political situation continued to deteriorate during the remainder of 1989 and 1990. Thatcher had maladroitly handled the demotion of Howe from Foreign Secretary to Leader of the House of Commons in July 1989, although it appeared to be his loss of the Chevening country house, which was one of the perquisites of the Foreign Secretary's job, which most aggravated him. This created another potential enemy in the cabinet. Speculation was growing that a more serious challenge for the leadership from a stronger opponent could be expected in 1990.[82] In September 1990 just before the Conservative annual conference, Thatcher was persuaded by her new chancellor Major to take Britain into the ERM. This reflected her political weakness. She was in no position to lose another senior minister. ERM entry at this particular point did provide her, however, with two other distinct benefits. First, it provided a propaganda coup about an active government, which diverted attention away from the Labour Party's annual conference which was then meeting. Secondly, it offered her the opportunity of fulfilling her passionate ambition of reducing interest rates, as the financial markets could now be convinced that there was an anti-inflationary strategy taking place. Even this decision was undermined by the announcement of a 1 per cent cut in rates simultaneously with ERM entry, which was a crude and clumsy attempt to seek the rewards before the policy could take effect, and served to question the sincerity of the anti-inflation strategy.[83]

The Conservatives secured one minor benefit in May 1990 when, despite losing seats in the local elections, the new party chairman Baker, who had moved from the education portfolio, managed to portray the party's retention of its 'flagship' and actively privatising councils of Wandsworth and Westminster, as a major political triumph.[84] This only provided a temporary respite, however, as an ineffectual campaign, 'Summer Heat on Labour' two months later, portraying Labour as a red-blooded socialist party was regarded even by its author as ineffectual.[85] Its theoretical basis had been that, with the return of two-party politics, dissident Conservative voters would have to be wooed away from voting Labour. This made it essential to secure the votes of so-called 'Essex man', which had been lost to Labour over the issues of rising mortgages and the Poll Tax. Baker's strategy was to retrieve the support of the upwardly mobile, who had lost their emotional attachment to Labour, and who could be frightened into voting Conservative if a successful propaganda campaign could sufficiently emphasise Labour's irrevocable socialism.

Baker's campaign could not override the objective political realities. Thatcher recognised the problems of high interest rates, rising inflation and party divisions over Europe; all of which were making Conservative MPs nervous. She also recognised two other revealing traits of the modern Conservative Party. First, its MPs were now professional politicians who were interested in office and career success. Those who had neither been given office under Thatcher, or who had been removed from it, were disgruntled with her. The newer MPs also judged ideological and leadership issues on the basis of whether they would contribute to winning general elections. The generation of independent 'knights of the shire' who were non-political loyalists and who had been selected for their seats because of their social position in their own localities, had finally passed in the 1970s. Secondly, while the party in the country was still contented with the ideological direction and leadership, Thatcher asserts that the rank and file influence over Tory MPs had diminished. She claims that 'the rank and file of the party were still with me, as they would show at the 1990 party conference, indeed perhaps stronger than ever in their support. But too many of my colleagues had an unspoken contempt for the party faithful who they regarded as organisation fodder with no real right to hold political opinions. And in the event, no one would seriously listen to them . . . though they were formally consulted and pronounced heavily in my favour . . . when it came for my fate to be decided.'[86] She identifies a feature of the modern party in which, while ministers aim for a favourable response from delegates to their speeches at the annual conference, the views of activists count for little in the rest of the year.[87] Yet while Thatcher had a close relationship with conference, and had an instinctive agreement with the prejudices of the delegates in a way that her predecessors in the leadership did not, she exaggerated her uniqueness in the cabinet. Others in her cabinet in 1990 claim that they too considered it important to send delegates home in good heart and with an understanding of why government decisions had been taken.

It is not necessary to reconstruct in detail the complex sequence of events which led up to Thatcher's loss of the Conservative leadership in November 1990. There is justice in Thatcher's comment that 'it's a funny old world', when a three-time election winner, who many believed had presided over a political revolution, should lose the party leadership while she was still Prime Minister. It is an event that can be partly explained within the context of Conservative Party history. There is earlier evidence of ruthlessness at elite level within the party towards failing leaders, even when the rank and file remained loyal.

The ousting of Churchill in 1955, Eden in 1957, Macmillan in 1963 and Heath in 1975, all with some degree of resistance by the deposed leader, provides clear evidence.

Was the perception of Thatcher as a failing political leader justified? By the autumn of 1990 there were many instances of policy failure; for example, the Poll Tax and the economy, and continuing controversy over Europe and the reforms to health and education. There were also signs of the poor management of the cabinet evidenced by the Lawson and Howe resignations. Thatcher had become more isolated from the parliamentary party and was paying few visits to the tea rooms to talk to back benchers. Most importantly for the Conservative Party at any time, but particularly with the newer type of professional MP, was the dire electoral situation in which much of Labour's strategy was based upon the claim that the country was exhausted by the style and content of Thatcher's leadership.

Lawson attributes Thatcher's enforced resignation to three main causes. First, the resignation of Foreign Secretary Howe, which took place at the very moment when a leadership election could be triggered. Secondly, Howe followed up his resignation with a devastatingly effective resignation speech in November 1990. After Thatcher had attempted to dismiss the importance of Howe's resignation by claiming that he merely disagreed with her style of leadership, he was provoked to respond. He denied to a packed Commons that he simply objected to her style.[88] He pointed to a difference in policy, and said that as the party had accepted her leadership for so long, it was assumed that everyone shared her opinions. It was necessary to make clear his rejection of her stance on Europe. He concluded with an invitation to rivals for the party leadership to declare themselves: 'The time has come for others to consider their own response to the tragic conflict of loyalties with which I have myself wrestled for perhaps too long.'[89] The obvious person to respond to Howe's cue was Heseltine. He remained cautious at first, not wishing to appear as a 'regicide' and unsure whether it was premature to launch a successful challenge. This leads to Lawson's third cause for Thatcher's downfall. As Heseltine was cautiously testing the waters to determine whether or not to challenge for the leadership, Lawson points to 'the black propaganda machine in Downing Street' which mishandled the situation by urging Heseltine 'to put up or shut up'. This left Heseltine with little choice since, if he were to hold back, any future challenge would appear still more opportunistic. Incidentally, Lawson considers that it was correct for

Thatcher to be removed. This was because of her style, her Poll Tax blunder, her ineptitude in splitting the party over Europe, but above all because she had become an electoral liability.[90]

Baker analyses Thatcher's fall through the impact of great events which had been caused by unrelated and bizarre happenings. He admits that the issues of 1990: the Poll Tax, Europe, the economy, the visible presence of Heseltine as an alternative leader and an ever-growing list of MPs with thwarted career ambitions, were decisively important. Yet there were also crucial short-term factors. The 1990 conference had been successful, and Thatcher was not fanciful in claiming that the rank and file demonstrated their continuing enthusiasm for her. It was here that she proclaimed the goal, which Major later plagiarised as his own, of 'an open classless Britain'.[91] Yet this minor revival only a few weeks before she lost the leadership was derailed by a series of short-term events. These included a heavy by-election defeat at the hands of the Liberals at Eastbourne in late October with a 20 per cent swing coupled with a substantial Labour lead in the polls; her emotional outburst in the Commons after the Rome summit when she cried, 'no, no, no', about Jacques Delors and his vision of a strengthened European Community, and her public attack on Howe at a cabinet meeting in early November for being laggardly in producing legislation which finally drove him to resign. Baker is also correct in identifying the inadequacy of her campaign to retain the leadership once Heseltine had raised his head above the parapet, as her campaign organisers were complacent and so she undertook little canvassing. In this respect Ian Gow's death mattered as Peter Morrison proved a poor substitute.[92] She even left the country on government business during the vital few days when MPs were deciding which way to vote. Baker also asserts that too much of the public face of her campaign was the preserve of dyed-in-the-wool ideologues such as Tebbit and George Gardiner, that there was no attempt to mobilise the constituencies to exert pressure on MPs and that her campaign team repeated the mistake Heath had made in succumbing to Thatcher in 1975 of believing the false promises of many MPs.[93]

Parkinson attributes Thatcher's downfall to the fact that, after a period in which she enjoyed the benefit of a supportive cabinet, by 1990 'she was once again in a minority in her cabinet and had been for some time'.[94] The 1970 and 1974 intakes including Hurd and David Hunt were now at the peak of their careers, and the 'more able' centre-right intake of 1983 including Michael Forsyth, Peter Lilley and Michael Portillo, although 'on the fast track', had several years to catch up. It was Thatcher's misfortune, therefore, to be surrounded by pragmatists rather than conviction politicians at the crucial moment. Parkinson also considers that Howe's resignation and subsequent speech were critical, and blames Howe's wife Elspeth, 'the doyenne of protective, committed ministerial wives'.[95] Nicholas Ridley's forced resignation in July 1990 further highlighted her isolated situation.[96] Parkinson implies a fatal concoction of ambition, back-biting within the party's elite, and external pressures, as interacting to force Thatcher's departure.

Alan Clark's *Diaries* also cast light on Thatcher's fall. Fearing a coup against her, he wrote in March 1990 that the situation had arisen because of the Poll Tax and persistent deficits in the opinion polls which 'rattled' MPs. But the real problem was that 'the party in the House has just got sick of her. She hasn't promoted her "own" people much. Her "constituency" in this place depends solely on her proven ability to win general elections. But now this is in jeopardy.'[97] Clark also confirms that she and her immediate courtiers, who were all outside the Commons, were failing to see the problem.[98] In early November he wrote, 'I don't think she realises what a jam she's in. It's the bunker syndrome. Everyone round you is clicking their heels. The saluting sentries have highly polished boots and beautifully creased uniforms. But out there at the front it's all disintegrating. The soldiers are starving in tatters and makeshift bandages. Whole units are mutinous and in flight.'[99]

The external pressures on the events of November 1990 are also significant. Political journalists stress personalities and short-term happenings, as indeed do some of the participants themselves. The Conservative Party is naturally sensitive to the economic and financial interests which fund it, and is responsive to the business community. Thatcher's rooted dislike of an integrated Europe, whether because of a desire to protect her own power and the 'revolution' which she had inaugurated, or on grounds of sheer nationalistic prejudice, led her uncharacteristically to be careless of business opinion on European issues. There is evidence that segments of business, and most particularly the City of London, favoured a more European strategy than Thatcher was prepared to accept. This damaged her position with some in the party's ranks. The City favoured Britain's entry into the ERM, as did some other sectors of business, because 'they were prepared to sacrifice large elements of sovereignty in order for the United Kingdom to enjoy a leading role in the creation and eventual operation of a far more united and centrally controlled Europe'.[100] The same City pressures which pulled her reluctantly into the ERM assisted her fall from power. Clark points to the poor reception she was given for her final speech at the Lord Mayor of London's banquet. In expounding her scepticism on Europe, 'She was greeted with almost complete silence . . . and got flatter and flatter.'[101] The business and financial interests represented at such an event may only directly speak for a minority in Britain, but this weakness is compensated for by their vigilance, effectiveness, resources and strategic economic position. The most serious external pressure, however, was the desertion of the electorate. Her departure demonstrated 'that in the age of polls, at least for a Conservative Prime Minister, losing a series of them had become tantamount to losing a general election, especially when there are nuclei of opposition within the Conservative Party'.[102] The differences between November 1990 and the two previous occasions when she was under threat were that unlike 1981 she could not blame the previous government for the state of the economy, and unlike 1986 her personal popularity was now lower than that of her party. The earlier threats to her leadership had been speculative, and she did not need to compromise to retain her position. Indeed her refusal to do so had been a strength. 'By 1990 this was not the case . . . It may be that she preferred defeat and rejection by her party rather than continue in office on the party's terms as a "kept woman".'[103]

The manoeuvring in the final days of Thatcher's leadership is not important in the long-term history of the party. After the first ballot results were declared on 20 November with Thatcher securing 204 votes against Heseltine's 152 and 16 abstentions, a mere 4 votes short of the required percentage of votes for her to be declared the victor. It was clear that her leadership had run its course. A few deluded supporters still thought that she would win in the second ballot and, advised by her immediate coterie who thought the same, she returned to London in a determined mood. Advice from party officials in the Commons, such as Tim Renton and Cranley Onslow was ambiguous, and even her campaign manager for the second ballot advised her to consult the cabinet. It was at this stage that the notorious 'men in grey suits' who represented the party's 'establishment' undertook the political assassination that they judged to be in the party's best interests. Two-thirds of the cabinet urged that she stand down, and four ministers: Chris Patten, Malcolm Rifkind, Kenneth Clarke and Norman Lamont, threatened to refuse to serve with her if she continued in office.[104] Most cabinet members uttered a prepared formula intended to be discouraging, which Thatcher thought both discredited the establishment of the party and male politicians. She subsequently described the plot to remove her as 'treachery with a smile on its face'.[105]

To describe Thatcher's downfall as the result of accidental events, or as an unnecessary plot, is to trivialise the event's significance. Lawson's resignation had resulted from conflicting theories of monetarism, the ambitions which ensue from an extended period in government and Thatcher's proclivity for relying on external advisers rather than ministers. It was the 'pre-play' to her downfall. The succession of unpopular policies after 1987 resulted from a Conservatism which was losing touch with its electoral base in a mass democracy. Howe's resignation reflected the renewed salience of the European issue after the Bruges speech. Europe retains the potential to split the party at the end of the millennium. The impact of opinion polls, by-elections and local election results demonstrates that intra-Conservative Party politics are now mediated by a sensitivity to the movement of public opinion, particularly as expressed through the mass media.

Thatcher anointed Major as her successor. To expiate its guilt, the party followed her advice, as all but three of the MPs who voted for her on the first ballot supported Major. He possessed other negative advantages. Unlike Hurd he was not an old Etonian and unlike Heseltine he did not threaten a return to pseudo-corporatist policies. Both realities explain how far the party had changed, partly owing to Thatcher, in the previous quarter of a century. It would be impossible for the party to re-establish its old deferential type of leadership.[106] Thatcher supported Major as a leader who would secure the future for her legacy. Was her confidence justified?

6

THE TRANSITION TO MAJOR

The removal of Margaret Thatcher from the party leadership in 1990 may have had many causes, but paramount was a fear that the Conservatives would lose power if she were to remain in office. This ensured that John Major's main preoccupation in the period between his succession to the leadership and the ensuing general election would be to secure his party's re-election. There was much discussion among the 'chattering classes' during the first period of Major's leadership as to whether he was continuing or altering the party's ideological stance from the Thatcher years, or whether he was simply changing the style rather than the substance of political leadership. Labour sought to maintain that Major was merely 'the son of Thatcher'. The question about the ideological nature of the relationship between the policies of the Major and Thatcher administrations is best determined after examining the entire six and a half years of Major's period as Prime Minister. In any event, Major subordinated such philosophical niceties to the central task of winning the election, whenever it would come. As Seldon expresses it, the key factor is 'the perception of the public mood. The desire to retain power remains paramount.'[1]

The mere change in the party's leadership was sufficient to make an impact on public opinion. There was a hint of desperation in the tactic of the Labour opposition in maintaining that Major would continue with Thatcherite policies. Given the continuing doubts about Labour's capacity to govern and about Kinnock's managerial competence, there was every likelihood that the substitution of Major for Thatcher would be sufficient to satisfy the public mood for a change in the country's political leadership. On the very day that Major captured the leadership, commentators were observing that the Conservatives had 'shot Labour's fox'.[2] The initial evidence supported this judgement. The polls had already shifted in the Conservative Party's direction during the leadership campaign, which had been generally attributed to the concentration of media attention on the Conservative Party's affairs. The first polls published after Major succeeded to the leadership gave him and his party the reassurance that they sought as the party moved into a handsome 11 per cent lead.[3]

MAJOR'S PREVIOUS CAREER

Some of the debate about Major's ideological position and his relationship to Thatcher's policies is understandable. His wife Norma says 'I'm not sure I entirely understand what makes him tick'.[4] A sympathiser remarked that Major inherited the leadership 'with remarkably little ideological baggage'.[5] To claim that any politician is bereft of political and social values is clearly false, since all political decisions are necessarily rooted in some system of values even if they are relatively inarticulate.[6] There are some differences evident, however, in the extent to which political leaders possess strategic direction and a clear intellectual underpinning for their actions. Major is rather like Heath in his concern to focus on policies which work, while Thatcher had a clearer sense of the direction in which she wished her government to proceed.

The enigma of Major's politics in 1990 is apparent. While some exaggerated his lack of ideological perspective, Thatcher and Tebbit joined the Labour Party in an outburst of wishful thinking with regard to Major's future direction. As Major moved into Downing Street she observed that 'the future is assured', and predicted that her policies would continue for a further eleven years.[7] Tebbit called Major 'very tough, very dry'.[8]

Were there any clues as to Major's politics from his earlier life? He was born on 29 March 1943 to relatively humble parents. Neither he nor Thatcher would have been chosen as Conservative leaders under the old system of selection which existed before 1965.[9] His family fell on harder times when economic circumstances forced his parents to move from Worcester Park to Brixton, 'a rough tough part of London'.[10] He had unhappy memories of his grammar school, and he appears to have passed few 'O' level examinations before he left. His examination performance at 'O' level became a subject of speculation and apparent secrecy in the early months of his leadership. If his school days were unhappy it is also suggested that his parents were elderly and he lacked a secure and loving childhood. Seldon concludes that despite a calm outer surface, he suffered 'a restless interior and a strong hunger for affirmation'.[11]

Major's first active involvement in politics was when he joined the Young Conservatives in response to a canvasser who knocked on the family door, and he soon took part in public speaking on a soapbox in Brixton market.[12] This was the style of politics to which he reverted during the 1992 general election campaign, which enabled him to improve his public image, with 'a genuflexion towards the campaigning style of yore'.[13] Major has since pointed out that it was by joining the Conservative Party that he saw the best opportunity for getting out of deprived circumstances and gaining a passport to personal advancement.[14]

After a period in the banking industry, which took him to Nigeria, he returned to south London, and in 1968 got himself elected as a local Conservative councillor in a Labour area. This was possible because the Labour government was unpopular at the time, and he then became chair of the Housing Committee in Lambeth. He worked closely with the Director of Housing, Harry Simpson, in a programme of slum clearance and the provision of social housing. Based on his experience in London politics at this time, the Labour left-winger Ken Livingstone argues that Major is a progressive Conservative with a social conscience. Major's political ambitions were encouraged at the time by a relationship with a divorcee thirteen years older than himself, Jean Kierans; and he was selected to fight the safe Labour seat of St Pancras in the two general elections in 1974. Subsequently, he sought a more winnable seat and found that his social origins were an obstacle to his adoption as a candidate. He suffered so many rejections at the hands of local Conservative Party associations that he and his wife decided that Huntingdon was to be his last attempt to secure a seat.[15] After a number of failures at selection conferences he complained to a friend, 'people like us with modest backgrounds and non-BBC accents, will always be at a disadvantage'.[16] The overspill population from the East End of London to the Huntingdon constituency was represented in the party, which assisted his selection. Major beat off competition for the seat from such future leadership figures as Michael Howard, Chris Patten and Peter Lilley. Despite his easy victory, however, the 'county set' within the local party remained unhappy.[17]

On entering the House of Commons Major did not appear to be an ultra-dry. His career began slowly, and something of his own attitude and of the social snobbery which fuelled some of the opposition which he faced in the party when Prime Minister was apparent when he attributed his failure to achieve a government post to his social background. Once he got his feet on the first rungs of the ministerial ladder, however, he benefited from Thatcher's patronage. His appointment as Chancellor of the Exchequer in October 1989, after only a few months as Foreign Secretary, revealed that Thatcher was grooming him as her successor.[18] He served successively in the Whip's Office, as junior minister at Social Security, as Chief Secretary to the Treasury, as Foreign Secretary and Chancellor of the Exchequer. While for much of this time he was considered a Thatcher loyalist, and this was evidently an attitude she shared, he never appeared a passionate 'true believer'. His views were clearly those of an economic liberal, but with a more pragmatic slant than Thatcher demonstrated. A fellow MP is convinced that Major demonstrated at the Department of Social Security that he 'cared about the quality of public services, and the importance of the public services for those who cannot pay. I doubt whether she (Thatcher) . . . had any idea about that side of his beliefs.'[19] Nigel Lawson considers that Major was a non-political technocrat of no fixed beliefs, but that his real skill was as a networker. The skill of 'being good with people and with back-bench colleagues', stood him in good stead when he cashed in on these acquaintances in the 1990 leadership election

It is Major's views on what proved to be the most vexed of the questions during his leadership of the party, the United Kingdom's relationship with Europe, which were the clearest for those who wanted to consult the evidence. It was his true attitude to Europe which excited most speculation during his years in Downing Street, as he attempted to hold a fractious party together on this divisive issue. Yet Seldon suggests that his views on the issue were captured by a statement he made in 1982, when he asserted that, emotionally, ' I am an agnostic on the subject of a united Europe. I've no longer-term vision of a federal Europe and I don't wish to diminish the languages and the cultures of the member states . . . I [am more] a European by logic than by emotion.'[20] This measured attitude towards Europe explains why he found it hard to accept that it was worth tearing his government apart from 1992 to 1997 on the issue.

MAJOR'S INHERITANCE

In considering the views which Major brought with him to Downing Street, it must be remembered that events and circumstances are vitally important. The circumstances in which Major had to operate were as important in determining his policies in government as were his own personal instincts. As a correspondent in the *Guardian* expressed it, Major had to prove that he was not merely a duplicate of Thatcher, without alienating the Thatcherites.[21] Seldon summarised the problems as 'lack of time to prepare, the Europe split, the ERM straightjacket, the recession, the difficulty of finding a post-Thatcherite voice, and Mrs Thatcher lurking in the background'.[22]

Thatcherism was indeed a difficult legacy for Major, as it had established a mood of high expectations among the party faithful. If previous party leaders had the opportunity of adopting a 'dispositional' Conservatism of merely protecting what they inherited, this was not a feasible opportunity for Major, because of the excitement and sense of forward movement which she had established in the 1980s. Thatcherism provided the rank and file with a yardstick against which they could evaluate Major's performance. While Thatcherism appears more coherent with the benefit of historical perspective than it did at the time, it was the dominating faction in the party, and Major was even seeking to appease it during the 1997 general election campaign. The debate about the nature of the legacy was still provoking splits in the party in 1999. Thatcher attributed the heavy election defeat in 1997, and the likely second term for Labour early in the new century, to her removal in 1990; to which Stephen Dorrell MP responded that it was the serious divisions within the party bequeathed by Thatcher to Major which were the real cause of the Conservative Party's subsequent travails.[23]

Major's problems were compounded by the change in the country's political values. If the British Social Attitudes Surveys demonstrate that there was a marked psychological movement of opinion in the country in the 1970s towards individualism and opportunity, and away from social solidarity and publicly provided support for the underprivileged, which Thatcher exploited in four general election victories, values were beginning to change even in the 1980s. By the 1990s there was a greater readiness on the part of voters to accept the need for higher taxation in order to fund social and public services. Thatcherite values had peaked in their electoral appeal despite a decade of a government theoretically able to control the agenda. By large majorities voters said that they preferred a society with state-provided welfare instead of individuals simply taking responsibility for themselves; and majorities even favoured a managed economy over one run on free-market lines. A clear majority also favoured social spending over tax cuts, and action by government to promote employment and greater equality.[24] A MORI opinion survey also revealed that a majority of 54 per cent supported a society based on socialist principles as against 39 per cent supporting Thatcherite values.[25] It is also apparent that the shift to the right in the late 1970s in Britain found some echo in other democratic states. Taken together with the impact of the collapse of Communist regimes in quick succession at the turn of the 1990s, British right-wingers gained in confidence and rectitude. In the 1990s, however, many countries had returned to social democratic rule. This was evident in Australasia, and in many western European countries. The erosion of the left in the 1980s now appeared to be less the 'tide of history' and much more a purely Anglo-American phenomenon.

The problem for Major was that he had to satisfy both intra-party demands for 'pure undiluted' Thatcherism, and to appeal to the mass electorate, many of whom had never accepted Thatcherite values. Even some of those who had done so for a period were falling out of love with it by the final years of the Thatcher government. The recession of the early 1990s was hitting hard at the Midlands and south of the country where the Conservative Party piled up its majority of seats. This contrasted with the recession of the early 1980s which had damaged the more Labour-inclined territories of the north of England, south Wales and central Scotland. Even some of the intellectuals who had swung to the right in the mid-1970s were altering their perspective. From being a keen Thatcherite, for example, John Gray converted from promoting a neo-liberal economic agenda to asserting the limits of marketisation, recognising that a deregulated and flexible labour market created instability in families and society, and urging Conservatives to rediscover their sympathy with family and community.[26] With Tony Blair's leadership he saw Labour as carrying the 'torch of innovation', and condemned Conservatives for failing to address 'the desolation of communities by unfettered market forces and the spectre of jobless growth producing an even larger, and increasingly estranged underclass'. The Conservatives had ignored the 'human need for local rootedness and strong and deep forms of community life'.[27]

Another Conservative and Conservative-voting intellectual who turned to Labour was A.N. Wilson. In 1989 he proclaimed that Thatcherism did not work particularly because of its unrealistic view that public services can be privately paid for by the individual. He criticised Thatcher and the former Thatcherite minister Cecil Parkinson for inflicting poverty on people when, from their own upbringing, they should have known what poverty is like. He deplored the introduction of charges for eye tests and for false teeth and the 'hopelessly inefficient' performance of the privatised industries, and praised the attempts by Labour councils to look after their local citizenry. The failure of Thatcherism could only be addressed by all who were critical of Thatcherism voting for the Labour Party. Only with Labour in power would it be possible to not 'face a future with dud trains, dud libraries, dud museums, dud hospitals, and the poor getting poorer – sans eyes, sans teeth, sans everything'.[28] The shift of intellectuals can sometimes signal a political change, as in the 1970s. Clearly, Major's dilemma was very real. Building what Gamble describes as 'the politics of support' called for very different tactics for the party in contrast to those required for the country, whether for the intelligentsia or the mass of the people.[29]

PREPARING FOR THE 1992 ELECTION: FORMING A GOVERNMENT

Major's first government from November 1990 to April 1992 was subject to varied fortunes. It achieved its central objective, however; that of winning the further term in office which most had thought was unlikely in the final months of Thatcher's leadership. He was fortunate in the immediate occurrence of the Gulf War as he could portray himself as a war leader, and he specifically avoided partisan bellicosity and sought to build a consensus in the country and in parliament in support of the war. Yet he was still able to gain good television footage by visiting and talking to British troops stationed in the Gulf, and to be seen joking and signing autographs.[30] He had the further advantage that with an election only a little over a year away, he could expect a closing of the party ranks.[31] Yet in the period before the general election he had less instinctive rapport with the membership than had Thatcher. He was more sympathetic to the party organisation than she had been, however, as was clear from the appointment of his greatest political ally, Chris Patten, to the post of chairman of the party, and John Cope as deputy chairman. Both men had risen to prominence through Central Office. Thatcher and her closest acolytes had tended to be suspicious of the party organisation as a haven of left-wingers and Heathmen. This was untrue as there was no disloyalty to Thatcher herself.[32]

Major's first task was to appoint a cabinet. The central question was what to do with Heseltine. To build unity and to harness Heseltine's talents he wanted him in the government; and yet to the Thatcherites Heseltine was tinged with treachery owing to his resignation at the time of the Westland affair and his challenge to Thatcher in the leadership election. In terms of policy, his positions on the Community Charge which he pledged to abolish, industrial intervention and sympathy for the European project, also made him highly suspect. Major handled the issue skilfully by offering Heseltine the post of Secretary of State for the Environment to make him responsible for carrying out his commitment to replace the Poll Tax. This suggested that Major had sensitivity as a party manager.[33]

Norman Lamont was appointed as Chancellor of the Exchequer, partly as a debt to his role as campaign manager for Major during the leadership election. Since he was a Thatcher follower it was a more questionable appointment. Friendship also contributed to the appointment of Chris Patten as party chairman who was left with the difficult task bequeathed by his predecessor Baker. Patten found little in the way of preparations for the election, and discovered deep financial problems. He took steps to address the party's organisational and communication difficulties, and as a close confidant of Major, was an inspired choice as chairman, despite his definition of Conservatism as European Christian Democracy. Certainly he would not create an alternative power base to that of the party leader. Such an outcome has always been a threat to the party's health.[34] Baker became Home Secretary, having learnt that the party chairmanship is rarely a route to the leadership: of twenty-seven former chairmen, only Neville Chamberlain secured the leadership in 1937.[35] Thirteen cabinet ministers remained in place. The main problem was that Major had failed to appoint a single woman to the cabinet which caused 'enormous indignation' from women MPs.[36]

Major also moved to set up a Policy Unit. He chose former journalist Sarah Hogg to head it. Until the 1992 election the unit was of central importance with Hogg mediating relations between the Prime Minister and individual ministers, including the chancellor, much to Lamont's chagrin. Hogg influenced such crucial policy decisions as the replacement of the Poll Tax and the forthcoming Inter-Governmental Conference (IGC) at Maastricht as well as overseeing the broad thrust of government policy.[37] Her competence and political sensitivity were not in evidence in this period, however, and Major also made a questionable appointment to head his political office, perhaps choosing another woman, Judith Chaplin, to compensate for the lack of women in the cabinet. Her relations with Hogg were poor and there was much conflict between them, in which Hogg emerged victorious.[38]

Major's first appearance at the despatch box was nervous, but in general the Conservative press welcomed a good start. The *Daily Telegraph* at this early stage acknowledged a good start, citing Major's astute cabinet selections, his vision of 'a classless society', his 'stealing Labour's thunder' by his review of the Poll Tax and his cooperative attitude towards Europe.[39] The same newspaper soon reverted to enmity. There were clear signs that Major was trying to stamp his own style, a rather gentler one than Thatcher's, on his early actions. He placed relations with Europe on a sounder footing. At the December Inter-Governmental Conference he established a sympathetic tone with Britain's European partners. He pledged that in European affairs Britain would be 'on the pitch and playing hard'.[40] A few months later he remarked in Bonn that 'Britain should be at the heart of Europe'.[41] A series of other early actions pointed in the same more consensual direction. He promised a concern for social cohesion and for the needs of the inner cities and the north of England. He proposed the goal of creating 'a country at ease with itself', and endorsed the candidacy of a black Conservative lawyer, John Taylor, in the Cheltenham constituency, against local party demands. He also expressed sympathy with those who 'needed a helping hand', and he announced the re-indexation of child benefits.[42] His style differed in his collegial attitude to the role of cabinet, in which he invited ministers to speak freely. One minister compared it with being released from prison into the sunlight.[43] Yet these were easy 'soundbite' statements or small acts of 'gesture politics'. Within four months the charge which opponents often made against him was first heard. As he failed to decide what should be done about the Poll Tax the Labour Party accused him of 'dithering'. In the aftermath of the Gulf War Thatcher began to voice her ideas. She adopted a markedly tougher line towards the Iraqis, particularly to Saddam Hussein, and when evidence mounted that there were massacres by the Iraqis against the minority Kurdish community, she expressed her concern that so little was being done to assist them.

To counter suggestions of dithering, and to avoid an outflanking by Thatcher, he strongly proposed the idea of establishing 'safe havens' to protect the Kurds, which ultimately the Americans helped to implement.[44]

Thatcher managed to avoid the excesses of the negativity which Heath had shown towards her leadership. Yet she accepted the presidency of the anti-European Bruges Group and the 'Conservative Way Forward' group to defend Thatcherite policies. She also told American television viewers, 'I see a tendency to try to undermine what I have achieved and to go back to giving more power to government'.[45] The Thatcherites were soon to make their voices heard. One admitted that there were those who were 'ready to be disillusioned and who duly arrived at that state'.[46] In substance, it was difficult for them to criticise Major, since with an election imminent it was obvious that he would soften the party's approach, and only the most 'dyed-in-the-wool' Thatcherites thought that there was no need for any modification of the Poll Tax. Despite strenuous efforts at ministerial and Central Office level, the officially named Community Charge was now universally dubbed the Poll Tax. In any event, given Major's personality, and for reasons of electoral appeal, it was sensible for him to emphasise policy differences from his predecessor.[47]

Some Thatcherite critics expressed themselves despite the complex inheritance with which Major was attempting to deal. Alan Duncan MP urged Major to persevere with the agenda of the 1980s, which he asserted was in harmony with the true Conservative tradition of combining 'the best elements of both the great political traditions of Victorian Britain: the Tory respect for time-honoured customs and institutions, and the Liberal emphasis upon individual freedom'.[48] From within the government Portillo maintained the Thatcherite perspective that governments should do what they consider right regardless of popular opinion, and be judged by results rather than succumbing to the familiar fallacy of so-called consensus politics. This required that the party should continue to win the battle of ideas and not to seek victory through appealing to voters' affluence. To win the battle of ideas required 'fidelity to the agenda of the 1980s: the independence of the individual, the free operation of the market, and the need for improved incentives. These ideas are scarcely questioned in Britain today.[49] Portillo also argued that Europe had to be 'a deregulated, freely-trading, single market . . . it is clearer than before that there are conflicting visions about the future of Europe. That conflict is not principally to be found in the Tory Party. The vision of a free-trading Europe in a free-trading world unites the party . . . Within the EEC we shall see a re-run of the competition of ideas already played out in Britain.'[50] Those former Thatcher cabinet ministers who were standing down: Tebbit, Parkinson and Ridley, were free to complain about Major's overly favourable attitude towards Europe and the ending of the Poll Tax. There were also a number of right-wing commentators who, whether for reasons of intellectual or social snobbery, or a futile longing for the re-emergence of Thatcher, never accepted Major. They included the former socialist turned enthusiastic Thatcherite, Paul Johnson, the *Times* journalist William Rees Mogg and Simon Heffer of the *Telegraph*. Their criticisms of Major were less about policy and more a determination not to be reconciled to the new *arriviste* leader. While Heffer condemned the Citizen's Charter as 'Pooterish', and as providing evidence that Major lacked vision, much of the detailed criticism which these commentators expressed was based on prejudice. They made no effort to conceal their scorn. In general, Major was able to disregard most of these comments although Thatcher's brooding presence was an irritant. There were two areas of criticism which led him to worry on policy issues. One was relations with Europe, where he was to convince himself that he had discovered the formula to deal with the problem in the Maastricht Treaty; and the other was the ballooning Public Sector Borrowing Requirement (PSBR) in the immediate run-up to the general election, which he tolerated for electoral reasons.

There were few intra-party counter pressures to the Thatcherite majority, but one of significance was the view expressed by Patten, Major's friend and party chairman. He advocated the identification of the Conservatives with a caring form of capitalism, arguing that they should offer a 'social market' message similar to that of the Christian Democratic parties in Western Europe. While the free market should generate and allocate wealth, the state should set aside resources for social welfare.[51] More controversially, Patten was interviewed by *Marxism Today*, in which he urged that there be no re-fighting of the old battles of the 1970s which were 'as relevant as talking about the battle of Bosworth field'.[52] He reiterated the need to add social responsibility to successful individualism. Seldon argues that Patten's concept of Christian Democracy instead of Thatcherism was stimulating and served to demonstrate 'the vacuum of similar strategic thinking from Major's cabinet'.[53] This is too harsh a verdict. The profoundly controversial project of importing continental types of capitalism, with their statist connotations, in contrast to the free-market Anglo-Saxon model which was well entrenched after the Thatcher years, would also only find support among a minority clique inside the party. Major lacked political vision, it is true, but it was his skills of party management which were most required at this stage in the party's history.

Major was far more likely to be affected by the electoral and polling evidence about his prospects for a further term of office in which he could secure his own personal mandate, than about producing a political vision. The polls fluctuated in his first year in office. After a good showing for the Conservatives after the Gulf War there was a decline, and the party fell behind until September 1991 when it regained its lead, producing serious discussion about a November 1991 election. The hard electoral evidence was discouraging enough, however, to dispel any real prospect of a general election during 1991. There were by-election setbacks, for example, in Ribble Valley in March, although the Poll Tax was a major issue there; and in Monmouth in May, where the National Health Service was the central controversy. Both results demonstrated substantial swings, to the Liberal Democrats in Ribble Valley and Labour in Monmouth. The local election results in May also led Heseltine to admit that while the Conservatives were within 'striking distance' of a fourth consecutive win, they were not quite there.[54]

The political issues which dominated Major's government from 1990 to the general election were Europe, the economy, the Poll Tax, the reform of the state and education. Whether through the lack of any such ideas, or because he was chary about a total commitment to either Thatcherism or to Patten's European Christian Democracy, Major avoided proposing a central 'big idea', although he claimed that there was a distinct vision underpinning his reform of the state.[55]

THE MAASTRICHT TREATY

It is now clear that the cleavage within the parliamentary party was one of the main reasons for the way in which MPs voted in the leadership ballot in November 1990. Major was the beneficiary of the votes of the Eurosceptics and he underestimated the extent to which the Eurosceptic MPs expected him to adhere to their preferences on reaching Downing Street. It also appears that Major overestimated his capacity to finesse the divisions within the party by compromise and party management. He recognised that after the fractious turn relations with Europe had taken at the end of the Thatcher regime, it was necessary for him to 'mend fences' with the European Union. It was also evident that the Conservative Party was ceasing to be the effective voice of the business community, since large swathes of British business took the view that their future depended upon European trade. He played down the significance of the opposition he encountered from sceptical MPs and from sections of the press after he talked of Britain being at the heart of Europe. He was also imprudent in underestimating the impact on the party's rank and file of Thatcher's public opposition to the European federalist 'Utopia', which she defined as involving any system of managed exchange rates such as the ERM.[56]

Given the pressures to which he was reacting, and his own pragmatic attitude to Europe, Major felt well placed to resolve the split in the party. He believed he could do so by attempting to blur the differences of opinion by the twin tactic of rejecting the federalist vision of Europe, but simultaneously stressing that Britain should be at the heart of European affairs, in order to fight to protect British interests. He advocated Britain striking the correct balance between 'closer cooperation and a proper respect for national institutions and traditions'.[57] As he expressed it in the Maastricht debate, Britain could leave the EU, stay in it 'grudgingly', or 'play a leading role in it, and that is the right policy'.[58] He also marked out the position on the single currency which unravelled in the 1997 election campaign, that while 'we cannot take that step now . . . we should not exclude it'.[59] The principle of 'subsidiarity' should also be 'enshrined' in the Treaty.[60] His ambiguities were necessary because of the growing splits particularly over European Monetary Union (EMU), whereas the divisions were less serious on the European social chapter on workers' rights, because only a minority of the Euro enthusiasts in the party were supportive of European social policy. Howe objected strongly to the idea that Britain was falling down 'some slippery slope' in its relations to Europe and accused the Eurosceptics in his party of misapprehending Britain's interests, and of being negative and fearful. One of the Eurosceptics in the same debate, Nicholas Bugden, exemplified this fear by raising the spectre of federalism.[61]

In his first conference speech Major managed to reduce Thatcher to the level of Heath and Macmillan as they were all three Prime

Ministers who took Britain down the European road. He stressed that Thatcher had signed the Single European Act. He continued to avoid any clear commitment to either of the factions. He argued that the idea of the single currency was, 'an uncertain prospect . . . It is our decision. A single currency cannot be imposed upon us . . . but in no circumstances . . . will a Conservative government give up the right, our national right, to take the crucial decisions about our security, our foreign policy and our defence.'[62]

Major was aware that the meeting of European ministers in Maastricht in December 1991 was likely to take a number of substantial steps in the direction of further European integration. He was aware that both the single European currency and the social chapter were unpopular in the party, yet there were a few MPs who were still prepared to accept the inevitability of both. Given the possibility of Maastricht widening the intra-party divisions this was, in Lawson's words, 'an acutely difficult period for John Major which he handled with considerable skill'.[63] Lawson also asserted that Thatcher's confrontational style on European issues was counterproductive even in her own terms, and added that Major passed the test of holding the party together, 'with flying colours'.[64] Lawson considered that in Britain there was the opportunity for a proper national debate on Europe which was denied to mainland European countries, where popular opposition was greater than political leaders were ready to admit.[65] Perhaps Lawson failed to grasp that European conservative traditions were very different from those of the United Kingdom, and that the issue of the social chapter symbolised the two different attitudes towards state intervention to protect workers' interests.

Many of Major's qualms about the currency were well founded. With both factions pressing him to declare for or against a single currency, Major would not be moved as he was determined to keep his hands free for the future. Among his concerns was a recognition that a single currency would be managed by a European central bank, independent of governments. He was also aware that, according to Jacques Delors, the European commission would oversee national budgets with 80 per cent of all economic decisions taken in Brussels.[66] Major worked in advance to set the scene for a special deal for Britain to help secure a compromise to sell to his party. It was his skills in face-to-face personal interactions which enabled him to get the best out of Europe's most influential statesman, Helmut Kohl. While Kohl's Christian Democracy made him more sympathetic to the principles of the social chapter, Major convinced Kohl that they believed in similar conservative values such as stability, individualism linked to responsibility to others and continuity.[67] At the same time, Major conceded that he would say nothing to prevent Kohl presenting his domestic audience with the interpretation that Maastricht constituted a real step towards a federal Europe.[68] In the period preceding the Maastricht negotiations, Tebbit and Thatcher began to cause serious problems for Major. The new theme they started to press was the need for a referendum on EMU.[69] Thatcher pressed this demand and as Major failed to respond she called him arrogant.[70] Opinion polling evidence at this time demonstrated that more voters were in sympathy with Major than with Thatcher. It took the many years of subsequent Eurosceptical press propaganda to shift popular attitudes to a more Thatcherite position on European issues.

The Maastricht negotiations were of the profoundest political importance for Major as the outcome involved the future of Britain's relations with the EU, the unity of his party, his own reputation and his party's electoral prospects. After lengthy and complicated negotiations Major secured a double success. First, he obtained the excision of the social chapter from the Treaty. The other negotiators understood that Major would use the veto to block the Treaty's passage unless the social chapter was removed, so it was agreed that there should be a separate protocol allowing the other eleven countries to endorse the social chapter. This removed the fears of the Conservatives that there would be the imposition of harmonised minimum wages, maximum hours and worker participation in industry which would affect industrial competitiveness.[71] Secondly, he obtained an opt-out from the final stages of monetary union.

Major's delight was considerable and it was reinforced by the statements made by Delors which made it apparent that he deplored Britain's obduracy over the social chapter.[72] Major claimed that the outcome demonstrated that subsidiarity was in and federalism out. Journalists endorsed this view and argued that Major's 'coup' had achieved his twin objectives of ensuring that Britain remained at the heart of European affairs while preserving Britain's freedom of action in an area where such latitude was considered important.[73] Even some of the Eurosceptics who were virulently hostile to Major in later years voted with the government at the end of a two-day Commons debate. Major possibly made a blunder in not 'whipping' the Maastricht Treaty through the Commons early in 1992, but he decided to delay owing to the scale of the parliamentary business which needed to be tackled, and to avoid provoking any pre-election party split.

It will never be known whether Major was fully aware, or even content, that the opt-out of the single currency was of necessity a temporary piece of sticking plaster over a serious wound within the party, and that he had every intention of Britain joining the currency in the future. His political secretary Judith Chaplin certainly took this view when she wrote in her diary, 'EMU agreed with the British opt-out which we all know is pointless for if (the rest of the EC) have single currency we will have to join'.[74]

MANAGING THE ECONOMY

In the 1992 American Presidential election Bill Clinton ran an election campaign guided by the slogan 'it's the economy stupid'. His view was that voters act on the basis of the performance of the economy, and that as the American economy was faltering under his opponent George Bush, the Republican president, his best opportunity to win the election was to concentrate solely on the state of the economy. The misfortune for the Major government was that as it faced the inevitability of a general election, the economic and the political cycles were out of synchronisation. One part of the unhappy legacy which Thatcher bequeathed to Major was an economy dipping into recession. The fragility of the economy was sufficient to convince Major that despite the benefit of his honeymoon with the electorate, which was enhanced by the Gulf War, the risk of facing the voters was too great. In the first budget of 1991 Lamont had been motivated primarily by the desire to throw money at the problem of the Poll Tax. By the autumn of 1991 the Treasury was more optimistic about the prospects of the economy and at the party conference Lamont claimed to detect 'the green shoots of economic spring'.[75] The recession proved to be more durable, however, and yet despite Clinton's maxim, and the absence of any synchronisation of the economic and political cycles, the opinion polls showed the Conservatives well ahead of Labour on the central issue of economic management. While Clinton was correct to argue that the economy was the main issue, in British politics in the 1990s the normal laws of politics were suspended. With the economy in recession the government was still perceived as the party of economic competence, while in 1995 with the economy growing and unemployment and inflation declining, the polls 'humiliatingly recorded that voters believed Labour would manage even the economy better than the Tories'.[76]

In the period before the election of 1992 the government was compelled to retain interest rates at a high level, and Lamont and Major were failing to delude the electorate by their stubborn refusal to refer to the existence of a recession. Yet they accepted the advice of both the Treasury and the Governor of the Bank of England and failed to cut interest rates. ERM membership was also a constraint on the British government's capacity to determine its own interest rates. The recession was increasingly painful and unemployment doubled from 10 to 20 per cent between 1990 and 1992; it was now hitting the affluent south-eastern middle classes. These groups, which had previously been relatively unscathed by economic downturns, were affected because the services rather than the manufacturing sector bore the brunt of the recession. The collapse of house prices led to the widely reported phenomenon of 'negative equity': that the price of recently purchased houses was less than the mortgage to which the owners were committed.

There were two main reasons for the Major government's success in escaping the blame for the economic recession. First, the Conservative leadership persuaded much of the electorate that the recession was world wide in character and was, therefore, not the responsibility of the government. The essential message was that recovery had been delayed by the fall into recession of Britain's chief export markets. A poll in January 1992 revealed that 50 per cent of voters blamed 'world-wide recession' for the state of the economy.[77] The second reason was that as the domestic roots of the economic difficulties were genuinely located in the public policy errors of the later Thatcher years, Major was forgiven owing to his unfortunate inheritance. The depth of the recession's impact on retail consumption was considerable and was exemplified by a dead car market. Even car dealers were indulgent towards the government and believed Major's propaganda that all that was required was the re-election of the Conservatives for the recession to end the following day.[78] Persuading voters to anticipate a better prospect for higher living standards was to prove a successful electoral ploy. Surveys of business opinion supported the respectively positive and negative views of Tory and Labour policy. In March MORI revealed that 90 per cent thought a Conservative victory would be beneficial for the economy, unlike a mere 6 per cent who were optimistic about the effects of a Labour government.[79]

Right-wing groups in the party were unhappy about the constraints which the ERM placed upon government's ability to cut interest rates, although Maastricht diminished the intensity of the party split over the European dimension of the issue. The European issue was replaced, however, by the central economic question of the burgeoning size of the Public Sector Borrowing Requirement (PSBR) which exceeded £30 billion. This was needed to maintain public spending in the run-up to the election. These critics on the party's right wing harked back nostalgically to the period when Thatcher brought the national finances 'briefly into surplus'.[80] The continued split was now between the party's mainstream, and those dogmatic neo-liberals who had been revivified by the Thatcher experience. Thatcher and Parkinson urged 'belt-tightening' to reduce the deficit in the public finances, while the government's position was that the PSBR necessarily rises during the recession to protect public spending programmes, and economic recovery would witness its rapid decline. The government was also anxious to maintain some scope in the final pre-election budget to cut taxes. The combined impact of both maintaining public spending, and finding money for alleviating the tax burden was to build up the public debt further, and was anathema to Thatcherites such as Parkinson and Tebbit.

As the final pre-election budget approached, the possibility of borrowing to finance tax cuts divided right-wing economists. Some monetarists resisted tax cuts based upon borrowing, while others allowed their ideological proclivity for tax cuts to prevail. Thatcher was herself horrified at the thought of financial imprudence.[81] The decisions over the budget obviously depended upon Lamont and Major, and it was apparent that for them, the electoral imperative of tax cuts took precedence over the views of the authentic deficit-averting Thatcherites. The budget's main proposal was politically astute. In order to offer tax cuts, but of the type which Labour would find difficult to oppose, Lamont's budget re-established the 20 pence tax band for the first £2000 of taxable income to assist the lowest paid. Labour was forced, after some uncertainty in Kinnock's instant parliamentary response, to adhere to its previously stated position of attacking the Conservative government's profligacy in neglecting the existing deficit. This forced Labour to oppose tax cuts to help the four million people who were among the poorest in society. Parkinson also criticised the decision from a fiscally prudent standpoint of reducing the PSBR.[82]

Lamont's skill was apparent in that the lower tax band opened the prospect of extending the rate for all taxpayers so that the party's ultimate goal of a 20 pence basic rate was in sight. A member of Labour's economic team considered the budget as 'tactically brilliant', in reducing the Shadow Chancellor John Smith's options to present to the electorate in the forthcoming election campaign.[83] While Lamont was praised for his political skill, the outcome was actually the result of a compromise between those cabinet ministers who wanted a direct cut in the basic rate, and those who argued either for an extension of the tax threshold, or for the view that in the financial circumstances tax cutting would simply appear cynical. The politically clever compromise, which provided a good launch for the election campaign, was the idea of Jeremy Haywood, Lamont's Principal Private Secretary.[84] Labour's decision to oppose the tax cuts proved a mistake, as it helped to focus on the Tory claim to be the party of tax cuts while Labour could be portrayed as the party of 'tax and spend'. It is notable that while tax experts argued that the 20 pence tax band was an inefficient use of money, it was retained by the Blair Labour government.

The economy was not in a healthy position, however, when Major was finally forced to call the election. The budget exacerbated the situation, and with expenditure increasing and revenue declining in the middle of a recession, the deficit was moving towards £35 billion, or 6 per cent of national income. Major took the risk before the election of letting public spending run and postponing economically sound decisions until after the election.[85] The strategy of generous pre-election budgets which have subsequently to be reversed was an old Conservative tactic. The 1955 budget presented by R.A. Butler is the most dramatic example. Yet the ballooning PSBR in 1992 was a dilemma for Labour as well as the government, as neither party could make generous promises in their election manifestos. The Conservative manifesto avoided firm spending commitments which enabled Major to condemn Labour's fiscal imprudence.

REPLACING THE POLL TAX

The replacement of the Poll Tax was a political imperative for Major in the period before the 1992 general election. There was a clear need to discover a more voter-friendly way of financing local government. In her period of hubristic behaviour after 1987 the greatest single example of *folies de grandeur* had been Thatcher's determination to introduce the Poll Tax rapidly, in violation of public opinion. One of the reasons for her removal by the party was her stubborn refusal to countenance any change to the Community Charge, as she preferred to describe it, so it was incumbent on her successor to re-think the funding of local government. The Poll Tax had not just become deeply unpopular, it was also not achieving its own goals. Some of the party's right-wing continued to share Thatcher's enthusiasm for the tax, however, so Major had to tread warily. Tebbit, Ridley and Parkinson were among those prepared to defend the tax. Major astutely appointed Heseltine, who had made such a strong public commitment to the removal of the tax, to find a means of replacing it. The problems involved in attempting to address the Poll Tax issue contained an early warning of the difficulties which Major was likely to face in the longer term with the unreconciled Thatcherites. While many Conservative voters recognised that the Poll Tax was a reform too far, the hard core of right-wingers in parliament, many of whom clung to the view that Thatcher was irreplaceable, wished to persevere with it. Faced with this opposition Major was unable to break free, and Labour could justly accuse him of 'dithering'. This charge was reinforced by a strong attack in the Commons from Nigel Lawson in which he lent weight to the charge of indecisiveness, by asserting that Major seemed incapable of choosing, when 'to govern is to choose'.[86]

It was clear in 1991 that a somewhat premature debate was beginning about the continuity or lack of it between Major and Thatcher. For some the change in the Poll Tax was already indicative that in continuing the Thatcherite project, Major was doing so without conviction or true radicalism. This jeopardised the future of the project.[87] Others argued that the specific policy changes as with the Poll Tax were exceptional, and that the difference between the two leaders was essentially one of style.[88] Major's problems arose from the Thatcherites on the one side, but also from Heseltine who initially wanted to return to the old rating system. This was anathema to many Conservatives who had long deplored the rates. After years of attacking the rating system many MPs remained keen to retain a personal element in whatever system was adopted to replace the Poll Tax. So Major had to attempt to satisfy a diverse range of groups. They included the old Thatcherites, the party mainstream who distrusted Heseltine's plans, Heseltine himself, the local authorities whose task it was to collect the tax and whose warnings about the virtual uncollectability of the Poll Tax had not been heeded, and the Treasury, which could provide the tax expertise which had not been exploited by the Department of the Environment previously.[89] The key for Major was to indicate to the electorate that the tax would go since a replacement could not be in operation before the general election. This was because there was insufficient time, but there were also political benefits to the government in postponing the costs of transferring from the Poll Tax to its substitute until after an election.[90] By the time of the election, while Labour propagandists listed the Poll Tax in their litany of what had gone wrong under the Conservatives, and despite the final Poll Tax bills landing on voters' doorsteps at the start of the campaign, the political damage had been removed by the promise of its abolition.[91] There was a perverse benefit for the Conservatives from the Poll Tax in the 1992 general election. Its introduction had led to many poorer voters not registering to vote in the hope of escaping the tax, so reducing the Labour vote.[92]

Heseltine considered a range of alternatives to the Poll Tax including local sales tax, local income tax and mixed taxes. Many Conservative MPs thought the answer was for central government to take over altogether.[93] In fact, the cabinet approached the issue by inviting Heseltine to undertake a review not just of the Poll Tax but of the structures and functions of local government.[94] Major lanced the boil of the Poll Tax by insisting that Lamont do in the 1991 budget what Lawson had refused to do at Thatcher's request, which was to throw money at the Poll Tax in order to lessen the bills. This reduced the average Poll Tax bill from £392 to £252 at a single stroke and kept open the possibility of a June 1991 general election.[95] The Treasury extracted the price of close involvement in the production of an alternative. If the Conservative local government conference in March 1991 strongly expressed the preference for retaining the Poll Tax, the party's heavy defeat in the Ribble Valley by-election a few days later, in which the Poll Tax had figured as a main issue, strengthened Heseltine's hand.

The new Council Tax ultimately emerged from the deliberations of the GEN 8 cabinet committee and was a compromise combining both property and personal elements.[96] Cabinet committees are often neglected when internecine policy disputes within government are analysed. In reality they are the crucial, if invisible, sinews of political decision-making. While they bind the entire government the decisions which emanate from cabinet committees are often misperceived as the individual decisions of a particular ministers.[97] Such committees are valuable to Prime Ministers, however, because they are used to ensure that a proposal enjoys a measure of solid ministerial support before it is brought to the full cabinet for ratification. During the difficult period when the policy was being prepared, Major dealt with the conflict by the repetition of the mantra that 'nothing is ruled in and nothing is ruled out'.[98] In April 1991 the cabinet accepted the GEN 8 proposal for a Council Tax which involved every household paying a two person tax band based on the value of the property, with a 25 per cent discount for houses with single occupation. Properties were to be assessed and allocated into seven bands, but residents in properties in the highest band defined as over £160,000 would not be required to pay more than two and a half times the amount of the cheapest.[99] Heseltine responded to protests that the rich were treated leniently by the banding system by introducing an eighth band for houses worth more than £320,000.

Patten considered the production of the new and electorally saleable Council Tax as the 'most brilliant piece of government I ever saw'.[100] At last the Conservative Party had produced a viable alternative to the rating system which Thatcher had excoriated nearly twenty years before. The Council Tax did not revivify local government, however, as it produced a mere 20 per cent of local authority revenue. This conflicted with some of Heseltine's stated ambitions to revive local government, as during 1991 he floated such ideas as locally elected mayors, only to find little support in the cabinet. As a result of the decision to locate the replacement of the Poll Tax within a wider context, however, the Local Government Commission was set up under John Banham early in 1992. Major had achieved his goal of removing one of the most serious political disasters inherited from the Thatcher years by playing a long-drawn-out political game, by careful compromise and by an emollient style. He perhaps wrongly inferred that such a technique could work over Maastricht and Europe. They proved to be quite different propositions.

THE REFORM OF THE STATE

Major was patently prepared to be radical in the area of reforming the state by continuing to implement the 'Next Steps' report of 1987 and to hasten the process of agencification in government. This policy may have been less visible to the electorate, but under the Project Director of Next Steps, Sir Peter Kemp, some radical changes were afoot.[101]

Agencies were conceived as capable of transfer to the private sector and much progress in this direction was achieved during the second Major government after 1992. The process of agencification also had the beneficial consequence from a Thatcherite perspective of fragmenting and weakening the previously large and potent Civil Service Association. The Thatcher goal of 'deprivileging' the civil service was thus able to continue apace.

The other main reform concerning the role of the state was, in fact, Major's 'big idea': the Citizens Charter. Major unveiled it at a meeting of the Conservative Central Council in March 1991. This policy was understood by many on the right wing of the party as evidence that Major was reverting from privatisation to a sympathetic view of the public services. Much press comment regarded it as a distraction from the true faith of privatisation.[102] Certainly some regarded it as a shift from Thatcherism since the lady found it hard to believe that anything of merit could come from the public sector. A quite different interpretation is, however, more convincing – one which recognises that in its consumerism, contractualism and individualism, its negative assumptions about public bureaucracies, its patent managerialism and its attitude that the public sector is merely an inefficient version of the private sector, it was foursquare with Thatcherism. The only dilution from pure Thatcherism was that, to use Hirschman's typology, it was an example of the user exploiting the method of 'voice' rather than 'exit' in relation to inadequacies in the public service.[103] Despite laying down minimum standards for the provision of services, however, the charters were not legally binding and were open consequently to the accusation of 'gimmickry'.

REFORMING EDUCATION

Major determined to make education a central issue in his government. This was surprising in view of the recent passage of the 1988 Education Act. Since he wished to reward teachers his government set up an independent pay review body which awarded substantial increases. This was vigorously opposed by Lamont and the Treasury who argued that it conflicted with the government's aversion to centralised pay bargaining and would become an expensive commitment. Major's views prevailed. He appointed Kenneth Clark as Secretary of State for Education. Clark had acquired a reputation as a strong man whose views prevailed over the opposition of strong vested interests. His reputation as a 'one nation' Conservative remained intact despite his proving to be a highly effective promoter of Thatcherite policies as, for example, when he pushed through the reforms of the Health Service which had defeated his ministerial predecessor John Moore. Reassured by Clark's political weight behind him, Major pursued further 'shake-ups' of the education system. Further education colleges were removed from the control of the local education authorities and became corporations, the distinctions between universities and polytechnics were abolished and both organisations were brought under the direction of a single non-elected body, the Higher Education Funding Council for England (HEFCE). Finally, a system of youth credits was introduced in place of the old Youth Training Schemes which provided the young unemployed with a credit to purchase training. This idea had long been promoted by the CBI and encapsulated many Thatcherite principles. It implied the sovereignty of the consumer over the producer, as young people could spend their credit with whichever supplier of training that they chose. It was designed to develop a training market, therefore, in which the producers and suppliers of training programmes were compelled to compete with each other in order to capture business. This was claimed to 'empower' the young trainees.[104] The reality was very different, however, with the young people unaware of their rights, of the choices available to them and often resident in an area where there was a single dominant training supplier. Further, the TECs as 'brokers' between the trainees and the suppliers had a clear role to play. It is also abundantly clear that when the TECs were set up to deliver training the government argued that it was the employers who should control the training market as the group best situated to determine their training needs, and the TECs were the instruments of the employers who ran their boards. Training credits were flawed, therefore, by the contradiction between giving the management of training to both employers and to young people.[105]

A further reform compatible with Thatcherism was the abolition of the old inspectors of schools (Her Majesty's Inspectors) and their replacement with a new organisation OFSTED which was independent from the Department of Education and Science (DES) and operated as a private sector body contracting with individuals for specific inspections. This was a policy pleasing to the right wing as it both weakened the central state by removing another function from its direct control, but it also accepted a long-standing prejudice that the

HMIs had been captured by the educational establishment, and were reluctant to risk unpopularity by reporting on just how poor standards were becoming in schools. Seldon is correct to comment that Major had succeeded in placing education on the fast burner in a few months, but in describing these reforms as 'undoctrinaire common sense' he fails to discern their strong ideological underpinning. That he could even offer such a judgement is testimony to how far the ideological parameters of British politics shifted during the Thatcher and Major years. A good example is the fundamentally different role of LEAs. From being all-encompassing providers, they have become bodies whose claims to be central in the provision of services now appears to be antideluvian.[106]

THE 1992 GENERAL ELECTION

It was Patten's responsibility as party chairman to prepare the party for the forthcoming election and he soon discovered that the chairmanship was a poisoned chalice. While most of his problems came from disaffected Thatcherites, the Charter Movement launched into one of its more assertive phases. As an intra-party group concerned to increase both the probity and the internal democracy within the party, with the democracy aimed at enhancing the party's probity, it had nuisance value. It had been formed in 1980, but its concerns had grown during the Thatcher years. In 1991 it condemned the party's inept financial stewardship, particularly for the three year decline in the proportion of funds derived from the constituency parties, whose contributions had fallen from 24 to 7 per cent. To compensate, the party had resorted to funding from such sources as the Greek millionaire John Latsis. More distressing was the overt use of Central Office organised offers to potential donors to provide access to the party's policy-making counsels in return for financial contributions. A Central Office letter asserted that, 'we will undertake . . . to keep you in touch with our thinking and give you the opportunity to tell us yours through meeting ministers'.[107] If only offering nuisance value it was a contribution that the Conservatives could well have done without.

There were many problems confronting the party as it looked towards an early election. It was deeply in debt, and the fact of it deriving its funds from questionable sources, intensified its problems. One MP described Central Office as 'coming apart at the seams'.[108] There was strong criticism of the legacy of Baker as party chairman.

While he had a propaganda triumph in portraying the 1990 local election results as a success for the Conservatives, his 1990 'summer heat on Labour' campaign was dismissed as implausible.[109] Many activists were also disgruntled about Thatcher's removal and had to be re-galvanised into action. So unhappy were some local parties that there was a spate of attempted deselections of those suspected of disloyalty to the pure milk of Thatcherism.[110] Patten prepared to turn the party round, and persuaded Major to continue to use the services of Sir Roland Miller and Sir Gordon Reece, who had respectively helped with speech writing and political advice. Patten dispensed with the services of some older hands, however, and introduced Shaun Woodward from the BBC as Communications Director and re-established Saatchi and Saatchi as the party's advertising agents in the hope of recreating the energy they had demonstrated in 1978–9. Contrary to his 'clean' image, he also brought over Sir Richard Wirthlin from the United States, who was an expert in negative campaigning techniques, such as personality attacks.[111] Patten also streamlined the regional and constituency level of party activities to introduce better technology and press communications, and so the party employed both traditional constituency and modern mass communications forms of campaigning.

As alarming as the electoral unpreparedness was the lack of policy preparation by Baker. As Patten expressed it, 'the cupboard was bare'. The party's strategists could not avoid the issue of whether or not Major was continuing or changing the Thatcherite agenda. The evidence from policy decisions was that Major offered a shift rather than a break with Thatcher's policy and style. One participant said that, 'in supermarket terms we want to sell an updated product, not a new brand'. Ministers stressed that they were building on, rather than 'ditching', Thatcherism.[112] This explains why Major accepted Saatchi's advice and avoided such terms as the social market and caring capitalism which would have implied a sharp break with his predecessor.

At the start of 1992 the opinion polls showed a significant Labour lead and the Conservatives decided to retrieve the ground with the help of a long campaign. As a result, the near term campaign, as it was described, began early in January 1992. Its main purpose was to counteract the unfortunate state of the economy by creating alarm over Labour's taxation policies. This consisted of the unveiling of one thousand poster sites displaying a 'bombshell' which revealed that under Labour tax would be more than £1000 a year higher for the average voter. This Saatchi image was expanded into the infamous 'double whammy' of both taxation and inflation which it was claimed would follow from the election of a Labour government. A party political broadcast in January further developed the theme with the slogan, 'You'd be worse off under Labour.'[113] The economic situation remained grim, however, and all the economic indicators pointed in the wrong direction. Yet most Conservative ministers expected to win narrowly, and their confidence helped carry them through as against Labour's nervousness about whether their opinion poll lead could hold. The secret Conservative weapon of unity had not yet broken down, as apart from a few rumblings on the margins by unreconciled Thatcherites, the real splits were to occur after 1992. While the Conservatives knew from the experience of 1992 that Labour would mount a professional campaign, press support was estimated to be worth £18 million for the Tories as against £6 million for Labour.[114]

It is evident in retrospect that Labour's narrow opinion poll lead at the start of the campaign was fragile, and that the campaign would matter. When the Shadow Chancellor John Smith presented his alternative budget, which proposed to raise national insurance contributions for wealthier voters and to increase the top tax rate, it gave credence to Conservative claims about Labour's tax and spend policies. By contrast, the Conservative election manifesto appeared unthreatening. It included progress towards stable prices, a widening of the 20 pence tax band, a promise to cut inheritance tax; and on public services, the Citizens Charter, further privatisation including the railways, tougher sentencing for criminal offenders, housing measures to encourage home ownership and private renting and a Millennium Fund to be financed by a national lottery.[115]

In the campaign itself it was only when Major abandoned some of the packaging propounded by his 'spin doctors', and took to the soapbox of his youth, that the Conservative campaign came alive. In contrast, Kinnock was so heavily packaged throughout, that his natural ebullience was not allowed to show through until, excited by the spectacular nature of a premature victory celebration at a rally in Sheffield, he became over-excited and lost the statesmanlike image which his 'minders' had so sedulously cultivated. Until the end of the campaign opinion appeared to be equally divided. A few more Conservative mistakes and fewer Labour errors could have produced a different outcome. That Labour could not oust the Tories after their thirteen consecutive years in government demonstrated that the

Conservative claims about the world-wide nature of the recession, and their proclaimed ability to remedy it, reflected the respective credibility of the two parties in April 1992.

Labour's strategists argued in their post-election analysis that Labour's opinion poll lead had always been false. Their argument was that the change from Thatcher to Major boosted the Conservatives and that the tax and leadership problems were always going to make the party unelectable.[116] This view was based on a Conservative victory, which while narrow in terms of seats, the Conservatives merely securing an overall majority of seventeen, gave them 41.9% of the vote against 34.4% for Labour. Certainly, the Conservatives continued to add the support of the aspirational working classes to its middle-class constituency. If in the nineteenth century, the spectre of 'the tyranny of the majority' terrified the middle and upper classes, in 1992 it appeared that the electors' verdict involved the tyranny of the comfortable and contented majority over the poor. The result led the political commentator Anthony King to make the rash prediction that the Conservatives had achieved permanent political power.[117] That this was a misjudgement at the time is now apparent, as neither Major's political skills, nor the extent of the divisions within his party, had yet been fully tested.

CHAPTER

7

BLACK WEDNESDAY TO BLACK THURSDAY

Thursday 1 May 1997 is the blackest day in the history of postwar Conservatism with the party suffering its worst electoral defeat since 1832. The roots of this disaster can be traced back to so-called Black Wednesday, 16 September 1992, when the pound was ignominiously forced out of the European Exchange Rate Mechanism (ERM), to which Britain had belonged since October 1990. This was a particularly humiliating event for the Prime Minister John Major, and for his Chancellor of the Exchequer Lamont, since they had spent the previous months strenuously defending Britain's ERM membership as the cornerstone of the government's economic policy. The significance of Black Wednesday is that it instantly destroyed the Conservative Party's reputation as the party of competent economic management. Many other problems, both self-inflicted and externally imposed afflicted Major's beleaguered government in the following four and a half years, but their impact was magnified by the collapse in credibility caused by the events of Black Wednesday.

INDIAN SUMMER TO BLACK WEDNESDAY

The fourth successive electoral victory by the Conservative Party in April 1992 led to a brief period of euphoria for the Conservatives and for Major personally, not least because during the election campaign he had shown one of his rare examples of political courage by ignoring the advice of his 'minders', and taking to old style campaigning by addressing public open-air meetings on his symbolic 'soap box'. In the early months of the government it was not apparent that the story of

163

Major's second term was one of a slow slide to disaster, although in retrospect it is apparent that the triumphs in the early months were balanced by events which foreshadowed the problems to come.

Major immediately reshuffled his cabinet and appointed the defeated party chairman Patten, who had lost his seat in Bath, to be the Governor of Hong Kong. In May 1992 the Tories also fared well in the local elections as demoralised Labour voters stayed at home. Anthony King proved rash in his speculation that Britain could now become a one party state, but it reflected the mood in the two main parties in the immediate aftermath of April.[1] The Major government's optimistic mood was strengthened by the events surrounding the first Queen's Speech in May 1992. Half of the party's manifesto was included in the government's programme for the first year, with sixteen major bills. They included proposals for the privatisation of coal and rail, reforms to health, education and housing, an asylum bill, a national lottery, curbs on trade unions and an expansion of the Citizen's Charter. In the debate following the speech from the throne, Major announced legislation to place the intelligence services on a statutory foundation and promised to reduce secrecy in government. He reaffirmed his closeness to Thatcher, by maintaining his intention to resist pressure from Europe to re-establish the handicaps on British industry that had been abolished in the 1980s. It has been argued that for Major, 'the speech and debate were a defining moment in the premiership; never again would he have so much power and so much ability to establish his own agenda and tone . . . He radiated quiet confidence . . . later in May Major was being spoken of as pre-eminent among European politicians . . . Major's stock, in both Britain and the European Community, was never to be higher.'[2]

Even in those early months there were signs of the depths of disaster to come. The size of the government's overall majority, which was a mere twenty-one despite a substantially larger lead of 8 per cent in the popular vote, was not a good augury, with contentious issues such as the degree of Britain's integration into Europe likely to cause serious internal party difficulties. Other harbingers of disaster also occurred: in May twenty-two Conservatives voted against the government, and four abstained, on the second reading of the Maastricht ratification which foreshadowed later parliamentary crises. The Danish rejection of the Maastricht Treaty in a referendum led to back-bench Tory demands to re-think Britain's commitment to the ERM and for a referendum on the issue. The National Heritage Secretary David Mellor refused to resign over sordid press descriptions of his affair with the actress Antonia de Sancha, but later did so after revelations that his family had enjoyed paid holidays at the expense of a woman with links to the Palestine Liberation Organisation. This event pointed to the problems to come concerning sleaze in the party. The election of John Smith as Labour leader in July 1992 demonstrated Labour's readiness to return effectively to the fray with a new and apparently more managerially competent leader. The sending of troops to Bosnia in August opened up a much more ambiguous British military involvement than ever the Gulf or the Falklands conflicts had been. But above all the continuing nuisance value of Thatcher's ideological carping was revealed.[3] A mere week after the election she revealed her true thinking; although like many both in the party, and among political commentators, she was never consistent in determining whether Major was continuing with her political project. She told an American interviewer that, 'I don't accept the idea that all of a sudden Major is his own man. He has been Prime Minister for seventeen months and he has inherited all these great achievements of the past eleven years which have fundamentally changed Britain, ridding it of the debilitating, negative aspects of socialism . . . There isn't such a thing as Majorism . . . Thatcherism will live. It will live long after Thatcher has died, because we had the courage to restore the great principles and put them into practice.'[4] Her former press adviser Bernard Ingham advised her to desist from making such statements if she wished to remain influential in the party.[5]

Black Wednesday was devastating for Major because of his constant reiteration in the weeks leading up to it, that it was vital to his whole financial and economic strategy that Britain remained in the ERM, and that to do otherwise was to fall for the attractions of 'fool's gold'. He added that such a devaluation would be a 'betrayal'.[6] Possibly Conservatives have a desire to portray devaluations of the currency as the type of inflationary panic measure to which Labour governments are prone. 'The perfidy of 1967 [Labour's last devaluation of the pound], however, continues to dominate the judgement of macho Conservative politicians. The prospect of repeating it is something they have ferociously, vainly, resisted.'[7] Major even boasted that the strength of sterling was becoming a threat to the predominance of the Deutschmark.[8] Major and Lamont staked their reputations on keeping the pound within the ERM, despite all the contrary signals from the international financial markets that the pound was overvalued. Enormous sums of money were spent shoring up the pound; for example, £10 billion on 3 September alone.[9] On 5 September, Lamont reasserted his refusal to modify Britain's exchange rate and maladroitly tried to pressure the German Bundesbank to lower its interest rates.[10] Clearly, despite years of Thatcherite preaching against financial incontinence 'the begging bowl' had still not been put away. The problem was that the exchange rate of 2.95 DM to the pound had been Major's decision as chancellor, which explains why he was doggedly determined to adhere to this same rate even as its unsustainability became more apparent in the late summer of 1992. Major remained convinced that this was the only way to contain inflation.

Maintaining British membership at this rate of exchange required the retention of high interest rates, yet it was these high levels of interest rates which were ensuring that the British recession lingered. Major was privately inclined to blame the Germans, who were maintaining a high level of interest rates to counter inflationary pressures, in the aftermath of German reunification. Yet Britain was forced to pursue the same interest rate strategy as Germany to retain the same level of the pound against the Deutschmark. There was an alternative way forward, although it could not be publicly discussed because it would precipitate an economic crisis, which was to negotiate a formal realignment for the pound within the ERM. Major had privately asked his political adviser Sarah Hogg to investigate this for him at the end of 1991 and she suggested the option of a new central rate of 2.78 DM, a lowering of 6 per cent. But Major did not raise this option with Lamont as the Treasury was sanguine about the recession and the Bank of England remained worried about inflation.[11] Major should have reconsidered this option in the summer of 1992 as the recession continued, but instead made the cardinal political error of allowing himself to be 'boxed in'. As speculators recognised that there was no serious prospect of an economic recovery in Britain without devaluation, the pressures increased. The denouncement arrived on Black Wednesday. Despite a dramatic raising of interest rates during that fevered day there was no impact on the calculations of speculators, and by the evening, exhausted and visibly discomfited, Lamont announced to the press in Downing Street Britain's departure from the ERM. One Conservative newspaper described the outcome as 'the biggest U-turn for decades'.[12]

The full extent of the electoral damage of the U-turn and the reversion to a freely floating pound on the international markets which it involved, was not immediately apparent. The precipitate nature of the withdrawal from the ERM, however, and the government's evident embarrassment over the episode was immediately appreciated. The *Sun* newspaper had fought so vigorously for a Conservative victory in 1992 that it boasted that it had won the election for the government. Betrayed by the failure over the ERM and the damage which it inflicted on Major, and implicitly referring to the Mellor affair, its headline on the day after Black Wednesday was 'Now we've all been screwed by the Cabinet'. Its analysis referred to 'the smell of panic' in Downing Street.[13] Many newspapers called for Lamont's resignation and described the political damage which the episode had inflicted on Major after his fruitless battles with the financial markets.[14] The *Times* argued that the ERM

> had blown up in his [Major's] face . . . The Prime Minister's pledge to take whatever action was necessary to defend the pound within the ERM was the main plank of his economic policy. Last night it collapsed. Not even James Callaghan and Denis Healey, whose economic policies were also found wanting by international and domestic holders of sterling, suffered the humiliation of raising base rates twice on the same day and then to admitting that it had all been a mistake.[15]

A Conservative writing in the *Independent* newspaper described it is 'the most grotesque day in the history of British finance, a day of crisis, disorder, confusion and mismanagement'.[16] Yet Major refused to scapegoat Lamont for a policy failure in which he shared. This proved to be misplaced loyalty as he later dismissed Lamont, who was then sufficiently aggrieved to turn against Major and to extract his revenge.

Conservative popularity declined immediately and never subsequently recovered. The party hovered around 30 per cent in the polls and Labour led by more than 20 per cent right up to the date of the 1997 general election. It was also evident that while voters continued to like Major as a person, they considered him 'a weak and ineffectual leader'.[17] The root cause of this persistent unpopularity was the disassociation of the Conservative Party from the possession of superior skills in economic management. On previous occasions during the Thatcher and Major years the Conservatives had lagged in the opinion polls, and had been regarded as less effective than Labour in a range of policy areas, but they had always led on economic competence. It was the careless frittering of this political advantage of economic competence which, intensified by other political difficulties after 1992, led to the party's electoral demise.[18] In October 1992 Labour took an 18 per cent lead on the issue. This stretched to 22 per cent in November, and while it narrowed subsequently, the Conservatives never regained their reputation as the party best suited to run the economy.[19] In a party system the performance of the other parties is also decisively important. It was unfortunate for Major that John Smith's and, after 1994, Tony Blair's reassuring credentials as managers of the economy, suggested that there was a real alternative to the Conservatives. The events of Black Wednesday were also decisively important because they raised the issue of Europe and emboldened Eurosceptics in the party and the press to exert pressure on Major.

It is implausible to argue that the 1997 defeat was inevitable after the events of Black Wednesday as other events might have intruded to revive the Conservatives. In practice, however, other events served mainly to reinforce the difficulties of the Major government. Events during the rest of 1992 ensured that the year was an *annus horribilis* for the government as well as for the royal family.

1992: THE ANNUS HORRIBILIS

In the parliamentary debate after Black Wednesday, Major was scoffed at for his previous predictions that the pound would be the strongest currency in Europe, and he failed to grasp that strong economies produce strong currencies rather than the reverse. Matters worsened, however, and Major described the autumn period as 'the worst period by far' of his premiership.[20] Some of the problems were a direct result of the European issue which Maastricht had highlighted. Among those who exploited his troubles at the Brighton conference that autumn, and played to the Eurosceptical gallery, were the recently sacked Education minister Baker, Tebbit and Thatcher herself. While Thatcher was well received when she entered the conference, there was ambiguity in the reaction of delegates towards a former leader who appeared to be undermining the incumbent. While Major's speech in which he promised to put Britain's interests first was also well received, the conference was a further warning that the party was becoming split over Britain's future European role.[21]

In October the government announced a programme of pit closures which amounted to a halving of the workforce. This was badly presented, as well as an inherently unpopular policy at a time of recession, although Major showed himself out of touch with reality when he attributed the unpopularity of the policy in its entirety to presentation.[22] The need for the policy was the result of the government's earlier privatisation of electricity, but it led to an unexpected upsurge of popular protest which unsettled many on the Conservative back benches. This outrage was a delayed response to popular anger about the ERM debacle, a reflection of a long-standing popular concern over the fate of the miners, the fact that many of the Nottinghamshire pits which had remained loyal during the prolonged 1984/5 dispute were now being terminated, but above all because of the additional burden which closures placed on the unemployment problem. The government was unintentionally conveying the message that it was unconcerned about the nation's social fabric as well as blasé about the country's future energy requirements. The minister responsible was Heseltine who had been appointed to the Department of Trade and Industry after the election, and many had thought that he would take this opportunity to pursue an interventionist strategy to promote industry and employment. Yet here he was presiding over a free-market approach to energy which also appeared socially uncaring. A number of local Conservative Party associations and a number of MPs were in rebellious mood. The fact that many were on the party's right can be explained by such factors as an instinct for populism, and sympathy for the Nottinghamshire miners whom they regarded as allies in the cause against trade union militancy, but above all it was an opportunity for Eurosceptics to embarrass Heseltine, who they regarded as the classic Europhile within the cabinet. The government was surprised by the reaction, but it rode out the storm by promising a review which ultimately reaffirmed the policy, and by stepping up the economic aid to the affected local communities.[23] Assisted by a policy of procrastination over the next couple of years, therefore, the pits were closed. The affair was so mishandled that one television interviewer pushed the normally assertive Heseltine on to the defensive by enquiring whether he was pleased that he had turned Arthur Scargill, President of the National Union of Mineworkers, into a popular figure.[24] The scale of popular protest was signalled by a march of over 50,000 demonstrators through London urging, 'Sack Major not the Miners'.[25]

The aftermath of ERM withdrawal obviously led to debate about new directions for economic policy. Eurosceptic MPs increasingly described 16 September as 'White Wednesday', as it gave the opportunity for Britain to resume control over its own interest rates, and for trade to expand as the value of the pound fell and overseas markets became more accessible. Lamont outlined two main objectives in his Mansion House speech in October: the promotion of growth through the protection of publicly funded capital projects such as the extension of the Jubilee Line on the London underground and the launch of the Private Finance Initiative (PFI) in which private money would be used to fund public projects through new forms of public-private partnerships.[26]

It was the need to secure ratification for the Maastricht Treaty, of which Major remained inordinately proud because of the opt-outs that he had secured, which most preoccupied him in the autumn of 1992. One of the most implausible political predictions of the year had appeared in *The Economist* in April. Analysing the significance of the Conservative victory in the general election it argued that Major 'will be able to put aside one issue that has preoccupied him since he took over from Margaret Thatcher: the Tories' divisions over the European community will now not count. For the first time since Britain joined the EC in 1973, its role in Europe can be framed without regard to the minutiae of domestic politics.'[27] Major decided to attempt to create such a situation, by introducing a 'paving bill' in November 1992, to demonstrate to Britain's European partners his earnest intention of persevering with the parliamentary endorsement of Maastricht. Such a Bill was not necessary, and Major's macho approach at this stage merely added another dramatic episode in the attempt to secure the bill's passage, which could have been avoided. As critics in the party became vociferous he initially threatened the dissolution of parliament and when that failed to silence his critics, including the majority of the 1922 Committee who thought such drama unnecessary, came up with the self-defeating ruse that the 'paving bill' would not actually mention the word Maastricht.[28] Despite the vigorous efforts of the Whips Office and the adoption of a more conciliatory tone towards the rebels, the paving bill only passed the Commons by 319 to 313 votes, with 26 Conservative MPs voting against the government and a further 7 abstaining.[29] The open display of the divisions within the party undermined the whole purpose of introducing the paving bill, and the development of the Tory split over Europe into a chasm was now plainly evident.

Given the scale and extent of the divisions within the party over Europe, it is necessary to understand the nature of the argument. There have been three periods in which the leadership of the Conservative

Party has appeared to be enthusiastic about Europe. First, when Heath's government secured British entry in the early 1970s. Secondly, when even under Thatcher there had been enthusiasm for the idea of the single European market in the early 1980s, and thirdly, when Major promised in early 1991 that he wanted to see Britain 'at the heart of Europe'. The problem was that the Euro-enthusiasts in the party rarely made the case effectively to the country, and the European cause became one of elites, in which the mass of the party in the country and the mass of voters were uninvolved. When the Conservative MP Emma Nicholson decided to defect to the Liberal Democrats in 1995, which provided yet another bombshell to the then tottering Major government, one of her reasons was the party's abysmal failure to inform people about the case for European membership. Even during the party's debates over the Maastricht Treaty she complained that

> the Conservative Party's continued refusal to brief either its supporters or the wider electorate properly over European issues had become even clearer to me. I spent considerable amounts of time during this period responding to invitations to speak to constituencies to explain the Treaty . . . I found that the constituency Conservative associations lacked even basic knowledge of the subject . . . All the material was readily available from Brussels; surely it should also be available from Smith Square? [Conservative Central Office] . . . Once again the Conservative Party deliberately left its supporters in ignorance, about a matter it was supporting.[30]

Even if some Conservative supporters of Britain's membership had a very instrumental view of the country's role, and were interested in bargaining within the EU in order to get the best deal for the British rather than having a strong ideological commitment to the European idea, there were some in the party who by the early 1990s had acquired an almost visceral dislike of Britain's membership, particularly if it involved any further integration.

Thatcher formed and inspired the party's Eurosceptical faction. Her mood changed in 1988. She then realised the full implications of the Single European Act, which she had negotiated through parliament in 1986, as interpreted by such enthusiasts for the Social Charter on employee rights as Jacques Delors. The enthusiastic ideological affiliation between Thatcher and Ronald Reagan, President of the USA, in the 1980s also served to reinforce the Atlanticism of the Conservative right wing. The ending of the Cold War and the spectre of a strong and reunited Germany also alarmed Thatcher and her followers in the early 1990s. Two other inter-related arguments were increasingly advanced in the Conservative Party in the early 1990s. 'First, it was argued to be more in the British interest to develop trade and investment opportunities with the dynamic Asian economies than with the sluggish European economies . . . Second, it became conventional wisdom that openness to inward and outward foreign investment was the key to developing the UK economy. EU rules, including, (but not only) its social legislation, created obstacles.'[31] Naturally, Britain's enforced departure from the ERM 'catalysed the controversy about European integration more broadly and made it the Achilles heel of Conservative European policy'.[32]

Seldon differentiates the Eurosceptics into four different groups. They were the long-standing all-out anti-marketeers like Teddy Taylor, the constitutionalists like Bill Cash who wished to protect national sovereignty, the free-marketeers such as Michael Spicer who regarded the EU as an unwelcome interference in Britain's newly restored capitalist economy and the populist nationalists such as Tony Marlow.[33] This typology is a useful aid to understanding, recognises the subtle differences in motivation by individual Eurosceptic back benchers and shows how the European issue touched so many sensitive Conservative nerves. It oversimplifies, however, like all such categorisations, and many of these MPs simply had a visceral and inarticulate objection to further integration. Some were also simply yearning for Thatcher's party leadership and regarded Major as a hopeless substitute. The groups often acted in concert, whatever their varying grounds for Euroscepticism, but were divided mainly on the degree to which they considered their position on Europe to be more important than keeping the party in power. In any event, they continued to pose difficulties in subsequent years.

Most of the problems which undermined the Major government had emerged by the end of 1992. The rest of the parliament was the playing out of a tragedy, the outlines of which were apparent by the end of that year. Before the year ended the issue of sleaze emerged with the arms to Iraq affair. A machine tools company, Matrix Churchill, was being prosecuted for shipping its products to Iraq in defiance of an arms embargo against President Saddam Hussein. The former Conservative minister Alan Clark made a statement in court which made it appear that

BLACK WEDNESDAY TO BLACK THURSDAY

the government had known of the breaking of the embargo, had not prevented it, and was now willing to let the innocent directors of the Matrix Churchill company go to prison. Some ministers were suspected of signing Public Immunity Certificates which might have sent the innocent men to gaol. Major's response was to announce in November the setting up of an enquiry led by the liberal judge Richard Scott. The enquiry lasted a few years and did not quite produce the clean bill of health for the government which Major had anticipated. When it ultimately appeared in 1995 it simply added to what appeared to be a crescendo of incidents involving Conservative MPs and ministers in sleazy episodes.

Major's attention was diverted in December 1992 by the need to negotiate, and to announce the divorce of the heir to the throne, Prince Charles from Princess Diana. This cast some doubt on the credibility of the royal family's capacity to set a moral lead, and contributed to the undermining of one of the main traditional institutions of British society. This is always a more serious problem for the Conservative Party than for Labour, and began to add to a mood of decay about the Conservative regime. Just eight months after its re-election the Conservative government was looking decidedly vulnerable. Its main assets of unity, economic competence, effective leadership and national self-confidence in British institutions were seriously eroded. Yet Major was not entirely to blame, and neither was his predecessor as leader guiltless about the situation. Major was disadvantaged in the legacy he inherited in three main respects. Thatcher had excited the Conservative Party into believing that Conservative governments are radical and purposeful, and Major's more balancing style of leadership, while not historically un-Conservative, now appeared so. Secondly, the heady cocktail of free-market economics and populist nationalism which had considerable electoral appeal in the 1980s was losing its salience with the people. Thirdly, she bequeathed a party becoming divided over Europe. Thatcher had begun to evoke Powell's British, perhaps even English nationalism, to enthuse an anti-Europe faction in the parliamentary party.

1993: FROM CHAOS BACK TO BASICS

One of Major's less convincing responses to the party's growing unpopularity and sense of ideological drift was to resort to redefining his own vision of Conservatism. His efforts during 1993 ranged from the banal to the dangerous. The party's financial difficulties also returned to the surface. It was also the year when the party's reputation as a tax-cutting party went the way of its image as an economically competent party, and when Major reached his goal of securing the passage of the Maastricht Treaty through parliament, but at a very heavy price. In January it was becoming clear that the cabinet was also dividing through personality clashes, but more politically important was a conflict between radicals and consolidators. This was more relevant than a dated left-right split, and was a tactical dispute which continued throughout the parliament. The debate between radicals who wished to proceed with a Thatcherite agenda, and those who sought a period of calm and consolidation, continued throughout the rest of the government's life. Major's problem was that both in words and actions he straddled the two positions, satisfying nobody.

From the beginning of his period as Prime Minister, Major had been under challenge to produce a 'big idea' to give his party a clear identity. That this was unfair can be shown by the fact that he inherited the job when the party was in office and so had no time to prepare. This contrasted with Thatcher's four years as leader of the opposition before her arrival in Downing Street. The main problem with his attempt to continue Thatcher's project of restructuring the British state was that he was torn between a desire to reduce the size of the state and to improve the quality of the public services which delivered health, education and welfare.[34]

Initially his intention had been to focus upon the Citizen's Charter as his own distinct contribution to redefining the British state, as well as to offering the party a 'big idea'. A concern with promoting a better quality of public service provision is not an issue which would have exercised Thatcher, and so it gave him a distinct identity, as the charter offered 'an agenda for action which neatly points up the difference between Thatcherism and the policies that the Prime Minister intends to make his own'.[35] On the other hand the conception of placing 'the customer' at the heart of the process, and the methods involved, appeared to be a continuation of the managerialism which Thatcher had introduced into the public services.

The charter was compatible with Conservative thought in the Thatcher years by its placing the recipients of the public services at the centre, and its replacement of accountability to citizens with consumer rights. The process was also compatible with Thatcherism as it provided no more expenditure. The initiative was a part of Major's continuing restructuring of the state. The stress was on better management in the public sector, the more efficient delivery of services through competition and market discipline, privatisation, contracting out and responding to consumer demand. Thatcher's NHS reforms were similarly an exercise in management accounting.[36] The charters were further developed in the second Major term after 1992 under the control of William Waldegrave at the new Ministry of Public Service and Science, and they were presented as being at the cutting edge of public service improvement.[37] They were also fully consonant with Major's concerns about competition, deregulation, privatisation, the market-testing of civil service functions, the introduction of performance-related pay and the extension of the Next Steps Agencies for the delivery of public services. This was adding momentum to changes which Thatcher had inaugurated.[38] Each of the Next Steps Executive Agencies were required to produce a charter, the utility of which was debatable given the lack of legal sanctions to enforce its provisions. The agencies complied with requirements, however, and the Employment Service's version promised to reduce waiting times, sought the prompt and accurate payment of benefits and introduced the wearing of staff badges. These reforms merely dealt with the procedures which users of the service experienced. Evidently 'unemployed people are not consumers able to move elsewhere if they are unhappy with the quality of the service, they are legally obliged to sign on, attend compulsory interviews and show that they are available and actively seeking work'.[39] The changes generated by the charters were largely cosmetic, however, and so did not impress those who were enthusiasts for better public services. At the same time the very concept of the charters was sufficiently orientated towards the public sector, and essentially trivial in nature, to earn the mocking opprobrium of the Tory right.[40]

Major's attempts to become philosophical did not alter the public perception that 'he has no sense of where he is going'.[41] His various efforts at presenting his Conservative vision patently lacked the detailed policy background to give them meaning'. Major's tendency was to produce these visions in speeches delivered at times when he was particularly under stress. His problem was that he was no philosopher. He was essentially a pragmatist and balancer concerned with the here and now of politics rather than long-term objectives. Lacking an ideological compass he veered between a stance of reassuring consolidation and pursuing a strategy which reeked of 'Thatcherism on autopilot'. As a product of 1950s culture he also often resorted to nostalgia for that decade.

In February 1993 he delivered a speech to the Carlton Club and hubristically proclaimed it as an attempt to draw together, 'the principles and values that underpin Conservatism, linking themes and thinkers of our past with the challenges which we must address in the last decade of the twentieth century'.[42] He defined the four principles of Conservatism as being choice, ownership, responsibility and opportunity.[43] In asserting that the free market did not disturb community he included wistful references to local bakers' shops, Rotary Clubs, 'meals on wheels', traditional villages and the monarchy as an institution which gave focus to British national life. This was in order to contrast Tory-voting small communities with Labour inner city areas where, with the state dominant, business had fled.[44] In what one writer called a 'telling phrase', he captured traditional sentimentalism by asserting that his Conservatism had 'an ear for history and an eye for place'.[45] He mentioned fresh policy ideas, but as some had not been worked out and he appeared to be 'kite flying' to test the response, a few controversies broke out. He urged the case for a new 'right to buy' campaign, proposals for road pricing including motorway tolls, a reform of the honours system to eliminate class-based distinctions and a new emphasis upon rewarding voluntary work. What proved most contentious was his phrase, 'I increasingly wonder whether paying unemployment benefit without offering or requiring any activity in return serves unemployed people or society well.' This suggested the adoption of the American idea of 'Workfare', or the unemployed being forced into some form of labour, in return for receipt of benefit.

A furore ensued as Gillian Shepherd, the new Employment Secretary, poured derision on the idea, and the Treasury clearly feared the cost implications of giving the right to work to everybody. The whole episode created a climate of confusion, linking Major to a policy which he was not able to produce, and highlighted the danger of developing new political ideas 'on the hoof'.[46] Still more derision came Major's way when he offered another nostalgic version of Conservatism, this time conceived to demonstrate to the Eurosceptics that his belief in Britain's role in Europe went hand in hand with a love of his country. In a speech in April 1993 he waxed lyrical about 'the country of long shadows on county grounds, warm beer, invincible green suburbs, dog lovers and pools fillers, and as George Orwell said, old maids bicycling to communion through the morning mist . . . Britain will survive unamendable in all its essentials'.[47] This was partly vacuous and partly a reflection of Major's own yearnings for a simpler era. In any event, it earned him ribaldry rather than plaudits for being an original Conservative theorist. One commentator observed that the speech reflected the exhaustion of Conservatism and proof that it offered nothing for the future. One newspaper headlined its report, 'What a lot of tosh'.[48]

Major's most disastrous attempt to redefine Conservatism occurred at the annual conference in October 1993 with his infamous 'Back to Basics' speech. His decision to make such a speech confirmed that Conservatives feared that they were, for the first time in fifteen years, losing the battle of ideas, and that Major was unable to offer solutions to the crumbling of his party's base. Major's theme was that Britain was suffering from a serious moral decline. He asserted that it was time 'to return to core values, time to get back to basics . . . to accepting responsibility for yourself and your family . . . and not shuffling it off on other people and the state . . . We must go back to basics, and the Conservative Party will lead the country back to these basics right across the board; sound money, free trade, traditional teaching, respect for the family and the law.'[49]

His invocation of a return to basics was well received by conference delegates despite being rather unclear in its meaning. It also appealed to Christian moralists such as John Patten and John Selwyn Gummer. Conservative Central Office (CCO) briefings to the press suggested it was about the restoration of social constraints and the need for improved personal morality. Evidently, it was about addressing the social ills which worried 'middle England', and looked to the family as the best social building block in contrast to single parents, who symbolised social disintegration. While some leading Conservatives tried to disassociate the speech from the behaviour of Conservative politicians, the speech was clearly a reference to 'law and order, the family and suspicion towards Europe'.[50] In a society which had become both multi-racial and pluralist in its religions, faiths and cultural identities, it was not at all clear whose basics were being invoked. Rank-and-file delegates certainly condemned state support for illegitimacy and single motherhood.[51] The CCO made it clear that the purpose of the 'back to basics' theme was to challenge fashionable theories on health, education and crime.[52] While many Conservatives felt that 'back to basics' was an improvement upon Major's big ideas at the 1992 conference, about the need for more lavatories and fewer cones on motorways, others continued to 'revile him privately'.[53] One claimed that Major's epitaph would be that 'He was the man who thought up the cones hotline'.[54] One Conservative commentator said that Major's approach made the country feel miserable.[55]

There were two main problems with the 'back to basics' speech. First, it lacked real substance and despite pleasing delegates as a piece of rhetoric, real politics soon came back to dominate the Major government's agenda.[56] The second difficulty came with the speech's aftermath, when a spate of resignations from his government after a series of misdemeanours suggested that this was a dangerous terrain for any political party to try to exploit. 'Those preaching strict morals to society must surely be above reproach – as a number of American television evangelists have discovered to their cost.'[57] Most of the revelations concerning the morality of Tory MPs which undermined the government in the wake of the 'back to basics' message took place in 1994, but it was soon enough for voters to make the associations, and the press ensured that they did so. The party's links with sleaze first reappeared, however, as its financial problems came to public attention.

HOW TO PAY FOR THE PARTY

The Conservative Party's expenditure in the 1992 general election led to a serious financial position in 1993. The party chairman, Norman Fowler, pointed out that party activists would have to undertake more campaigning efforts as spending freely to revive the party's falling popularity would now be more difficult.[58] The party's willing propagandist, Jeffrey Archer, tried to make light of the financial problems by reasonably pointing out that there were always shortages of money in the year following a general election. This resulted from the twin problem that much money had been spent and activists and business contributors to the party were not yet geared up to raise funds for the next battle.[59] Archer could not deny, however, the reality of the problem then confronting the party. The party's deficit reached £19 million by mid-1993 since the recent substantial outgoings were followed by a downturn in corporate and constituency association donations.[60]

The decline in income led the party to seek funding elsewhere and the Middle and Far East became promising areas. While Major entertained foreign financiers in Downing Street, in the hope that their experience of proximity to power might entice them into funding the party, it was ironic that the name which most embarrassed him during 1993 was Asil Nadir, whose generosity to the party had taken place during Thatcher's era. Nadir had controlled the Polly Peck company which had traded with both sides during the Iraq–Iran war. He donated one and a half million pounds to the party in 1992, but was then charged with eighteen offences of theft and false accounting, which led to his escape to Cyprus.[61] Unfortunately for Major, the close involvement of Nadir with government ministers came to light in 1993. The most damaging example was that of Michael Mates, a junior minister at the Northern Ireland Office, who, it was revealed through a leak to the press, had interceded on Nadir's behalf with the Attorney General. Major temporised for a while, but Mates deemed it politic to depart from the government. Some on the more left-leaning wing of the party accused Major of failing to defend Mates because of pressure from the party's right wing, as Mates had been a close associate of Heseltine.[62]

It also emerged in 1993 that another businessman, Octav Botnar, who had been arrested for tax fraud, had given large sums to the party and had previously had links with Lords Parkinson and Tebbit. Tebbit was on record as stating that the country owed Botnar a debt because of the role he had played in helping the government to persuade the Nissan car company to set up in England.[63]

Fowler took tough measures to address the party's financial problem by downsizing Central Office, and 140 staff lost their jobs in the 18 months up to April 1994. The party was outspent by Labour in the 1994 European election campaign, and it was only through a considerable reorganisation at CCO that the situation was painfully turned round, so that the party obtained a £2 million surplus by May 1997.[64]

A major reason for the victory of the Conservative Party at the polls in 1992 had been their success in portraying the Labour Party as the party of high taxation. In his March 1993 budget, Lamont, who was already unpopular and the object of a negative press campaign because of Black Wednesday, presided over a tax-raising budget. He increased taxes on alcohol and tobacco by more than the rate of inflation, announced a higher national insurance contribution for employees, froze personal tax allowances, reduced tax relief for mortgage holders and married couples and extended Value Added Tax (VAT) to the maximum of 17.5 per cent on domestic fuel. The combined impact of these measures was a significant rise in the tax burden.[65] Lamont was persuaded to increase taxes because of the continuing financial deficit and the signals from the markets that it was necessary to cut the PSBR. While this may have been a credible policy in the circumstances, it was the combined impact of the recession and the government's pre-election reluctance to tackle the deficit in 1991/2 which had created the problem.

The budget caused the government serious unpopularity. Its image after this budget was of a high tax and spend party which was simultaneously perceived as restricting public service provision.[66] There were political problems resulting from the backlash against a party which had won office by portraying itself as a low taxation party. In April 1993 a Gallup opinion poll discovered that only 16 per cent of respondents believed that the Conservatives were truthful about taxation and 70 per cent of those questioned thought that the chancellor was 'doing a bad job'. The situation was such that one of the normal rules of British party politics was broken as Labour was now regarded as 'the best party on taxation', an advantage it maintained right up to the 1997 election. It was the increase of VAT on fuel which most damaged the party, however, as it had previously ridiculed the Liberal Democrats for advocating it, and it appeared to attack the old and vulnerable.[67] One left-wing Conservative MP voted against the budget because of the imposition of higher VAT on fuel, and even a Thatcherite commentator doubted the wisdom of this policy, asserting that 'all factions and none are united by mounting fear of losing their seats'.[68] It should be added that these unpopular tax rises were occurring while the recession continued. It had now bitten so deeply that Kingston upon Thames, Luton, Folkestone and Southend were all seeking designation as assisted areas. One newspaper pointed out the irony that those MPs who were urging assisted area status had once referred to the policy pejoratively as 'the begging bowl' and 'state handouts'.[69] The overall competitiveness of the British economy was also causing angst as a Department of Trade and Industry report stated that it would take many years for the country's manufacturing base to recover, and that despite a competitive exchange rate after departure from the ERM, the main source of new products was still that of imports.[70]

In these circumstances it was likely that Major would resort to sacking his chancellor, who was by now deeply unpopular. Lamont's prestige had never recovered from the debacle of 'Black Wednesday', and his insensitive comment that when he went home that night 'he was singing in the bath'. As one Tory commentator expressed it, 'this represented the problem that the Conservatives suffer from an inability to see what they look like to other people'.[71] When in the course of campaigning in the Newbury by-election Lamont told reporters, '*je ne regrette rien*' about his economic policy, this proved one gaffe too far.[72] When the subsequent Newbury by-election was lost to the Liberal Democrats on the same day that the party also lost control of fifteen county councils, the extent of the political damage was apparent.[73] Lamont's sacking appeared unfair to him because the first signs of economic recovery were beginning to dawn and his successor as chancellor would reap the credit. He was also conscious that the ERM fiasco had also been Major's policy. His resignation speech was deeply damaging to Major as it struck a convincing chord. Lamont informed the Commons that there was 'too much short-termism, too much reacting to events, not enough shaping of events. We give the impression of being in office but not in power.'[74] This was remarkably like a comment of Thatcher's at Ridley's funeral a couple of weeks later. 'It was sometimes said that Nick was short on presentational skills, but he was never short of policies *worth* presenting, a much more difficult and creative side of politics.'[75]

Lamont's successor was Kenneth Clark. This appointment alarmed the right as many MPs felt the political balance in the cabinet was shifting away from full-blooded Thatcherites. It was ironic that by the autumn conference the disillusion of the party's right with Major was such that many were promoting Clark's credentials as an alternative leader. By then Clark was indeed reaping some benefit from the economic recovery, as the country's economic indices moved in a favourable direction. It was also his strong personality which appealed. One right-wing commentator cited Clark's aggressive approach to the Eurosceptic right wing with great approval, even though highly sceptical about Europe himself, and quoted Clark's comment that were he the Prime Minister, 'What I think is that they're a bunch of complete f....rs and if only I didn't have a majority of seventeen I'd kick their heads in.'[76] Clark was seen at this stage by many elements in the party as 'the only natural leader when the party cries out for one'.[77] Such speculation was ended at the conference, however, when Clark declared that any 'enemy of John Major is an enemy of mine'.[78]

THE FINALE OF THE MAASTRICHT CRISIS

Major should have learnt from the problems surrounding his attempt to secure the passage of the Maastricht paving bill in 1992, that the party's unity over the treaty immediately preceding the April 1992 general election had occurred in quite different historical circumstances. Critics warned him of his petulance on the issue and stressed that those who were discontented with the treaty were not just 'the usual suspects' from the Thatcherite wing.[79]

Before the Act could arrive on the statute book there remained the hurdle of a vote on the social chapter of the treaty. Two votes were scheduled for 22 July 1993, on a Labour amendment to prevent ratification without the social chapter, and a government motion simply noting the opt-out. There was much speculation that the Eurosceptic rebels would vote with Labour on its motion, to sabotage the treaty. Major worked hard to secure the support of the Ulster Unionists to counter the expected seepage of votes from his own back benches, although there is disagreement about whether any policy concessions were made to the Unionists on Northern Ireland issues. When the final vote was taken the government defeated the Labour motion on the speaker's casting vote. The second vote was lost by 324 to 316 votes, however, with 26 Tories voting against. The government then arranged a vote of confidence for the following day which it duly won, although the Eurosceptics were satisfied that they had made their point. They were not prepared, however, to bring the government down on the issue.[80]

This was a Pyrrhic victory for Major. Although he secured the treaty's passage, which led some to praise his courage, the party was deeply split. The rebels were regarded as speaking for the party, and it was reported that when the government's defeat was announced, cheers rang out in the Conservative clubs and letters ran twenty to one against Major.[81] Major's subsequent misfortune was when he revealed to an ITN interviewer his true feelings about Thatcher and the Eurosceptics. He had mistakenly thought that the microphones were switched off, when he asserted, 'Just think about it from my perspective. You are the Prime Minister, with a majority of eighteen, a party still harking back to a golden age that never was, and is now invented . . . You can't think of ex-ministers who are going around causing all sorts of trouble. We don't want another three more of the bastards out there.'[82] This was an exasperated reference to his three cabinet colleagues, Lilley,

Portillo and Redwood. Major's comments deepened the sense of a chasm in the party over Europe. It is difficult to dissent from the perspective of one Thatcherite that 'the Conservative Party is split from top to bottom on the issue of British membership of the EU. During the passage of the Maastricht Treaty through the House of Commons, open divisions created what was little short of a civil war within the party. Indeed, it was one of those rare constitutional occasions when the government had to table a motion of confidence to ensure that the legislation to ratify the treaty was passed; had the Conservative rebels not backed down, a general election would have ensued.'[83] Certainly the rebels with their different motives for opposing the government had acquired a common identity, and they were now able to spread stories about Major's 'nastiness' because of the bullying to which they claimed to have been subjected. The disagreements in the party were now so profound that some Conservatives were prepared to contemplate withdrawal from the European Union rather than get sucked into the sort of federal union which they feared was the corollary of Maastricht.

The government had some achievements in the autumn of 1993, including the passage of the bill to privatise the railways. This passed despite the anxiety of some on the Conservative benches, and it was only in later years that some of the ensuing problems with the rail system came to the forefront. In November the first unified budget, which sensibly linked spending and revenue raising in the same government statement, occurred. Finally, although it was only a first tentative step, there was a joint Anglo-Irish Downing Street Declaration which suggested that Major might have the statesmanship to solve one of Britain's most intractable political dilemmas.

By the end of 1993 the various forces which were to lead inexorably to the party's defeat at the ensuing general election were all in place. They included a deep 'fault line' over Europe, the loss of standing as the party of low taxation and economic efficiency, a sleazy image and an apparently drifting leadership no longer able to control the agenda.

1994: SLEAZE AND MORE SLEAZE

There was one brief interlude in the summer of 1994 when the pressures eased on the Major government. Hurd could then claim that the party's divisions over Europe were over, and Major could warn his party in apocalyptic terms that they had to unite. Both statements could be made without immediate contradictions or denials.[84] This was a brief respite in a troubled year which was dominated by the unravelling of 'back to basics' in an orgy of Tory sleaze.

The problems began in the New Year with news that a junior minister in the Environment Department, Tim Yeo, had fathered a child with his mistress, herself a Conservative councillor. This led Major to observe that 'back to basics' had not been about personal morality after all, which merely added to the press's delight. In any event, a Thatcherite back bencher protested about people 'bonking their way around London', and Yeo was forced to resign.[85] A week later three more scandals broke out. A wealthy Tory MP, Alan Duncan, admitted purchasing a council house, the Earl of Caithness resigned from his post as Parliamentary Private Secretary to the Health minister because his wife had shot herself, it was alleged, on hearing that he was leaving her for another woman, and another MP was reported as sharing a bed in a French hotel with a male friend. As the scandals continued, one CCO official remarked that every Saturday night there was an expectation that another scandal would break in the Sunday newspapers.[86]

As the scandals continued, Major was forced to abandon 'back to basics', as his attempt to decouple it from the personal behaviour of MPs had clearly failed. If the ERM forced him to jettison his economic strategy so the conduct of many of his MPs compelled him to overthrow his social agenda. His government sought to retain some elements of 'back to basics' through the passage of bills to strengthen the powers of the Home Secretary to exert greater influence over the behaviour of the police and the magistrates courts through the Criminal Justice and Public Order Bill. This may have enhanced the government's reputation as a force for law and order, but only at the expense of arousing disquiet in many circles about the centralising threat to civil liberties that it entailed.

The question of party finance continued to cause concern in 1984 just as it was becoming clear that the party had a membership crisis. In the 1940s there had been over two million Conservative Party members, but by 1994 this had fallen to below half a million. There were dire predictions that on the existing trends membership would be less than 100,000 by the end of the century.[87] More disturbing still was the discovery that half the membership was aged sixty-six or over, only 5 per cent were under thirty-five years old and the mean age was sixty-two.[88] The consequent problems for the party were very real. Many local constituency associations were in difficulty by 1994, and this was symbolised by the Conservative Association in Major's own seat of Huntingdon selling its buildings. Further research revealed that local party associations were continuing to decline in importance as sources of funds for the party nationally. This further compelled the party to depend upon individual donations, which enhanced the risk of charges of corruption being levelled against it. The message was becoming clear, 'the Conservative Central Office needs either to develop new sources of income or to revive the ability of local associations to meet targets, these findings also show a worrying situation regarding local organisation: the clear implication is of alienation and atrophy, in a party whose membership is already dominated by old people'.[89] Political parties require a local presence in order to fight elections despite the mediazation of politics, and local activism still has some impact on the election results in individual constituencies. It was the signs of decline and the resulting inability to raise funds, however, which most alarmed the party as it simultaneously faced serious problems in government.

The dependence on individual donations also caused further difficulties in 1994 with the revelation that Nazmu Virani, who was in prison for his role in the downfall of the Bank of Credit and Commerce International (BCCI), had given substantial donations to the Conservatives over many years.[90] The intricacies of the links between business and the Conservative Party were beginning to unravel. One episode highlighted what appeared to be an increasingly unsavoury link between finance and the Tory Party. In July a Sunday newspaper ran a story revealing that two MPs had each accepted £1000 to ask a parliamentary question. Graham Riddick and David Tredinnick had patently been set up by investigative journalists but had fallen into the trap.[91] Major was angry, they lost their jobs as Parliamentary Private Secretaries and Major expressed his concern about the falling standards of British public life.[92] Other similar problems occurred in the autumn. First, Tim Smith MP resigned following his failure to declare payments he had received from the Al-Fayed organisation. More seriously, because the affair continued to cause significant problems during the 1997 election campaign, Neil Hamilton MP resigned his ministerial post shortly afterwards over the same issue.[93]

As the problems intensified, a MORI poll published at the end of March gave Labour a lead of over 20 per cent and press speculation grew that Major would be removed. He was strengthened by the fact that it was Heseltine and Clark who were the obvious contenders, as both were seen as more Europhile than Major. Thatcher herself, despite her periodic undermining of Major, preferred him to the alternatives.[94] Commentators proclaimed that 'the Tory jackals have had their day'.[95] Disastrous performances in the municipal and European elections followed. Securing 27 per cent of the vote in the local elections and 28 per cent in the European elections in May and June respectively proclaimed the deep hole into which the party had sunk.[96] The situation was even less favourable as there were early signs that the likely succession of Blair to the leadership of the Labour Party, after the early death of Smith in May 1994, would enhance the Labour Party's electability.

Party divisions over Europe appeared more rather than less intense after the Maastricht debates, although it is an over-simplification to argue that there were evident signs that 'the question of sovereignty versus interdependence, rather than left versus right or "wet" versus "dry", was the crucial source of the party's difficulties'.[97] This is not to contest the view that the party division over Europe had become unbridgeable, but to recognise that Europe is just the single most important part of the chasm. The conflicting attitudes towards Britain's integration into Europe symbolise 'a darker right–left split between nationalism and internationalism behind which lies the ideological confrontation over the balance between market forces and the managed economy'. In the final years of Major's government there was an anti-European integration, nationalist, and free-market faction characterised by Portillo; and a more pro-European, socially concerned and economically interventionist faction symbolised by Clark. Certain policy issues reinforced the European question. Eurosceptics reject the ERM, for example, because it prevents a national, and often free-market, approach to economic management, and they associate the ERM with the corporatist and collectivist style of economic policy which they consider prevails on the continent. Whatever its origins, and boredom from having been in power so long may also have played some part, the dispute intensified as the Major government headed towards its final doom. Whatever criticisms can be made of Major's leadership it was his misfortune that the conflict had made the Conservatives 'a beastly party to manage'.[98]

Certainly it was Europe that was at the heart of the party's factional difficulties in 1994. Major had one success in the summer of 1994 over the appointment of a successor to Jacques Delors as President of the

European Commission. The candidate favoured by the French and Germans was Jean-Luc Dehane, the Belgian Prime Minister. The Eurosceptical press in Britain did not respond sympathetically and Major sought to win a success by blocking his appointment. Major justified his opposition with the remark that Dehane was unsuitable because he came from 'a tradition of big government and of intervention . . . that's not my position . . . We need a commission president whose instincts are for enterprise, openness and subsidiarity.'[99] By standing firm against a united Franco-German initiative, Major actually won some support from other countries, and the compromise candidate Jacques Santer was appointed. Major was able to unite his party for a brief period round the perspective of Britain battling to protect its own interests and its vision of a multi-speed Europe in which different countries were integrated at different times.[100] One pro-European commentator was unimpressed, however, classifying the event as an example of a 'game nested in party factionalism'.[101] Major sought to exploit the new popularity which he was attaining with his own right wing by a speech in September which he regarded as his 'set text' on Europe when critics exhorted him to define his views. He rejected the idea that the European parliament had the democratic legitimacy to speak for Europe, and citing the low turn-out for European elections, he argued that it was the twelve national parliaments which conferred democratic authority on the Council of Ministers.[102] He tried to reaffirm this position in his speech to the 1994 annual conference and asked for freedom from his party to address the European question as he thought fit; a position he would plaintively reiterate during the 1997 general election.[103] If he thought that all reasonable people would gather round this definition he was to be disappointed, however, when despite securing the passage of the European Finance Bill in November 1994 by 330 to 303 votes, 8 of the Eurosceptics carried their opposition to the point of refusing to vote for the Bill. If by abstaining they had anticipated 'calling the government's bluff', they proved to be in error. The whip was duly withdrawn from Nicholas Bugden, Christopher Gill, Theresa Gorman, Tony Marlow, Richard Shepherd, Teddy Taylor and John Wilkinson. This was a drastic step for Major to take, but he was offended that what he considered to be a good financial deal for Britain which he had negotiated was being rejected. For their part the rebels were motivated by a contempt for Major's leadership.

The battle between the 'consolidationists' and 'the clear blue water' school of Conservatives who wanted a more radical agenda to differentiate them from Labour had not been stilled by these successes. David Willets adjusted his previously Thatcherite ideas by arguing that the harsh cutting edge of the market should be softened by a stress on community, although better provided by strong local communities than by the central state, and another Thatcherite, Alan Clark, warned of the danger of alienating all public sector workers.[104] The Employment Secretary David Hunt warned that young people were becoming 'atomised' and urged a return to one nation Conservatism, and the Financial Secretary to the Treasury, Stephen Dorrell, echoed Burke's tirade against 'solitary, unconnected, individual, selfish liberty'.[105] The Scottish Secretary Ian Lang warned against the government appearing to offer a pastiche of Thatcher's ideology. He claimed that her ideology had been an afterthought, 'cobbled together to give a spurious air of consistency to an otherwise disparate string of measures'.[106]

The announcement of an IRA ceasefire to give Major's peace process in Northern Ireland an opportunity to succeed in August, and the launch of the National Lottery in November, were minor breakthroughs, but did not much affect the internal party argument. Blair's arrival as Labour Party leader in July heightened the problem, since the apparent ideological confusion within the Conservative Party was inextricably linked with a debate about how the Blair threat should be handled. Some asserted that he should be portrayed as unreconstructed old Labour with a mere veneer of moderation, which Major favoured, others argued that he should be portrayed as a closet Conservative who would say anything to win votes. This ambivalence, like the general confusion as to the nature of post-Thatcher Conservatism was never resolved even by polling day in 1997.[107] Certainly Major did not appear to have either the intellectual capacity or the ideological certitude to resolve the problem, even if the party had been ready to accept decisive leadership. One minister complained that Major 'is always all things to all men'.[108] His concessions on Europe suggested that he wished to be perceived as a reasoned Eurosceptic; Blair accused him of capitulating to his left-wing opponents in the party by resisting Post Office privatisation, however, which he interpreted as the 'death of Thatcherism'.[109] This decision upset the party's right wing and may have led to the eight 'whipless ones' as they became known, defying the government on the European Finance Bill.

The year ended, as it had begun, on a negative note. The government was defeated in December on its proposal to increase VAT on fuel to

17.5 per cent, lost the Dudley by-election to Labour and on one Gallup poll trailed Labour by 40 per cent. A final blow to Major was the loss of Sarah Hogg as head of the Policy Unit. While she had not managed to overcome the government's problem of strategic indecision, her departure exacerbated the vacuum.

1995: THE RE-ELECTED LEADER

Major began the new year with the hope that the improving economic statistics would begin to produce the political dividend which had not materialised during 1994. The fog did not lift for his government, however, and in the summer he felt compelled to embark upon the 'shrewd and desperate' re-election process among his constituency of Conservative MPs.[110] The result of his bold experiment proved as ambiguous as his government's ideological stance, however, and the year ended with an embarrassing defection of Emma Nicholson MP to the Liberal Democrats. She listed many policy disagreements, but inevitably Europe was top of the list. As a Europhile, she objected to 'the complete failure of leadership on European issues'.[111]

The improvements in the economy were becoming notable, although they were as attributable to the natural economic recovery of the business cycle, as to government policy. At the same time the Major government, under the orthodox policies of Clark as Chancellor of the Exchequer, avoided some of the policy errors of their predecessors since 1979. Clark avoided the extremes of deflation and reflation and ran the economy pragmatically. He resisted the monetary insouciance of the 1979 to 1982 period, when the government appeared to consider that the protection and revival of industry was of no account as long as monetary targets were attained. He equally avoided the view that it was unnecessary to pursue an anti-inflationary strategy, as had happened between 1985 and 1989. Clark's policies did not address the fundamental paradox, however, that as the British economy integrated further into Europe, British governments continued to follow a neo-American policy of deregulation, free markets and an enterprise economy.[112]

The main political problem was that the government seemed to gain no political dividend from the economy's performance. In 1995 the truth began to dawn that even with the economy and political cycles working synchronously, which they had patently failed to do in 1992, the Conservative Party was heading for a likely defeat. This was partly because in 1992 it had denied any responsibility for the recession, attributing it to world-wide forces beyond its control. It was difficult to claim total credit, therefore, when the economy revived. More importantly, the fiasco of Black Wednesday appeared permanently to have shattered the view that the Conservatives had superior skills in economic management. In any event, the general intra-party divisions and the problems of sleaze were taking media precedence over the country's economic performance, and the economic debate itself was becoming dominated by the issue of whether or not Britain should join the single European currency, which simply emphasised the divisions.

The debate over the single currency broke out in February 1995. Major reiterated that Britain had every right not to join, although he did not rule out future membership. He stressed that he would continue to resist any further moves towards a more centralised Europe at the next inter-governmental conference. A briefing to the lobby emphasised that both Clark and Hurd, now the Foreign Secretary, had agreed the document.[113] Clark undermined this new-found unity in a speech on 9 February. He contradicted Major's carefully contrived unity position by arguing that it was possible to have monetary without political union, although he also defended the idea of political union. This reflected his true position, but he spoke out now because he was tired of having his attitudes cited by briefings from 10 Downing Street, without any consultation. This ensured that Clark was no longer regarded by the right as a better potential leader than Major.[114] In April the whip was restored to the rebels, without them giving the guarantees of good behaviour in the future, which might have vindicated the initial decision.[115] The whole episode, which had been intended to demonstrate a firmness of resolve on Major's part, had done him more harm than good. During their absence the government lost its formal overall majority thus making it the more dependent upon the whims of individuals. The expelled MPs also formed a group of their own while they were outside the party, and so secured themselves far greater prominence. For example, they issued their own manifesto on Europe, which received an attention that they would not have received had they remained within the party's ranks. It was their desertion of the government in the VAT on fuel vote in December 1994 which ensured the defeat which forced the government to find alternative sources of revenue. This was described as 'the revenge of the Eurosceptics'.[116] Blair turned this debacle to Labour's advantage when he told Major at Prime Minister's question time that he had secured nothing from the rebels as reward for their return to the fold. When Major responded that there were divisions within Labour's ranks Blair produced the ultimate 'put-down'. He asserted that 'There is one big difference. I lead my party. He follows his.'[117]

As the conflict continued Major's leadership was being criticised on all sides. Lord McAlpine, who as party treasurer, had been successful in raising money for the Conservatives in the Thatcher years, regarded Major as both 'stupid' and 'nasty'. He publicly stated that 'Major' had 'stuffed' the party.[118] As the criticisms mounted, fewer commentators appeared ready to recognise that the problems were partially beyond Major's control because of the hand that he had been dealt when he inherited the leadership. The 1980s blending of free markets and the individual, coupled with a greater emphasis upon law and order, was becoming an inadequate foundation for governance for a new century. Whenever Major tried to strengthen his leadership by an outburst of sceptical language about Europe, he did not help his position, because many of the party's supporters in the City sought the economic opportunities provided by Europe. The party was landing itself in the anomalous situation of advocating free trade, but appearing to suggest that it could not abide the people with whom we had to trade.

Further criticisms of Major's leadership were generated by the publication of the Nolan report on standards in public life in May 1995. The party was simultaneously awaiting with trepidation the Scott report on arms to Iraq which was investigating the Matrix Churchill affair, and many MPs thought it an error to have allowed that investigation to proceed so far. But Major's immediate acceptance of 'the broad thrust' of the Nolan report caused him dire problems in the parliamentary party. Nolan's proposals that there should be a quarantine period between the resignation of ministers and their accepting jobs in the private sector, and for restrictions on ministerial appointments to sit on quangos, led to many MPs feeling that in the event of an election defeat, it would be hard for many of them to earn a decent living.[119]

Thatcher continued to snipe at Major's government from the sidelines and even to praise Blair, and this encouraged the party's right to continue to complain about the leadership. There was further talk during the spring of 1995 about a challenge. In attempting to defuse the situation Major attended a meeting of the Fresh Start group of Conservative MPs in June where he was heckled, and one MP demanded that he rule out the single currency as long as he was Prime

Minister. The tone of the meeting so angered him that he decided that the situation could no longer continue.[120] After discussing the matter with his aides he called a press conference in Downing Street on 22 June. Protesting that he was no longer prepared to see the government wrecked by a minority, and that there had been repeated threats to his leadership, he announced his resignation as leader of the party, but stressed that in the ensuing election to find a successor he would be a candidate.

This was a dramatic gesture which revealed the extent to which the party had degenerated. At first it appeared a bold and clever move as no strong opposing candidate declared, but after some agonising, one of the 'bastards', John Redwood, did resign from the cabinet and challenged Major. Redwood stood on a platform of opposition to the single currency and more tax cuts. While he was undermined by the vociferous support of the formerly 'Whipless' MPs, he produced an effective slogan, 'no change, no chance'.[121] His candidacy changed the perceptions of Major's wisdom in putting himself up for re-election, which began to look like a blunder. Major began to fear that he would be embarrassed by failing to secure a healthy majority of the votes cast. Stories began to circulate of MPs casting votes for Redwood in the first ballot so that other candidates could enter the race in a second ballot. Though the cabinet protested its loyalty to Major a few were preparing to contest the second round if Major did not secure a strong majority.[122] Some Thatcherite supporters in the media argued for a vote which would necessitate a second ballot in which both Heseltine and Portillo would stand, to give the party a real choice, and to clear the air.[123] It might alternatively have split the party wide open in having to select between a Europhile and Portillo, who made his reputation with the party by promising 'to stop the rot from Brussels'.[124]

The result was declared on 4 July. Major secured 218 votes against 89 for Redwood, with 20 spoilt ballots or abstentions. Major had stated privately that if more than 100 MPs refused to back him he would stand down. When precisely that outcome happened, he 'wobbled' and had to be persuaded to stay on. His campaign team led by Lord Cranborne was sent out immediately to praise the result as a total vindication of Major's leadership, even though one third of the parliamentary party and half the back benchers had failed to support him. Despite some media manipulation to make the result appear as a triumph, which it most certainly was not, it was apparent 'that there was no strong body of Majorites to bang the drum in support of his beliefs and leadership'. A by now frightened party largely accepted 'the spin' put on the result, however, despite 109 MPs being unwilling to vote for him.

After the election he reshuffled his government. The appointment of Heseltine as deputy prime minister with a range of new powers, including the chairmanship of a number of cabinet committees, fuelled speculation that Heseltine had come to an arrangement, so that thirty of his followers voted for Major to carry on as leader. The evidence was that Heseltine had held a three-hour meeting with Major in the morning of the leadership election and that he and many of his supporters did not cast their votes until the afternoon.[125] Heseltine's newly dominant position, together with the other changes to the cabinet, appeared to represent a shift to the left. Many of Major's Eurosceptic right-wing critics continued to mutter against his leadership as a result, so much so that little seemed to have been resolved. Major attempted to re-launch his leadership with the announcement that he would listen more to the party, and seek advice on such issues as tax cuts and the proper balance to be struck between the public and private sectors.[126] Complaints that important areas of policy on which the Major government had been expected to advance radical proposals, such as welfare reform, failed to move Major now. This was clearly a policy sphere on which he could only offer a continuation of the status quo, while uttering the morality and efficiency goals which a Conservative government would ideally like to pursue with regard to the welfare state.[127] Even the Conservative press was unmoved by yet another re-launch, and commented that Blair had positioned himself to offer a 'sanitised, rejuvenated Tory Party' and that he could 'sweep the country' with a conservatism which promised greater success than was currently on offer.[128] Major's response was to call for the party and the country to stop judging the policies of his government from the standpoint of Thatcherism and to develop a Conservative philosophy for the next century.[129] Unfortunately, all of Major's previous efforts to produce such a new philosophy had been derisory.

Major hoped to use the 1995 conference as a further opportunity to re-launch his party. On this occasion he was upstaged by the Labour Party's orchestrated announcement of the defection of the left-wing Conservative MP, Alan Howarth. Major recognised that Howarth had been agonising over the decision, and it was the Labour Party which had arranged for the defection to occur at a time when it would cause maximum disruption at the start of the conference. Howarth had opposed the government's Jobseekers Allowance Bill in January 1995 which he considered a dismal attempt to attack unemployment with a mixture of compulsion, accompanied by a euphemistic renaming of the unemployed. He hoped that Major's re-election might have led the party in a direction he would have found more amenable. As it was, it had merely led to the 'abolition of capital gains and inheritance taxes. A crackdown on DSS fraud and more sport in schools.'[130] This defection from the party's left warned Major that there was potential embarrassment from that small wing of the party, and ensured that he had to maintain a careful balancing act.

The conference itself might have been hijacked by a nationalistic speech from Portillo who had been moved to the defence ministry after Major's re-election in July. Portillo attacked the EU, and suggested that Britain's defence policy must remain independent from that of Europe, suggesting that there was a real likelihood of British troops being conscripted by the EU to fight on its behalf. The speech was rapturously received, but neither the left nor the right of the party were really content with his performance. The left obviously condemned his rampant hostility towards Europe, while the right were suspicious that although he had not had the courage to challenge Major for the leadership, his speech was causing more damage than if he had done so. Major's speech to the 1995 conference was well crafted for the occasion. He welcomed the coming together of the party in the aftermath of the July leadership contest and managed to establish some 'clear blue water' between the government and the Labour Party by asserting the goals of Britain becoming 'the enterprise centre of Europe', a reduction of state spending to below 40 per cent of national wealth, a reaffirmation of opposition to devolution to Scotland and Wales and a promise of more than 5000 policeman 'on the beat'. While this was a litany of past commitments plus the ritual easy applause gainer at all party conferences of more police on the beat, it cheered up delegates. The press considered that the speech had distanced the party from the disputes which had weakened it for three years and Major was upbeat about the party's prospects for winning the election.[131]

As always appeared to happen in the Major government after 1992, any remission in the government's problems was soon followed up by new blunders, and by 'chickens coming home to roost'. The problems in the autumn were the result of past decisions: the establishment of civil service agencies, economic mismanagement, the aftermath of the Nolan report, the tendency to pacify the right and, as always, Europe.

The problem generated by the establishment of agencies was the result of the Home Secretary Michael Howard's refusal to take responsibility for errors in prisons policy, and his determination to 'privatise' the responsibility for such errors by blaming Derek Lewis, the Director of the Prison Service. In October, Howard dismissed Lewis after the publication of the Learmont report into a prison break-out which had blamed prison management for the escape. This was not an isolated problem for Howard, who had seen many of his immigration and parole rulings overturned by the courts, and some of his other legislation was strongly criticised by judges.[132] These problems mattered for the Conservatives as Labour was becoming a serious contender as the best party to deal with law and order. This was partly the result of Blair's 'soundbite' about the need to be 'Tough on crime and tough on the causes of crime'. The shadow Home Secretary, Jack Straw, was also effectively freeing Labour of the slur of being soft on criminals.

The economy came back into focus with the November budget. Owing to the demands placed on the social security budget by high unemployment, increases in expenditure on the police and defence and the voracious demands of the public services, the tax burden had increased for the average family in the Thatcher and Major years. The right of the party had hoped for big tax reductions in the November budget, but Kenneth Clark felt constrained, and only reduced income tax by one penny from the following April. One commentator calculated that this still left the tax burden markedly higher than when the Conservatives had first come to office. 'You Ken not be serious' was the response in the *Sun*.

Major's problems with Nolan now reappeared. He had delayed the decision of how to respond to Nolan's recommendation that MPs should reveal all payments received for giving advice to outsiders, by setting up a Commons committee to consider the issue. With their in-built majority, the Conservatives on the committee managed to propose a ban on paid advocacy, a compromise acceptable to most Tories. This proved another 'own goal', however, as the Labour Party was more in touch with the anti-sleaze mood in the country in supporting Nolan's original proposal; and many Conservative MPs joined Labour in rejecting Major's compromise. So any credit to Major for being a 'sleaze-buster' in having set up the Nolan committee, and for accepting the proposal that there should be limitations on the opportunity for former ministers to take posts in the private sector, was dissipated. He was becoming more blasé, however, about parliamentary defeats; blaming the tendency of his own MPs to rebel against him as the result of an extended period in office leading to frustrations about promotion and demotion. This led, he argued, to the protest of 'the dispossessed and the never possessed'.[133]

Europe reappeared as a major issue with the formation of the Referendum Party in November 1995. Major was failing to satisfy either wing in his party. The right's disaffection was apparent when Sir James Goldsmith launched what was obviously going to be a well-financed party to demand a referendum on Britain's continued membership of the EU. This was likely to be a threat to the Tories by taking important votes in marginal seats. In the following year two leading Conservatives, Lord McAlpine and Sir George Gardiner MP, whose contempt for Major was the most open of secrets, defected to the Referendum Party.[134] Major was beleaguered by the change in the party's composition in parliament. The 'neo-liberal Thatcherites' had increased their representation in the government under Major and were 'the most powerful ideological cohort on the right wing of the party elite in the 1990s'.[135] Yet to remind Major that he also faced opposition to the left, his advocacy of the use of a 'fast track' approach to permit Church schools to opt out of local education authority control was not only opposed by the bishops, on the grounds that it would transfer power from parents to governors, but was also contested by the Education minister, Gillian Shepherd. Her view prevailed.[136] Major was also reminded of the danger of defections from his left if he veered too far in a Eurosceptic direction, when Nicholson joined the Liberal Democrats. As the date for the general election drew near it was looking doubtful whether Major's leadership gamble in July had transformed the party's prospects.

MORE FALSE DAWNS: JANUARY 1996 TO MARCH 1997

Major veered between a conviction that his party could still win the general election and a despairing recognition that although he would probably lose, it would be possible to limit the damage to a small deficit in seats. This period alternated between more difficulties provoked by the same divisions and issues as before, and some short-lived successes which appeared to offer hope of electoral success. There was a great deal of planning for the election campaign and the launching of poster campaigns during 1996, but here too there were divisions over strategy. External events had their continuing tendency to undermine the government, but the main difficulty flowed from the continuing ideological divisions in the party fanned by European problems.

The first open split took place in January, when a Euro-enthusiast Conservative MP, Hugh Dykes, threatened that his faction could work with Labour, to secure a majority for the single currency. Another left-wing Conservative listed such measures as rail privatisation, nursery vouchers, and the abandoning of the Family and Domestic Violence Bill as evidence that the party was moving rightwards. A Conservative commentator from the party's right wing complained, 'Mr Major is a shimmier, a man who likes to creep on tip-toe between the ideological poles of his party in the vain hope of pleasing most of the people most of the time.'[137] The same commentator complained that the only cabal in the party was on the left, which had a 'blind faith in the European project and high public spending'.[138] The main, albeit often unwitting, orchestrator of the right-wing rebels re-entered the debate at this point. Concerned about the possibility of any 'backsliding' in the direction of so-called 'one nation' Conservatism as the election approached, Thatcher condemned the Euro-enthusiasts in the party as 'no nation' Conservatives. This came shortly after Major delivered his justified warning to the party that disunity was the main threat to its electability, and few MPs now thought that the Conservatives could win, as this latest phase in the argument broke out.

Northern Ireland rarely offers political rewards to the party in government, as the cleavages between the aspirations of the two communities run so deep. Major had made some progress, but the parliamentary arithmetic of his disappearing majority led him to rely on the Ulster Unionists. Before he could promote further progress, therefore, Major was adamant that the IRA should decommission its arms. This delay in making progress inevitably caused frustrations, and on 9 February a bomb at Canary Wharf announced the ending of the IRA's cease-fire. The prospects of Major achieving a dramatic coup in the context of Ulster finally evaporated with the Canary Wharf explosion. The Manchester bomb in June 1996 demonstrated that little concrete progress had been achieved in the Major years.

The main problem in February, however, was the publication of the Scott report after three years of investigation. It revealed a secretive and confusing culture in Whitehall. Scott also criticised a minister, William Waldegrave, for misleading the House, although apparently unintentionally, and the former Attorney General, Sir Nicholas Lyell, was also criticised for his mishandling of Public Immunity Certificates. The parliamentary debate was once more held in tense circumstances. The government's overall majority was now down to five, but some MPs were promising to vote against the government over its failure to take responsibility. Ultimately the government won the Commons vote by one. A MORI poll showed three voters believing that the criticised ministers should have resigned for every one who supported their continuation in office.[139] This was despite a huge 'spin doctoring' attempt by the government to persuade the public that the ministers concerned had done nothing wrong.

Sleaze stayed on the agenda throughout the year, however, with other episodes. While adultery was not of itself a matter for ministerial resignation, the party was open to the charge of hypocrisy particularly after 'back to basics'. Rod Richards, a minister in the Welsh Office, was forced to resign over an adulterous relationship, partly because he had listed 'family' as his main recreation.[140] The Neil Hamilton affair also persisted when he brought a libel suit against the *Guardian* newspaper. When in September he suddenly withdrew his action the newspaper headlined their front page with a story about him, 'A Liar and a Cheat'.[141] Evidence then emerged that David Willetts from the Whips Office had tried to influence the Members' Interests Committee to obtain a swift and favourable outcome to the affair by 'exploiting the good Tory majority' on the committee. When Willetts appeared before the new Standards and Privileges Committee of the House in December 1996 he was condemned, and further accused of dissembling by the manner in which he had presented his own defence.[142]

In March 1996 some Labour supporters were becoming concerned that Major could yet win an election. Reporting that the Labour Party was 'extremely nervous about the next twelve months' one Labour supporter, Nyta Mann, pointed out the main economic indicators were moving in the right direction and that the forthcoming budget would be 'a real election pump-primer'. The remarkable phenomenon in 1996, however, was that despite economic improvement the government reaped no reward. A few hours on Black Wednesday, exacerbated by continuing recession and middle-class job insecurity, lost the Conservatives their long-standing reputation for economic competence and financial probity. Mann also added, however, that while the Conservatives were mired in sleaze, 'Major himself is seen as squeaky clean – an honest man fallen among Tories'.[143] Labour also recognised that the endorsement of the *Sun*, if Major could secure it, could also be vital.

It was fairly representative of Major's political fortunes that just as this nervousness began to surface in the Labour Party a new problem blew up in his face. On 20 March the issue of 'mad cows' surfaced and brought discredit on the government. It had the effect of ensuring that Europe was back on top of the political agenda. The government was forced to admit to a link between the cattle disease of BSE and the human variant CJD. A world-wide ban on British beef followed. Clark bemoaned: 'Why the bloody hell we should suddenly get a scientist's report on mad cows coming out of the wide blue yonder right now just has to be put down to incredibly bad luck, of a quite extraordinary kind.'[144] Clark's comment neglects the fact that it was Thatcher's passion for deregulation which had lifted the restriction on the feeding of dead sheep to cattle, which was widely thought to be the cause of BSE. The cabinet decided to keep calm and to be guided by scientific advice, and it became a ministerial media mantra that everybody's reactions to the situation should be determined by 'the science'. Consumers at home proved immune to such curious defences of the quality of British beef and ceased to purchase it in large numbers. The responsible minister, Douglas Hogg, 'shuttled hopelessly back and forth between Britain and Europe. The government railed against the ban but, despite some minor relaxations, was unable to get it lifted.'[145] Major's blustering threats and promises of reprisals did nothing to alleviate the ban, and the government appeared lacking in competence and effectiveness.

Privatisation also lost its sheen by 1996. The privatisation of water had never been popular, and the inability of Yorkshire Water to avoid drought conditions in its region in 1996 generated hostility. Despite increased charges and high salaries to its executives, its only response was to urge its customers not to take baths.[146] The privatisation of the railways was at the centre of the parliamentary timetable at this stage, with the sale of Railtrack and of the franchises to operate the services, but one MP famously described it as 'the poll tax on wheels'.[147] Polls consistently revealed that the people did not wish to see the break-up of the rail network, although some of the worst consequences of privatisation on the quality of the services only emerged after the general election of 1997. While privatisation was undergoing a phase of serious unpopularity the government surprisingly decided to announce its intention of privatising the London underground.[148]

The loss of the mid-Staffordshire by-election in May 1996 proved a decisive turning point in the right's loss of patience with Major. Redwood and Lamont were in conversations with Goldsmith's Referendum Party about arranging a deal with the Conservatives. As they were not empowered to act in this way, it demonstrated Major's loss of control.[149] In June 1996 Conservative MPs supported the holding of a referendum on membership of the EU and a minister, David Heathcott-Amery, resigned over the issue.[150]

Given these disasters it is surprising that Major ever went through periods when he thought he could win again, and in retrospect his optimism was unjustified. There were times, however, when matters took a turn for the better. Once more the party engineered an effective conference in October. This was partly around a peace, brokered by party chairman Brian Mawhinney, between Major and Thatcher. She duly appeared on the platform, kissed him, urged the return of a Major government and said, 'let's get cracking'. Clark's speech to conference stressed the success of the economy and the threat to its further development that a Labour government would involve. Ministerial speeches were also coordinated to ensure the spelling out of a common view on Europe. Major's own speech was also effective as he teased Blair: 'It simply won't do for Mr Blair to say, "Look I'm not a socialist anymore. Now can I be Prime Minister please?" Sorry, Tony. Job's taken. And anyway it's too big a job for your first real job.'[151]

Once more the optimism was short-lived. In the November budget Clark only reduced income tax by one penny as he calculated that the heat had gone out of the tax issue and so voters could no longer be bribed. More serious was an outbreak of conflict within the cabinet on the issue of the single currency. It was motivated by ministers jockeying for position for the succession to the party leadership after an election defeat. Ministers who were previously considered sympathetic to the cause of European integration, such as the Foreign Secretary, Malcolm Rifkind, now appeared to furbish their sceptical credentials. The pretext for this December outburst of quarrelling was the single currency. The motive of the various participants must have been long-term and personal, since the argument was about what might happen in the future, when all the tests of public opinion revealed that it would not be the Tories who would be in power when the decision would be taken.

The Conservative Party appeared to have solved its financial problems by the summer of 1996. There were suggestions of Serbian funding, which were never finally proved, and continuing comments about controversially acquired money donated by Asil Nadir.[152] The party was back in surplus, however, and it decided to attack Blair with a demonic poster with the slogan 'New Labour, New Danger'. The campaign was not a success and a majority informed pollsters that they did not like the posters.[153] The problem for the Tories was that while their research demonstrated some reluctance to risk a change in government, particularly among female voters, the Blair effect had been positive for Labour. While Labour had been disadvantaged since 1983 in having less highly regarded leaders than its opponents, Blair actually led Major on all the criteria. This made it vitally important for the Conservatives to discern an angle of criticism that would not appear totally implausible. Until the election they were uncertain whether to attack Blair as a secret socialist, an opportunist without principle, or a decent man who was simply the front for an unreconstructed socialist Labour Party. While Major tended towards consistently attacking Blair for lacking all beliefs and principles, rather than accusing him of socialist extremism, his party also sought to frighten voters on the theme which had been most effective against 'Old Labour', that of high taxation.

Some Conservative thinkers sought to chart a way forward for the party. Tessa Keswick and Heathcott-Amery argued that the two Conservative traditions of encouraging the individual and the free market on the one hand, and providing firm government and care for the weak on the other, must be preserved.[154] They wanted an extension of the post-1979 change in the state's role from an interventionist to an enabling body, and on the European issue, they asserted that a law should be passed to define certain key areas in which British law would take precedence over European law.[155]

At the start of 1997 Major toyed with the idea of an early surprise election. In reality he held off until 1 May as most commentators had predicted. Two main events occurred in January. First, in order to attempt to create a united front the cabinet agreed that British entry into a single currency in 1999 was unlikely.[156] Different ministers nuanced this agreement in varying terms but, however interpreted, the statement was the most sceptical stance which the party had yet adopted. Secondly, the shadow Chancellor Gordon Brown removed the high taxation propaganda line from the Conservatives, by pledging to adhere entirely within the Conservative Party's public spending limits for two years.[157]

Stephen Dorrell also argued for a Conservative strategy based on a synthesis of sound money, low taxes, individualism and good public services. He was similarly compromising on Europe, and urged that Britain remain 'foursquare' within the EU, but reject the Social Chapter as a tax on jobs.[158] John Patten justified his contribution to the debate on the grounds that as Lord Blake expressed it, parties 'seldom philosophise in office. Their leaders are too preoccupied with administrative concerns.'[159] His main thrust was with morality and the need to underpin family life, protect middle-class values and teach children the difference between right and wrong. He feared that 'we give videos not time, condoms not the ethic of self-restraint'. There should be a moral strain running through the activities of government and civil servants would benefit from learning ethics.[160]

Willetts wrote the official publication on the Conservative case. Reflecting his shift from the excesses of the Thatcher era, he argued for community as well as the free market. He added that the suburb 'is not a place of rootless miserable apathy. People do assume their material aspirations . . . to own their own house, to be able to afford a good holiday . . . but they are not immoral or shameful.'[161] Willetts said that the Conservative vision is of an enterprise culture with an open labour market, free trade, limited government, high private savings; and that British Conservatism 'draws its strength from a kind of forward-looking memory'.[162]

Despite the imminence of the general election the Conservative Party found it as difficult in 1997 as it had previously to concentrate on electoral considerations. Some ministers sought to make sceptical noises to promote their position in the party, as if anybody outside a tight Westminster Conservative circle cared. A curious dispute opened up about the rebuilding of the royal yacht, with Portillo's advocacy contradicted by the unlikely alliance of Heath and Redwood. Equally arcane and diversionary was an argument about whether a future Conservative government would abolish any Scottish parliament that a Labour government might set up.[163] More valuably, Mawhinney tried to secure an agreement about what the party should do in the course of an election campaign in which Conservative candidates would put out dissident manifestos locally about their view of Britain's membership of the single currency. The party failed to pay sufficient attention to the issue which duly unravelled during the campaign itself when different candidates, including some who held government office, put out manifestos which deviated from the official 'wait and see' line.[164]

That this would be an area of controversy should have been obvious from yet another spat within the cabinet. Perhaps the failure to adhere to a common view at cabinet level made party managers aware that the matter was unsolvable, and that in a key policy area 'many different flowers were allowed to bloom'. The cabinet dispute was initiated by Malcolm Rifkind's statement that he was 'hostile' to the single currency. Clark's response was 'puckish', remarking that Rifkind's comments were 'a slip of the tongue under pressure from a very skilful interviewer . . . Howe weighed in . . . saying he would find it very difficult to back a government "that is in principle hostile to the concept of a single currency" . . . Major's response was that the government was not "hostile in its attitude to a single currency – the position remains that we have an open option".'[165] Among the other quarrelsome comments in February and March was Thatcher's unhelpful remark that 'Blair won't let Britain down'.[166]

Shrugging the problems to one side Major addressed the party's central council in mid-March. Apart from the uninspiring 'better the devil you know' argument for voters to remain with the Conservatives, although dressed up as 'you can only be sure with the Conservatives', the speech was another attempt to define Conservatism. This time he was back on the 'one nation' theme of representing the underdog and the have-nots. He claimed that what he had always wanted to do was to work for those for whom 'life is a struggle, for those who don't have the best education, don't have a decent home, don't have a safe neighbourhood, don't have a job'.[167] For a politician who had been a progressive Chair of Housing in Lambeth in the 1960s this may have been an authentic personal political credo. For one who had risen to dominance in the Thatcher government, however, and who had been busily pacifying the hard Eurosceptic right of his party for years and who had taken the 1980s agenda still further with rail privatisation and widespread 'market testing' in the civil service, it was less credible. Did he truly know where he stood or did he, as Thatcher accused him of doing, simply 'drift with the tide'? Was he now returning to his true principles, or was it a pre-election speech calculated to win him back some votes in the centre of the spectrum where the party had lost ground? It was Major's dilemma that he had led to the verge of an election campaign a party which had behaved as if the voters no longer mattered, in comparison to its own internal feuds. It was his own weaknesses, however, which increased that dilemma since he was never entirely clear where he wished to lead the party. Mainly, he just wanted to lead it.

The general election campaign itself was a sorry spectacle. Temporarily, the Labour Party was forced on to the defensive, on issues such as trade-union rights and its readiness to proceed with privatisation.[168] The Conservatives were much more alarmingly disadvantaged on the other hand because the issue of sleaze would not diminish in the first fortnight of the campaign. Labour accused the Conservatives of calling the election early in order to avoid the publication of the Downey report with its conclusions about the Hamilton affair. As it was, the case was now *sub judice*, but the opposition parties kept it in the forefront by agreeing to support one single Independent candidate, the journalist Martin Bell, to stand as an anti-sleaze candidate against Hamilton in Tatton, Cheshire. A crucial turning point was the decision of the *Sun* to support Labour. This was psychologically damaging to the Conservatives as well as a positive help to Labour. The newspaper's reasons were consistent with many of the views of defecting Conservative electors. It described the Tories as 'tired, divided and rudderless. They need a rest and so does the country. . . . They have all the right policies, but all the wrong faces.'[169] Once again it was the European issue which seriously wrecked the party's already negligible prospects of victory. As it emerged that candidates were putting out different manifestos on the subject, Major determined to take over a press conference and give his own personal credo on the issue in an attempt to restore authority. Major described it as the defining moment in the campaign. He stressed that he would protect Britain's interests rather than simply pursue party interest, and clasping his hands together appealed to his back benchers: 'Like me or loathe me, do not bind my hands when I am negotiating on behalf of the British nation.'[170] This did not remove the contention and the party almost imploded on the issue. 'If Europe was an obsession for many Conservatives, victory was the obsession for Labour.'[171] Some election campaigns have an impact on the result, and 1992 was an example. In 1997 Labour's lead held steady and the campaign changed little.

The Tories defeat was unexpectedly large: 419 MPs was an all-time record for Labour and 165 was the lowest Conservative tally since 1906; the Labour majority of 179 was the biggest since 1935, and the 10 per cent swing from Conservative to Labour was the largest two-party shift since 1945. The electoral system distorted the vote as Labour secured 44.4 per cent of the vote and the Conservatives 31.5 per cent. This was a massive reversal in political fortunes since 1992, in which many of the candidates expected to succeed Major also lost their seats.

The Conservatives did not lose simply because it was perceived to be time for a change, but because despite four successive victories they were always vulnerable to such an outcome. The party had not secured even 45 per cent of the vote since 1979, it was constantly vulnerable to by-election, local and European election defeats, and polls revealed that large majorities gave a comparatively low approval rating to the Thatcher and Major governments throughout the period. Its victories were attributable to a reputation for sensible government and effective economic management. That reputation was destroyed within three hours on Black Wednesday. This also strengthened longer-standing concerns about the Conservative attitudes to the public services.[172] Sleaze was of some importance but was probably well down the hierarchy of issues. Europe was unlikely to be a high salience issue for the bulk of voters, but its impact upon party disunity was of central importance. The final factor was that there was now an opposition party, and party leader, who voters were ready to support.

THE DEBATE ABOUT THATCHERISM

Much effort has been expended upon analysing Thatcherism from a theoretical perspective, and while the subject is prone to ideological bias, the various views which have been advanced cast light on the events of this crucially important period in modern British politics. All the interpretations have shortcomings, and so collectively leave open the possibility that the only meaningful way to explain the phenomenon is that 'Thatcherism' was simply 'the Conservative Party led by Mrs Thatcher'.

THATCHERISM AND THE NEW RIGHT

One interpretation is that Thatcherism was a product of the New Right which burgeoned in the late 1960s as an Anglo-American phenomenon. Many of the New Right's values were neo-liberal or neo-conservative, in that as an intellectual movement it fully understood that the world had altered substantially since the nineteenth century when liberal and conservative values first appeared in anything like a recognisably consistent form. Right-wing ideas needed to be re-invented in order to make them relevant for a world in which even the terms liberal and conservative had been distorted; liberalism into a form of social democracy and conservatism into a 'soft' consensualism associated with leaders such as Macmillan. As the Anglo-American intellectual elite increasingly adopted a left-wing perspective on politics from the 1930s to the 1960s, so the right attempted to retrieve the situation. Funded by large corporations, right-wing 'think-tanks' began to appear to challenge the supremacy of the left. They included the

Centre for Policy Studies (1974), the National Association for Freedom (1975) and the Adam Smith Institute (1979).

The New Right drew from contemporary writers and social scientists and its 'gurus' included such advocates of neo-liberal *laissez-faire* economics as Schumpeter, Hayek, Friedman and Joseph. Their emphasis was upon individualism and free markets. The other strand to the New Right was neo-conservatism, drawing upon the ideas of the Conservative Philosophy Group (1975) and the Salisbury Group (1977). These groups emphasised the values of hierarchy, authority and nation.[1] Elements of New Right theory would have appealed to the party because it explained what appeared to have gone wrong with Keynesian and social democratic policies. The rise of inflation in the early 1970s could readily be explained by the economic liberals just referred to, but also by American public choice theorists such as James Buchanan and Gordon Tullock. They described democracy as a system of vote buying through public expenditure. Their views were popularised for Conservative thinkers by Samuel Brittan, who pointed out that 'the cost of these handouts, whether met through taxation or inflation, will not necessarily accrue to the groups who benefit from them'.[2] Such spending commitments are necessarily inflationary. Even 'stagflation' was attributed to government intervention. Conservative newspapers popularised these ideas by suggesting that satisfying special interest groups who were becoming dependent on government and the buying of votes from electors, was being achieved only by the extensive use of the printing presses, and that monetarism offered the only way out.[3]

The interpretation that Thatcherism equals the New Right in operation has been most strongly advanced by King. He tends to over-emphasise the ideological coherence of Thatcherism and to link it too directly to the revived New Right of the 1960s and 1970s. The succession of Thatcher to the party's leadership in 1975, he argues, led to the party's espousal of 'the superior virtues of the free market in contrast to the state interventionist policy characteristic of postwar policy'. The economic doctrine of monetarism and criticisms of welfare state institutions were adopted at this time. The party was also committed to individual liberty and to the support of traditional institutions like the family; this recalled the individualism of the pre-Keynesian welfare state era.[4] King links the Thatcher government's monetarist policies to Friedman's influence, and the attack on the trade unions and the rolling back of the state to the impact of Hayek.[5] He accepts that Thatcher's government was unsuccessful in the outcome of its New Right ideas, but still assumes that the origins of its policies lay with the New Right thinkers. ·

King's linkage between the ideas of the New Right and Thatcher's politics is exemplified by his publications on training policy.[6] He asserts that the abolition of the Manpower Services Commission (MSC), and its replacement by Training and Enterprise Councils (TECs) in the late 1980s, represented a reversal of policy from statism to neo-liberalism.[7] This neglects the reality that much of the MSC's activity before 1987 was driven by neo-liberal considerations; for example, its officials described its work as 'catalytic', to produce the conditions in which a 'pure' labour market could operate.[8] As Alice Brown argues, 'the need to change market behaviour requires or implies intervention of a specific nature by government'.[9] Another commentator observed that the MSC marginalised opposition and 'effectively by-passed national and local representative government', and so 'the return of *laissez-faire* has assisted the birth of a new form of central state intervention'. If the MSC was used for neo-liberal purposes, King also exaggerates the extent to which its replacement by TECs represented a turn to neo-liberalism. The growth of the TECs does not involve the jettisoning of the older style tripartism which prevailed under the MSC. There is no genuine devolution to the market since TECs do not operate as autonomous entities. In the Major years the government remained anxious to maintain its control over training policy, and so funded and supervised TECs to ensure that they delivered training schemes to manage unemployment. At the local level also the TECs often engaged in limited local tripartism, working with local government, educators, and even 'tame' trade unionists.[10]

King unduly homogenises New Right and neo-liberal thought and certainly the degree to which it directly informed all government departments. He neglects the phenomenon of internal government fragmentation. Far from all government departments which had a link with training policy sharing the same neo-liberal view of TECs, TEC leaders deplored the ignorance about their purposes by government departments other than that of Employment. Since many departments in government play a role in training policy, for example the Department of Trade and Industry, the Home Office and the Ministry of Defence, this lack of understanding about TECs cautions against exaggerating the coherence of neo-liberal ideology across the entirety of government. It is interesting that one of the themes of the Blair government has been to re-establish 'joined-up' government, as he argued that there was cross-departmental fragmentation leading to a lack of unity in the Thatcher and Major years.

The New Right undoubtedly played a role in government thinking in the Thatcher years, but it is unconvincing to relate the entire phenomenon of Thatcherism to the ideas generated by the so-called New Right.

The remaining interpretations of Thatcherism are weakened by their tendency to focus on particular aspects of the phenomenon, or by interpreting it largely on the basis of being broadly sympathetic or unsympathetic.

THATCHERISM AND PRAGMATIC POLITICS

All governments are driven by events, but those governments which have a stronger sense of ideological direction are more likely to be protected from being 'blown off course'. If the Thatcher government had been highly ideologically directed, then its readiness to compromise with a pragmatic approach to events would have been very much reduced. Riddell argues that while the Thatcher's government was affected by values, they were less intellectually coherent than those developed by the New Right ideologues. Instead Thatcher was responding to the values which would have been prevalent in a small middle-England town in the 1920s, in her case Grantham, where she grew up. This explained her commitment to work, family, deferred gratification and patriotism. Riddell further argues that even to the degree to which Thatcherism was concerned with liberal free-market economics it failed to follow through the policy implications of such a position. In short, Thatcherism was a set of instincts, and an approach to leadership, rather than a set ideology.[11]

There is merit in Riddell's analysis. Its weakness is that he attempts to demolish the idea of there being a Thatcherite ideology by utilising a very restrictive conception of the term, apparently confining it to rigid and coherent sets of ideas, when ideology can be described more inclusively as simply 'values'.[12] Without making the definition of the term explicit it is difficult to determine whether or not Thatcherism is an ideology. Riddell also tends to over-personalise Thatcherism. Her personality and personal values played a part in political decision-making between 1979 and 1990, and her government's criticisms of the welfare state and her Victorian commitment to family and self-help are evidence of this phenomenon.[13] It is an over-simplification, however, to regard Thatcher herself as the dominating element in Conservative politics after 1975 when many other external factors also influenced events. If King exaggerates the theoretical fundamentals of Thatcherism, Riddell ignores the intellectual climate in which the Thatcher governments operated.

THE WILLETTS INTERPRETATION

David Willetts asserts that Thatcher's politics involved no departure from the paths of British Conservatism and was fully in harmony with the pattern of postwar Conservative policy. It was the interventionist and managerial style of the Heath government from 1972 to 1974 which departed from the true paths of Conservatism, to which Thatcher returned the party. Heath's interventionism was the exception, in an otherwise consistent party history, in which the core values of individualism, the free market and a commitment to a strong community were the guiding principles. Thatcher and Major were at one with Edmund Burke in advancing this agenda. British Conservatism had never been solely concerned with the promotion of the free market, fiscal prudence and monetary control, but has also had a strong concern with social order which is best secured by preserving a strong community. Conservatism has always regarded people as more than economic units and has recognised the need for loyalty to a higher entity. It is through the development of national identity that strong communities can be fostered and Thatcher understood that her emotional commitment to the country made her a Eurosceptic and a true Conservative. Willetts suggests that 'the real Conservative fear must be that our sense of Britishness, even, dare one say it, our Englishness, is eroded by the EC'. Paradoxically he supports the ERM as an anti-inflationary device while opposing economic and monetary union. He was at one with the former chancellor Lawson, however, since by upholding the ERM he was adhering to 'automatism'; the search for a rule of economic management to disregard the need for discretionary political decision-making.[14]

It was in Thatcher's regard for the nation rather than the welfare state that she expressed her preference for a strong community. Willetts exemplifies the Conservative Party's concern that all citizens should become part of national life by such devices as the National Curriculum and the Department of National Heritage's attempt to sustain a national cultural identity.[15] The problem with the European Union is that it lacks an underlying culture to sustain it.

Willetts rejects the view that a group of free-market *arrivistes* have changed the historical party of authority and deference, as the party has always promoted two different discourses: the individual, initiative, enterprise and freedom; alongside community, order and deference. He is too procrustean in maintaining, while allowing some slight deviation in Heath's case, a perfect symmetry in Conservative politics in which Thatcher is included. This view is closer to reality than the idea that Thatcherism was an alien importation into the Conservative tradition. Willetts is too inclined to dismiss the impact of the so-called *arrivistes* in the party in the 1970s, as the older generation of leaders was dying off. Skidelsky observed that the social composition of the Conservative Party's elite was changing. He stimulatingly argues that

> The postwar settlement had been underwritten by the ability of established money and social position to work with a trade union baronage and a Wykhamist intelligentsia. This wary, but complacent and inefficient, corporatism had given way, by the 1970s, to the fierce ideological antipathy of two groups of lower-middle class *arrivistes* – those who had risen through the private sector, and those who had done the same through the public sector. The theory of 'embourgeoisement' has a long history, but few of its proponents in the 1950s foresaw that its political fruit would be polarisation, not convergence.[16]

LETWIN: THATCHERISM AS CONVICTION POLITICS

Letwin's argument is, like that of Riddell, based upon an assumed and implicit definition of ideology. In her case ideology is a type of abstract, dogmatic and eternal doctrine. Her account of Thatcherism locates it within an ideological framework, if a more inclusive definition of the term is adopted. Vincent suggests three types of Conservatism which are non-ideological, although none of them would accommodate Letwin's description of Thatcherism. The three types are pragmatic Conservatism, or the readiness to adopt any idea which both works and is electorally popular; positional Conservatism, or a defensive posture towards whatever economic and political arrangements are in place and finally a Conservative disposition, or a scepticism about rational theorising.[17] In Letwin's terms Thatcher was never a pragmatist or a mere defender of the status quo, and she had a programme which was rational.

Letwin regards Thatcher as having a mission rather than an ideology which was to address the particular problems of late twentieth-century British society. Thatcherism was 'a bundle of attributes, held together by time and place'.[18] Letwin claims that Thatcher wished to promote the vigorous virtues of uprightness, energy, adventurousness, self-sufficiency, independence, loyalty to friends and resolution against enemies. These were the virtues which Thatcher wished to see families nurture and as a result national life would be re-invigorated.[19] The vigorous virtues which the British economy and society required were contrasted with the 'soft' virtues of kindness, humility, sympathy and cheerfulness, all of which prevented people from taking responsibility for their own lives, and had brought Britain to the sorry state that it was in when Thatcher arrived. Letwin also claimed that traditional social distinctions were altered as a result of Thatcher's impact as she judged people on their individual qualities and not their profession, education, achievement, wealth, social position, marital status or beliefs. As a political programme, Thatcherism had no faith in the capacity of the state to achieve worthwhile objectives, except to concentrate its power against those institutions which checked or restrained those vigorous, individual virtues which were sorely needed. This explained Thatcher's animus against such institutions as local government, the civil service, nationalised industries, trade unions and the BBC. Equally, some of her policies can only be understood as contributing to the promotion of these same virtues, as privatisation was aimed at increasing the ownership of shares to encourage popular capitalism, and the sale of council houses was to assist the family to operate as a property-owning unit. Letwin considers that the 1980s produced more risk takers. She is less than convincing in combining her claim that Thatcherism succeeded, and yet that Thatcher fell from power because the people were tired of her commitment to vigour. As Letwin expresses it, when Thatcher kept repeating 'there is so much more to do', they concluded that 'with that woman around there never would be any peace'.[20] Letwin also concurs with Willetts that there is an incompatibility between Britain and Europe, as was demonstrated by Thatcher's failure to identify with the bureaucratic monolith of the European Community, from her own individualistic perspective.

Letwin does succeed in reconciling the two components of Thatcherism, the free economy and the strong state – which Gamble finds contradictory – since both were valid means towards the end of disseminating vigorous virtues across the country. Letwin neglects the dominance of economic policy, rather than the promotion of vigorous virtues, in the first Thatcher period until 1987. There is also merit in the critique, that while Thatcher was inside the Conservative tradition, she distorted it by overemphasising the individualistic element at the expense of other components.[21] In her focus on the circumstances of the time as the distinguishing feature of Thatcherism, Letwin is guilty of tautology. All leaders produce policies which they consider relevant to their time in office. Since Letwin agrees that Thatcher promoted particular values and virtues, it is curious that she adamantly denies that Thatcher had an ideological focus.

THE CONSERVATIVE WETS

The Conservative 'wets', as Thatcher dismissed them, produced one of the least convincing analyses of Thatcherism. They were the most determined to deny any ideological element to traditional Conservatism and to criticise Thatcher for having the temerity to possess an ideology. It is ironic that willing participants in Thatcher's government in the early years can be so critical of activities in which they participated. Lord St John of Fawsley (Norman St John Stevas) argues that 'the bones of Thatcherism' reveal 'a fairly repellent skeleton'.[22] Ian Gilmour has developed the 'one nation' position most thoroughly, and his critique reads like one produced by a left-wing historian.[23] This suggests that it is the 'one nation' or 'wet' Conservatives who were outside the Conservative ideological tradition, and not Thatcher herself. The conviction of such 'wets' as Gilmour, Prior and Pym that the Conservative Party is non-ideological is almost a neurosis. Yet their own rejection of socialism, fascism and anarchism can only be based on ideological grounds. Ideology is as much about rejections as prescriptions.[24] Gilmour rests his case on Thatcher's predilection for the free market as the guide to policy-making. He asserts that the limits of government should rather be 'a matter of judgement and prudence. There is no place at all for dogma.'[25] Yet it is as ideological to defend a centrist position on the debate about the respective roles of the state and the market as it is to be the advocate of just one or the other. Gilmour would be comfortable with European Christian Democracy, which is as ideological as Thatcherism. Pym objected to Thatcher's unbalancing of Conservatism because he claimed that it departed from the party's finest traditions.[26] Those fine traditions almost appear to be synonymous with 'muddling through', however, which patently lacks intellectual force.

BULPITT: THATCHERISM AS STATECRAFT

This analysis overlaps with that of the 'wets', in that Bulpitt suggests that Conservative governments have always reacted to circumstances with the policies needed to retain social order, preferably under Conservative rule. He asserts that 'statecraft' drives the performance of Conservative governments with the aim of 'centre autonomy'.[27] This involves the party winning power and achieving a relative degree of autonomy on issues of high politics. It is always ready to delegate in the less important areas of low politics, which might explain the setting up of agencies and quangos.

Bulpitt maintains that before the 1960s Keynesian demand-management provided a strategy for 'statecraft' and in the 1960s economic modernisation took its place. As it became clear that economic modernisation benefited Labour electorally the party turned against it, but after two general election defeats in 1974 the Conservatives were left without any clear macro-economic strategy. This led them to revive the quantity theory of money and to ideologise it as monetarism. Labour had its own version of 'statecraft' with its Social Contract with the trade unions, and after 1972 monetarism offered the Conservatives an instrument to tackle inflation. This was excellent news for a party which had been traumatised by its attempts to experiment with incomes' policies, all of which had led to destabilising confrontations with organised labour. While the monetarist theory linking money supply increases to subsequent inflationary surges offered a policy framework, Bulpitt convincingly argues that it offered the Conservatives, in the circumstances of the mid-1970s, 'a superb (or lethal) piece of statecraft'. Many cautious Conservatives, and particularly the 'wets', had feared in the later 1970s that with Thatcher as the leader of the opposition, moralism, populism, nationalism and confrontational industrial relations legislation were electorally damaging themes for the party to stress. The Winter of Discontent helped the Conservatives, however, as it vindicated monetarism rather than incomes' policy.

Bulpitt is forced to recognise that the Conservatives talked about much else other than monetarism. He neglects the fact that many believed that monetarism was actually the cure for inflation and adopted it for economic rather than purely political reasons, and fails to recognise that the 'automaticity' involved in monetarist solutions to inflation does not effectively depoliticise the issue. This is because monetary policy will frequently dictate high interest rates. Yet interest rates were politically sensitive for Thatcher because of their effect on mortgage repayments and her vision of a property-owning democracy. Bulpitt is correct, however, in saying that the party needed an alternative 'guru' to Keynes, and a credible strategy for inflation which could liberate them from detailed negotiations with the trade union movement.

THATCHERISM AS A CENTRALISING PROJECT

This interpretation has been most strongly advanced by Jenkins. He is convinced that both intentionally, and as an unintended consequence, the impact of Thatcherism has been to promote a state with a more centralised structure and a greater democratic deficit than previously. He regards Thatcherism as the result of the leadership of a 'tense, intelligent, bossy woman'.[28] He points to the weakening of local government and the arbitrary abolition of the Greater London and the Metropolitan authorities and the transfer of many of the powers previously exercised by elected local government to such non-elected quangos as the Urban Development Corporations (UDCs). Such bodies can be manipulated centrally. In education policy he discerns the same trend, with the national curriculum in schools, and the nationalisation of the university sector through the more rigorous controls exercised by the newly established funding council for higher education. Jenkins even argues that the regulatory regimes set up to oversee the newly privatised industries, such as OFTEL and OFWAT, facilitate a greater degree of central control over those industries than was ever practised in the more benign era of nationalisation. He asserts that the rail privatisation merely threw the railways 'up into the air' and that they landed 'in the Treasury's lap'.[29]

Each of these measures of centralisation produced a dearth of accountability. If Bulpitt perceives Thatcherism as ensuring the autonomy of the centre, but by central government actually seeking to do less but doing it more effectively, Jenkins regards Thatcherism as having enhanced the role of the central state, and rejects the fashionable argument that the state is becoming 'hollowed out'. Jenkins argues a persuasive case, since transferring many of the powers to other bodies did not prevent the centre powerfully 'steering' the country; and Thatcher's animus against the public sector did not preclude an extension of the powers of her own office. Thatcher herself commented, 'we are strong enough to do those things which government must do and only governments can do'.[30] The central institutions of the state, particularly the Treasury, seized the opportunity that she provided, and the magnetism of power prevailed over neo-liberal ideology.

MARXISTS MANQUÉ: THATCHERISM AS HEGEMONY

As Marx went out of fashion so British neo-Marxists rediscovered the work of the Italian Marxist Antonio Gramsci. They consequently developed the idea of 'projects' in politics which seek to attain an ideological hegemony in their society. The rhetoric and style of Thatcher was sufficiently striking to make it appear that here was a new project, disassociated from traditional Conservatism, which the latter-day British Gramscians could analyse better than any other political group. They produced stimulating analyses which were, however, flawed; both by an undue sympathy for Thatcherism because of a predilection for 'projects', and a tendency, shared with Letwin, to associate Thatcherism with transient circumstances rather than the history of Conservatism. The Marxist theorists also shared the view of the 'one nation' Conservatives that Thatcherism divided the nation, and damaged the weak and poor to benefit the rich.

Hall deliberately introduced a closure into his analysis, by his use of the concept of hegemony. This was to demonstrate that Thatcherism was not simply another name for 'the exercise of the same old, familiar class domination by the same old, familiar ruling class'.[31] Hall's definition of Thatcherism as 'authoritarian populism' attempted to answer the paradox that the disciplinary and directive use of the power of the state was accompanied by populist politics which exploited the popular discontents of everyday experience.[32] This included pandering to popular prejudices in a manner that the Conservative Party had not done previously, on such issues as immigration, crime and welfare scrounging. This tactic enrolled the support of the poor for policies which in reality promoted the interests of business and capital. Hall's interpretation is most effective in explaining the party's political strategy in opposition before 1979. In attempting to reconcile the social authoritarian and economic liberal strands in Thatcherism, it neglects the changing emphases of Thatcher's policies at different stages during her time as leader. As with King's New Right analysis, it over-homogenises Thatcherism.

Gamble draws attention to the contradictions between the free economy and strong state elements of Thatcherism, exemplified by the simultaneous pursuit of a deregulated labour market and a rhetorical emphasis upon family values. Yet he neglects the reality that these two strands can be reconciled within the circle of petit bourgeois moral values. Gamble takes issue with Bulpitt's version of Thatcherism as 'statecraft'. He regards 'statecraft' as potentially aggressive rather than simply defensive. He argues that once the state's authority has been successfully re-established, 'no compromises with the enemies of Conservatism or freedom are necessary'.[33] Conservatism under Thatcher was not, as with the New Right theorist Hayek, about promoting political liberty through the mechanism of the free market, but about the creation of a strong state to establish the conditions in which a truly free market can function effectively. While the state was rolled back to generate greater economic freedom through privatisation and deregulation it was also rolled forward with the intention of enhancing social discipline and removing the impediments to *laissez-faire*. It is true that some real decentralisation of power did occur under Thatcher, and Major continued the process. The transfer of power from unions to employers, and from central and local government to 'quangos' run by businessmen and accountants, however, was in order to facilitate an economy based on direct exchanges between employers, employees and consumers, unmediated by public organisations.

Gamble seeks a multi-dimensional analysis of Thatcherism linking economic, political and ideological considerations. He properly draws the distinction between a shift in the terms of the national policy debate, which Thatcher and Major succeeded in achieving, and a change in the nation's basic values. While the country at the end of the twentieth century still favours more welfare and public service provision than Thatcher, the policies of New Labour reveal the continuing impact of Thatcher's contribution to the national policy debate. Gamble examines the government's economic policies, or its 'accumulation strategy', as he describes it. The Thatcher and Major governments presided benignly over the decline of British manufacturing. They favoured newer forms of wealth creation, such as a *rentier* economy based upon a portfolio of overseas investments, internationally tradable services and the encouragement of inward investment by foreign transnational companies assembling products, designed and developed elsewhere, to be sold in the European market. Gamble considers this a credible strategy for British capital, and offers three explanations for the abandonment of traditional staple industries. First, it was correct to understand the need for change in individual national economies, rather than artificially resuscitating declining industries. Secondly, modernising the nation's industrial base did not expand the political interests likely to support the Conservative Party. Thirdly, the emerging global economy made new ideas obligatory.[34] Gamble realises that a strong state can assist the free market, as it can maintain 'effective surveillance and policing of the unemployed and the poor', 'confront and defeat any union challenge' and 'contain any upsurge of terrorism and public disorder'.[35] Gamble has been unjustly criticised by Marsh for offering a 'uni-dimensional analysis of Thatcherism'.[36] This is fair comment about some of the other writers examined here, but not so of Gamble. He specifically asserts that 'hegemony is often misrepresented as meaning simply ideological domination, but properly understood it involves the successful inter-weaving of economic and political as well as ideological domination'.[37]

Jessop argues that Thatcherism was a 'Dual Nations Hegemonic Project'. He argues that bourgeois capitalist society is sustained by the promotion of ideas, in the form of common sense, which serve to conceal the rampant contradictions of the capitalist system.[38] Jessop shares the illusion of the particularity of Thatcherism, but while he analyses it as a discrete phenomenon, he recognises distinct stages and perceives the need to periodise it.[39] The concepts needed to analyse Thatcherism must change as Thatcherism itself changed. Jessop distinguishes four main phases. Before 1979 it was a doctrine aimed at addressing the perceived economic crisis and the threat of ungovernability, and at winning office. From 1979 it was concerned to take control of the government machine, a phase which lasted until 1982. From 1982 to 1987 it was concerned to create and consolidate a new political and social base for itself and mainly addressed the country's economic difficulties and the problems of production. The final phase from 1987 extended to intervention in society and was concerned with the politics of consumption. This is a useful analysis, although it suffers from confusing a *post hoc* interpretation with a pre-planned project. It is only in retrospect that Thatcherism appears to be so neat. If Thatcher and Major did not entirely make policy up as they went along, neither did they follow a totally consistent and conscious blueprint.

Jessop argues that Thatcherism restructured the economy to advance the interests of those segments of business best able to exploit the possibilities of footloose international capital at the expense of those interests best able to profit from a manufacturing Fordist economy. Thatcherism divided the nation economically and politically, even 'denying basic rights to those outside the electoral block'.[40] Jessop argues that in the postwar period 'one nation' politics was possible and concessions were offered to the entire population to gain popular support for capitalist interests. After the economic crisis of the 1970s the Thatcherites resorted to a 'two nations' strategy, creating an antagonistic cleavage between the productive, who became the favoured nation, and the parasitic.[41]

Thatcherism's strategy for capital accumulation prioritised financial and international capital over the domestic industrial sector. The south of England was freed from the relics of the Industrial Revolution and the trade unions tied to it, and the north became de-industrialised. The economy was internationalised and Britain became an offshore location for investment, insurance and speculation. This type of global service economy was different from the Thatcherite rhetoric of representing a revolt of small and medium capital against both big business and labour. In government there was some limited support for business start-up schemes, but Jessop argues that the small business focus was a disguise for advancing City of London and multi-national interests. In reality, Jessop exaggerates, as government was supporting both sectors of business in an incoherent way, but ultimately it was the interests of international capital which carried the greater weight. To attract global capital the Thatcherite governments reduced costs on business, and while Major claimed that this was a social policy as it saved jobs, it also created the dual labour market. The unacknowledged commitment to a dual labour market was discernible in the 1985 White Paper, *Employment: The Challenge for the Nation*.[42] Clearly the Thatcher and Major governments did not build their accumulation strategies on monetarism alone. Their economic policies were evidently socially divisive, and Jessop claims that Thatcherism produced a vertical social cleavage between the productive groups and the parasitic, such as the unemployed, the disabled and pensioners. The final stage of Thatcherism extended itself into the welfare state, therefore, and reformed social security so as to attack the dependency culture into which the disadvantaged 'nation' was being forced.

Jessop agrees with those who perceived the emerging economic interests in the Britain of the 1980s as being linked to a post-Fordist economy with its more flexible and diverse forms of production and consumption. Fordism was built upon collective bargaining, public credit and state intervention, while post-Fordism privileged individual and plant bargaining, the privatisation of the delivery of welfare and the consolidation of a two-nations society. Labour had benefited from Fordism and its 'smokestack' industries, but Thatcherism represented the expanding tertiary and service economy, and developed a coalition to unify the more substantial economic and social forces in the country which constituted a post-Fordist contented majority. But if, in opposition, Thatcher was a rallying force for anxious sections of the establishment as well as for discontented sections of both the bourgeoisie and the working classes, in power she advanced the demands of those likely to benefit from the internationalisation of the economy. Jessop correctly identifies Thatcher's encouragement of an open economy, a trend that the subsequent Labour government finds difficult to reverse. His error is his assumption that opening up the economy was at all incompatible with the ideology of the Conservative Party. In reality, Treasury officials had anticipated the policy of removing exchange controls, it proved an easy policy to implement, and became a bipartisan policy soon to be emulated by other governments. Harold Lever, who had been an economics minister in previous Labour governments, described the removal of exchange controls as 'a considerable encouragement to a great trading, insurance and banking nation'.[43] Jessop correctly points out the skewed results from this strategy, the encouragement of a *rentier*, alongside a low-wage service economy. The British state was thus put at the service of capital operating in Britain. Thatcherite economics forced Britain into a strategy of satisfying the demands of international capital in order to finance its balance of payments deficit on manufactured goods. Jessop argues that no other major capitalist economy exhibits 'such a high degree of internationalisation in its leading sector'.[44] There was an alternative, if Heseltine's theory of single-mindedly concentrating on the European dimension had been followed. It would have involved an active policy for the promotion of high-tech sectors, a micro-corporatist approach to labour relations and a shift towards a European strategy of defence procurement and planning.[45] In claiming the existence of this alternative Conservative strategy Jessop lacked the advantage of seeing how little active intervention Heseltine pursued in practice when he had the opportunity as Major's Secretary of State for Industry from 1992 to 1995. Jessop conceded that the success or otherwise of the Thatcherite 'project' would be determined by its economic outcomes.

Thatcherism shifted during the 1980s from a defensive to an offensive accumulation strategy, aimed at benefiting transnational corporations, and supported by an increasingly authoritarian state. The election victories of 1983 and 1987 were marked by nationalist rhetoric, but were used to endorse an internationalist and capitalist-orientated set of policies. While Jessop hits a number of targets convincingly, there was little in Thatcher's policies which was inconsistent with the Conservative Party's traditional orientation towards capitalist and propertied interests, in whatever form they presented themselves, at any given historical moment.

CONCLUSION

Most of the commentaries on Thatcherism tend to be uni-dimensional, that is to say influenced by one part of the decade rather than its entirety; they are convinced that Thatcherism represents a deviation from true Conservatism, and is thus an expression of New Right ideology. A more persuasive interpretation, however, is that Thatcherism lies within the Conservative tradition. As has been argued elsewhere, the history of the party allows for anything: 'the setting up and the dismantling of empire, and the creation as well as the dismantling of public ownership. Thatcherism is thus part of the great delta of Conservatism.'[46] In emphasising self-help, individual responsibility, independence and freedom to make money, Thatcher reflected a doctrinal continuity within Conservatism.[47] The view that Thatcherism represented some new departure is undermined by the argument of Marsh and Rhodes, that if Thatcherism is measured against the yardstick of policy implementation, then the outcomes are less than overwhelming.[48] Moon argues to the contrary, however, that the policy impact of the Thatcher years was unusually substantial.[49] Yet even Moon contests the idea of the Thatcher era being the fulfilment of a clear 'New Right' ideological blueprint. He suggests that 'the test of coherence and consistency, which no government can meet, ignores the possibility of rolling agendas and of governments learning to improve their capacity with the experience of office'.[50]

Insights into diverse aspects of Thatcherism at different periods between 1979 and 1997 do emerge from these theoretical perspectives, provided the continuities with the development of British Conservatism are appreciated. In reality, Thatcherism was a *melange* of crisis management, U-turns, abnegations of some aspects and concentrations of other aspects of state power and responses to pressures from those who wished to pursue a more rigorous right-wing agenda. The privatisation of the railways is an example of the Major government responding to right-wing pressures. Thatcher herself, far from being a rabid New Right ideologue, was often cautious as, for example, when she initially resisted Lawson in his desire to bring to an end the Dock Work Labour Scheme. This was an untenable legacy of the age of greater trade union power in the 1970s, and was widely condemned for its favouritism towards the Transport and General Workers' Union. Thatcher was unnecessarily fearful that abolishing the scheme would lead to a docks' strike and had to be pushed into acting. Lawson cites this episode as evidence of Thatcher's political caution.[51] Despite this caution it can safely be asserted that Thatcherism was a crusade against socialism, and that its impact was the result of exercising political power for eighteen consecutive years. Ultimately, Thatcherism was the Conservative Party demonstrating, successfully under Thatcher but much less so under Major, both the breadth of its ideological inheritance, and its capacity to adapt to changing circumstances.

CHAPTER 9

THE IMPACT OF THATCHERISM: CONSERVATISM AND NEW LABOUR

Any evaluation of the impact of Thatcherism on British politics should primarily explore the extent to which it determines the policies of Blair's New Labour government which, barring unforeseeable accidents, is likely to dominate politics for several years. Despite its apparent marginality at the end of the decade, however, it is also necessary to analyse briefly the nature of the Conservative Party led by William Hague in the aftermath of eighteen years of governments led by Thatcher and Major. The Conservative Party continued to reel from its heavy defeat for two years after 1997. It was so suffused with Euroscepticism that it proved impossible to elect such dominant and experienced figures as Kenneth Clark to the party's leadership, and in June 1997 Hague emerged as the candidate with the strongest support among Conservative MPs. Thatcher's continuing potency within the party was demonstrated by the fact that Hague considered it useful to secure her endorsement of his candidacy. To many in the party the day when Thatcher was deposed from the party leadership in November 1990 was a much bleaker day than the election of a Labour government in May 1997.[1] Apart from continuing hostility to further European integration and to Britain's early membership of the single currency, it is unclear where the party stands in relationship to Thatcher's legacy. Hague has shown some tentative signs of endorsing a more libertarian style of politics than Thatcher in the area of social and personal morality, but reveals little sign of embarking upon the fundamental re-theorising of Conservatism which is now clearly required.

FROM OLD TO NEW LABOUR

Thatcherism's lasting impact on British politics is amply evident from the transition in the Labour Party to New Labour. This was an incremental process between 1983 and 1997. One of Thatcher's overriding political goals had been to eliminate socialism in Britain while recognising that the Labour Party would survive as a political force, and to ensure that the main parts of her political project remained intact after her departure from the political scene.[2] This chapter demonstrates the considerable measure of success that she achieved through her party's role in the creation of New Labour. It is too simplistic to argue that the Blair Labour government is performing identically to that of a Conservative government elected in 1997. It is also too mono-causal an interpretation to suggest that Thatcherism has been the sole influence on the emergence of New Labour. The policies of the Labour government since 1997 are indisputably closer to those of the Conservatives, however, than they are to traditional social democracy. The transition from old to New Labour was a process which occurred very gradually between 1983 and 1992, stalled somewhat from 1992 to 1994 and then accelerated significantly after 1994. It was only in this final period, which coincided with the arrival of Blair as party leader, that the party began to identify itself formally as New Labour. Blair acknowledged in his 1996 conference speech, however, that the true author of the New Labour Party was Kinnock who had begun the process of ideological adaptation to accommodate the political, economic and social changes of the 1980s.[3] Kinnock publicly proclaimed his intention of 'modernising' the Labour party and commentators frequently made reference to the Kinnock's New Model Labour Party. Kinnock and not Blair was indeed the founder of New Labour.

Between the elections of 1983 and 1987, under Kinnock's leadership, the Labour Party reacted to the threat of electoral meltdown. Its narrow avoidance of falling into third place behind the Social Democratic and Liberal Alliance in the popular vote at the 1983 general election had a traumatic impact on most of the party. While many Labour Party members remained committed to traditional socialism and resisted Kinnock's attempts to adjust to the new political realities of the post-Falklands Thatcher era by abandoning some of its more unpopular policies, Kinnock obtained some alteration in Labour's ideological position. He achieved the abandonment of Labour's opposition to Britain's membership of the European Economic Community and overcame resistance to the sale of council houses. The party also came round to the need to lower taxes and to jettison its faith in old-style nationalisation.[4] Kinnock also disassociated the party from the extreme positions adopted by the Militant Tendency when he lambasted the militant leaders of Liverpool City Council at the 1995 party conference and set about the expulsion of those suspected of infiltrating the party from a Marxist or Trotskyite perspective. He also kept his distance from supporting all the actions of the National Union of Mineworkers during the 1984–5 strike, recognising that it was the last overtly political strike likely to occur in Britain. These steps merely constituted the removal of some of the negatives in Labour's position, however, rather than a major adaptation to the new political realities which the result of the 1983 election had so ruthlessly exposed.

In the 1987 general election Labour fought a highly effective media-driven campaign, under the management of its new head of Campaigns and Communications, Peter Mandelson. A visually attractive television campaign and the abandonment of some of the worst shibboleths of old Labour policy were insufficient to improve its electoral position significantly, however, and the party leadership realised that still further ideological adaptations were required. In the 1987 general election the party's share of the vote was an abysmal 31 per cent. Remarkably little progress had been made since 1983 in climbing the electoral mountain confronting Labour. 'Privately funded research after the election showed that, for all the moderation of the leadership and the manifesto, the Labour Party in 1987 was still widely perceived as committed to high taxation, untrustworthy on defence, and beholden to the trade unions.'[5] Doubts about the party's managerial competence were clearly widespread.

In the 1987 to 1992 parliament Kinnock inaugurated a policy review in an attempt to respond the more effectively to the obvious shift in the ideological centre of gravity which Thatcherism had produced. This caused some dissent within the party. In particular the 1988 conference refused to abandon the long-standing, sentimental attachment to unilateral nuclear disarmament. This still left Labour with an unpopular policy commitment, and many party members appeared ready to countenance the status of permanent opposition rather than abandon this sacred principle. Under the guise of consultations with major world leaders, however, and strengthened by the collapse of Communism in 1987, Kinnock persuaded his party that because the international circumstances were now sufficiently altered, and as a consequence of his recently acquired personal knowledge of the attitudes of the leaders of other countries, Labour could remove unilateralism from its list of electorally unpopular commitments.[6] The 1989 party conference duly abandoned unilateralism, although Kinnock's credentials as a man of the left, who had once been a passionate unilateralist, assisted the party to swallow the medicine. It was to take a fourth electoral defeat in 1992 before a more right-wing party leader was able to convince his party to make still further adjustments to the new *zeitgeist* of Thatcherism.

Labour's search for electability also persuaded Kinnock to launch a more far-reaching policy review at the 1987 conference. This turned into a major re-education campaign for the party. If the replacement of the red flag with the red rose with all the symbolism that it implied during the slick election campaign of 1987 had yielded so few results, then most of the party accepted that it was the product which the party was attempting to sell which was at fault. The old left was sullen and resigned rather than enthusiastic about a major policy review but events, as Thatcher launched into her third term of office with a mandate to pursue an even more radical right-wing agenda, were no longer on their side. It is true that there was a paradox, that while sufficient electors voted Conservative to ensure Thatcher's continuation in office, Thatcherite values had not become hegemonic in the country at large. Majorities in the population still appeared to prefer state provision of welfare and professed themselves ready to pay increased taxes for improved public services.[7] Yet when electors cast their votes, they did not behave in accordance with the values that they proclaimed. Votes in real elections are the route to power, however, and Kinnock and his acolytes were convinced that more needed to be accomplished before Labour could draw comfort from the limited impact which some of Thatcher's values had made on the population, and face the electorate with confidence. The acquisition of power was an understandable objective because the party in government possesses all the resources to set the political agenda and to determine the directional nature of the political and legislative process. The resources available to government are the Queen's Speech setting out the parliamentary legislative timetable, Prime Minister's question time where the Prime Minister always has the final word, ministerial statements and the annual budget to distribute national financial resources. Also the media pays attention to government statements rather than to the reactions of the opposition.

Kinnock's policy review was part of a grander plan to make Labour electable again. It reduced the scale of the trade union influence over policy decisions at the party's annual conference, moving to 'one member one vote' as a basis for party decision-making, lessened the role of annual conference in the party's affairs, by setting up policy commissions to examine issues in greater depth, and ensured his dominance over the party's National Executive Committee (NEC).[8] It is evident that the greatest symbol of old Labour was the party's constitutional commitment to public ownership, through Clause 4, which had been absorbed into the constitution in 1918. After the 1992 election when he was no longer the leader Kinnock produced a revised version of Clause 4, although he had effectively abandoned the policy of nationalisation in practice. It was left to Blair's leadership after 1994 to accomplish the party's acceptance of a rewritten clause to remove a formal commitment to public ownership.[9] Abandoning the policy in practice and securing its formal removal from the party's constitution were two different activities, however, and the 1987 party conference reaffirmed its enthusiasm for Clause 4. Even Blair recognised the constraints at the time, by remarking after the 1987 decision that it mattered less whether the party overthrew the offending clause because the issue is 'how you implement those things in practice in the modern world today'.[10] While slightly disingenuous in view of his later position, Blair was evidently drawing the attention of a suspicious party to the question of what it meant to give effect to Clause 4 and thus to launch a debate which would ultimately lead to a rewriting.

The policy review was aimed at bringing the party back to the centre ground of British politics where elections are won and lost, and to enhance the party's appeal to groups which it had conceded to the Conservatives, particularly the skilled workers of the south and Midlands of England. The theories of Anthony Downs about the behaviour and tactics of political parties in two-party systems, which leads inexorably to their convergence in the centre of the spectrum, clearly remained pertinent.[11] Labour was being compelled to react to the political dominance of Thatcherism, as the Conservative Party had itself been forced to adapt to Labour's landslide victory after 1945.

Another response to the defeat in 1987 would have been for the party to merge or combine tactically with the SDP/Liberal Alliance. Blair reflected Kinnock's thinking in 1987 by considering this to be a deflection from what needed to be accomplished. He considered that collaboration with the SDP/Liberal Alliance, or proposals for proportional representation, to be excuses for 'avoiding decisive choices about the party's future . . . There is no decision that it would be justifiable for Labour to make in order to win power in a coalition that it should not be making anyway for itself.'[12] This demonstrated that, as a new MP, Blair was solidly behind Kinnock's review, realised the limits to its ambition given the mood of the party at the time and was concerned to win over the wavering centre voters rather than to do deals with the centre parties. His most overt challenge to the party in 1987, foreshadowing the degree to which he would later move its position to accept much of what the Thatcher years had effected, was signalled in his judgement that Thatcher's government had been able 'to challenge the postwar consensus because it was weak and people were tired of it . . . Labour has failed to recognise this and shift its ground'.[13]

The policy review after 1987 led to a programme, 'Meet the Challenge, Make the Change', in 1989. This was subsequently revised to produce the final version, 'Looking to the Future' in May 1990. As the press began to speculate about a change in the popular mood away from the selfish individualism of the Thatcher years, towards 'a caring, sharing nineteen nineties', Labour appeared to have captured the ideological tide. While stressing its compassion with its promise to increase pensions and child benefits the document was otherwise a model of fiscal rectitude. No more would the party leave itself open to the charge of fiscal and financial irresponsibility, or so it believed, as it stated that all other spending commitments would have to wait on economic growth. On taxes there was to be a bottom rate of 20 pence in the pound with a top rate of 50 per cent. Kinnock's introduction to the new programme emphasised prudence: 'We will not spend, nor can we afford to spend, more than Britain can afford . . .' 'Making comes before taking.'[14] The policy review left Labour in a contradictory position in which it was trying to reconcile 'the options presented by the external world and the demands presented from within the Party . . . it maintains a policy of increased spending on education, training, health and pensions but commits itself to fiscal conservatism and limited tax increases . . . The Policy Review has produced change but also contradictions.'[15]

Despite some ambiguity in its position, therefore, the policy review had led to significant compromises with the ideas and language of Thatcherism. Even so Kinnock was still reported as feeling that 'the review was less successful in looking towards the 1990s, in getting the party to respond to the kind of society that Britain was becoming.'[16] While welcoming Labour's attempted shift from being a high tax party, unsympathetic to the market, to one stressing partnership between government and industry; and from one using the language of 'workers' and 'spending', to one which referred to 'consumers' and 'investment', Kinnock still considered that the modernisation project had further to run.

Evidence was soon forthcoming to support Kinnock's view that insufficient change had been introduced to assuage the electors' fears about Labour as a high taxation party. As the recession deepened between 1989 and 1992, and as the Conservatives mounted their 'tax bombshell' campaign to convince the voters that Labour would be a profligately taxing government, so the positions which Labour had adopted in 1989 which it convinced itself were sufficient to remove the tax and spend slur, appeared to have moved insufficiently from Labour's old image. By the time of the 1992 general election, the previous commitment to increase pensions and child benefit by raising income tax and national insurance was sufficiently radical for a country reared on thirteen years of Thatcherism to take fright. Many prospective defectors from the Conservatives were thus anxious to return to the fold.

Equally, the so-called 'prawn cocktail' circuit which the shadow chancellor John Smith and his then acolyte Gordon Brown had embarked upon, with a series of lunches in the City to reassure business and financial interests that Labour was now 'sound' on the economy, were not adequate to reassure the City that Labour had truly become a friend of business and finance. Blair tried in vain during the period immediately before the campaign, to get the party to rescind the 1989 pledge, that tax rises were needed to pay for the pensions and benefit increases. By 1992 this had a somewhat 'musty' feel to it. In any event, these proposals were irrelevant to any programme for national economic recovery which the deepening economic recession clearly called for. Kinnock had also hinted to journalists, to reassure business interests, that a Labour government might in practice phase in national insurance increases on those earning over £20,000 a year, only for Smith to refuse to move on a commitment which had been determined in very different circumstances.[17]

The modernisers in the party, for example, Blair, Brown and Mandelson, recognised a paradox about Labour's ideological stance in 1992. On the one side the policy review had produced some spectacular changes. One journalist commenting on the absence of any commitments to public ownership referred to the death of socialism. 'This is an historic moment in the evolution of British politics; yet one that is in danger of passing unremarked.'[18] This represented the fulfilment of Kinnock's aim since becoming leader in 1983 of appealing to 'homeowners' as well as the 'homeless', the 'stable family' as well as the 'single parent', 'the employed' as well as the 'unemployed' and the 'majority' as well as 'the minorities'. That this appeal was still incomplete in 1992 for the goal of electoral victory to be fulfilled was the result of commitments entered into in 1989. From the perspective of the arch-modernisers Blair and Brown, the outcome of the election demonstrated the further need to come to terms with business.

The disappointment of a third successive defeat did not lead immediately to a further bout of modernisation to parachute the party further in the direction appropriate for a post-Thatcher world. Within three days of the election Kinnock resigned and Smith duly succeeded him as leader. This was rather surprising as the general prediction had been that, in the event of a fourth successive defeat, 'Kinnock will be replaced by a leader of the centre-left or the right who after a fourth defeat will have the authority to take the Kinnock reforms even further. This might include cutting the links with the trade unions altogether and accepting the need for electoral reform.'[19] In reality Smith remained close to the unions, opposed electoral reform and came close to subscribing to the 'one more heave' theory of how to displace the Conservatives. He was no moderniser.[20] It was with his death in May 1994, and the arrival of Blair, that the next phase of modernising and adjustment to the post-Thatcher world took place.

THE THIRD WAY

New Labour claims to have developed a new ideology, equidistant between traditional social democracy and Conservatism. This is the Third Way. It rejects undiluted capitalism and old-style social democracy. It is this desire to be at the centre of the spectrum which is its driving force. It is not so much ideologically vacuous as usurping the political territory previously occupied by the Liberal Democrats. The main theorist of the Third Way is Anthony Giddens who defined old style social democracy as based upon the patriarchal family, mass production, an elitist state run by small groups of experts and 'national economies . . . contained within sovereign boundaries'.[21] Blair's conception of the Third Way claims to have overcome contradictions by its political inclusiveness. In many respects it differs from a centrist ideology, in that it does not consistently pursue policies which are mid-way between right and left, but rather decides upon a policy decision which is drawn from the right and then follows it with another which appears to have a left-wing inspiration. It is clearly an ideology with at least a short-term electoral appeal, attracting those in society who have always hankered after coalition politics. It suffers from two philosophical flaws, however, whether analysed from a pluralist or a Marxist perspective. First, much pluralist analysis recognises that all political decisions involve gainers and losers. Secondly, Marx warned that one form of bourgeois ideology is to attempt to conceal contradictions in capitalist society by denying their existence. This appears to be the strategy of the Third Way. The arguments of the British left on the viability of the Third Way will ultimately prove less significant, however, than the economic fortunes of the Blair government. Or as Bill Clinton's Presidential campaign guidelines in 1992 campaign expressed it: 'it's the economy stupid'.

The Blair government certainly rebuts the charge that it is a continuation of Thatcherism, although there have been times, when Blair has praised Thatcher and she has returned the compliment.[22] Giddens argues that the Third Way is about the renewal of social democracy and he convinced one social democratic commentator that the Third Way is indeed about 'the left, the renewal of social democracy'.[23] It is argued here, however, that Blair's position is that of a centrist, and that the jury remains out as to whether his governments can produce significant reforms.

Blair believes with some justification that elections are normally won in the centre of the political spectrum, and in a vague alliance with the Liberal Democrats, his project is to keep the Conservatives out of power. Other commentators endorse this analysis. 'New Labour is neither a radical nor a conservative labour party; it is no longer recognisably much of a labour party at all. Instead it is a catch-all party of a familiar kind, a party of the centre which seeks to remain autonomous from all interest groups.'[24] Shortly before the 1997 general election a leading Labour Party strategist urged the party to 'win the trust of the centre'.[25] This is only one of many perspectives on

231

the character of the Blair government, however, although it shares with most the idea that Blairism involves only a limited departure from Thatcherism.

A conference on the theme of the Third Way, with the ambitious title 'Towards a Radical New Century', explored the idea that the Labour government is pursuing a new political project which cannot be compared with what has happened before, and which is 'beyond left and right'. This perspective rather assumes that 1997 comprised a political year zero. The 'Third Way' also appeared in the United States during Clinton's presidency and he defined it in an equally vague way. 'My fellow Americans, we have found a Third Way: smaller governments and a stronger nation.'[26]

While the idea that Blairism lacks any historical forerunners is unconvincing, this was the assumption of many at the conference, 'Towards a Radical Century'. For example, the Financial Secretary to the Treasury, Stephen Byers, pointed to the decision to establish student fees and yet simultaneously to tax the utilities to provide prospects for the unemployed to secure training and employment under the New Deal, as exemplifying a readiness to take decisions influenced by the traditional preferences of both right and left. He also cited the freeing of the Bank of England to conquer inflation, which demonstrates the fiscal prudence of New Labour contrasted with the government's simultaneous attempts to challenge the cautious economic principles of such major international economic institutions as the World Bank and the International Monetary Fund, as evidence of the new ideologically inclusive politics.[27] The Labour MP Alan Johnston argued that old trade unionism in Britain had mainly campaigned for free collective bargaining and the closed shop, while the type of modern trade unionism associated with New Labour is closer to the European mainstream, in urging the minimum wage and greater employee rights through the social chapter of the Maastricht treaty.[28] The Health minister, Tessa Jowell, stressed that the main purpose of health expenditure should not be, as in the past, simply to hope to solve problems by throwing money at them, but rather to address through preventative medicine the needs of the socially excluded. People compelled to live in 'sink' council estates, for example, and who are denied basic shopping facilities could be helped by the provision of good subsidised local shops to have access to a healthy diet of fruit and vegetables. It was wrong that they should have to depend upon distant supermarkets.[29] The minister with responsibility for the regions,

Richard Caborn, emphasised that New Labour would be different from previous Labour governments, by its readiness to eschew centralisation and to transfer power to the regions, through the mechanism of the Regional Development Associations. This regional focus would combine the goals of economic regeneration through the encouragement of private enterprise, previously a right-wing concern, with a socially motivated strategy to overcome social exclusion by improving the lives of the least fortunate, which was previously the ideological territory of the left.[30] A motif running through the contributions of all speakers to the same conference was the readiness to utilise the public sector for the delivery of services, together with a revival of the whole idea of public service so excoriated by Thatcher. Unlike the old left, however, there was to be the proviso of strict accountability for the quality of the services provided.

A similar synthesis of right and left is apparent in the policies of the Chancellor of the Exchequer, Gordon Brown. While adhering to the Thatcher government's spending limits for the first two years of the Labour government elected in May 1997, his longer term Comprehensive Spending Review plans to increase spending subsequently on health and education, and he also produced a modest redistribution in the 1998 budget statement, which set minimum income guarantees for families delivered through the tax system. While Brown was similar to Blair in his acceptance of the policy constraints imposed upon Britain by the global economy he sought to 'take the lead on . . . a new code of practice for international finance'. Blair also called for the G7 industrial states to coordinate the management of financial and economic turmoil and for the remodernising of the International Monetary Fund and the World Bank.[31] A similar compromise between traditional Conservative and Labour views was patently implicit in the Blair 'tough on crime, tough on the causes of crime' soundbite. New Labour similarly offered both a communitarian resistance to Thatcherism, and a strong 'tendency to authoritarian social conservatism (curfews for kids, compulsory workfare, the appointment of a 'Drugs Czar').'[32] Blair argues that the old left championed indiscriminate and often ineffective public spending, while the Third Way concentrates on ensuring that public spending delivers the required results. New Labour seeks the 'dynamic market' of America but also the 'social cohesion' of Western Europe.[33]

A case could be made that New Labour has pursued a radical departure of policy in the area of constitutional reform. It is evident that if the series of reforms; for example, devolution to Scotland and Wales, House of Lords reform, elected mayors for major cities, a Freedom of Information Act, Regional Development Agencies, the application of the European Convention on Human Rights to Britain and a somewhat more proportionally based electoral system all occur, then a virtual constitutional revolution will have taken place. Two important riders must, however, be recognised. First, there is an attempt by New Labour to control the degree of autonomy enjoyed by these organisations through a central determination of eligibility of the candidates to stand for the new organisations. Second, the constitutional reform agenda is traditionally Liberal in nature rather than socialist.

It can be argued, therefore, that all of the policy decisions discussed illustrate a synthesis between Thatcherism and traditional social democracy; that is to say that New Labour is cautiously escaping the policies of the Thatcher era but is content to continue putting much of it into practice. The Labour Party's process of adjustment, enabling it to continue much that Thatcher had set in motion, began under Kinnock's leadership. Blair merely accelerated a process which had temporarily stalled during Smith's brief consolidationist phase as leader. The modernisation of the party had developed to such a degree under Kinnock that the added impact of Blair's further changes substantially altered the party's entire ethos from that which had prevailed under earlier Labour governments.[34] Blair's changes were specifically concerned to take account of the shift in society's values which had resulted from the impact of Thatcherism.[35] New Labour had to deal with a society which had become more bourgeois and individualistic. Certainly much of social life had become more privatised with the rise of the video and the 'take away' replacing the cinema and the restaurant. Even the leftist intellectuals who produced the journal *Marxism Today* had been preaching the rise of post-Fordism, which they portrayed as the demise of mass production and consumption and the rise of more individualised activities. They identified the times as characterised by globalisation, postmodernism and a new form of identity and citizenship and implied that Thatcher had more effectively pre-empted this agenda than had Labour.

Recognising the significance of these changes in the environment of British politics, Blair successfully cajoled his party into accepting the rewriting of Clause 4 of the constitution to remove the commitment to nationalisation, made it clear that the trade unions could expect no favours from a Labour government and reached beyond Labour's traditional vote to forge a progressive coalition. He invoked the spirit of Liberal reformers such as Keynes, Beveridge and Lloyd George. Party activists accepted this change because Blair appeared to have the potential to take them to victory.[36]

The view that Blair is a centrist, whose main project is to establish a new hegemony in British politics which excludes the Conservatives, is less ambitious than the project which Giddens predicts for New Labour. He argues that social democrats in other states have also embraced change, for example, Norway's Freedom Debate in 1988 and Germany's Basic Programme in 1989.[37] Giddens accepts that the rise of globalisation is a reality, particularly in world financial markets, and that states and business corporations have encouraged the process. While nation states retain considerable economic, political and cultural leeway he argues that protectionist economic policies are no longer viable. Rejecting the neo-liberal response of freeing up capital markets still further, Giddens argues that the response should be to resort to collective action involving many countries and groups. He advocates an international solution including macro-economic coordination and greater global governance.[38]

It is in this area of globalisation, and the Labour government's response to the phenomenon, that most of the criticism from the left has emanated. One left-wing Labour MP urges a resistance to globalisation and an alliance with green and socialist groups outside the party.[39] Another critic suggests that Blair's invocation of globalisation provides an excellent pretext for him to downgrade ideological expectations as globalisation is presented as an irrevocable process, despite the fact that it is a right-wing phenomenon.[40] The view that it is a right-wing phenomenon is supported by another critic who attributes to globalisation, 'the restructuring of economic sectors and workplaces . . . [and] the insistent pressure for labour flexibility'.[41]

It is Blair's apparent acquiescence in the impact of globalisation which most identified the critique of the New Labour government by *Marxism Today*. It asserted that Blair is too pessimistic.[42] The global economy 'is here to stay' but Blair failed to perceive, it argued, that its operation need not be identical to *laissez-faire*, the actors in the global market can only function smoothly with the assistance of non-market institutions. The power of certain states to control what happens within their own economy remains, as '10 states . . . contain three-quarters of global GDP'.[43] In short, 'New Labour deals with globalisation as if it is a self-regulating implacable Force of nature, like the weather'.[44] What was worse was Blair's desire to set the lonely individual free to 'face the hazards of the global weather alone'.[45]

The consensus in *Marxism Today* about Blair's unnecessary acceptance of globalisation as an objective phenomenon was mainly expressed in a purely negative form, with few ideas as to what would be an alternative. One commentator did attempt to be more positive, however, and argued that there were signs that Blair's approach was already outdated, as throughout the world, 'free-market ideology is now in retreat and is likely to retreat much further . . . Without a certain amount of government intervention, global capitalism generates booms, busts and crises . . . This is the real significance of the capital controls now being introduced in Asian countries, of the abandonment of monetary orthodoxy by the IMF and of the successive defeats of right-wing political parties.'[46] Another writer also offered alternative policies such as greater regulation of the international financial markets which merely sought short-term gains, a new coordinated economic agency working both at regional and a world level, more international regulation of social conditions, the reduction of third world debts and the re-imposition of a measure of national capital controls.[47]

The problems with the critiques offered by *Marxism Today* are twofold. First, they advanced few substantial practical proposals, and the ones they offered, such as the control of capital flows, were distinctly unradical. Secondly, the journal had been in the vanguard of urging modernisation upon the Labour Party throughout the 1980s and had even praised Thatcher for being more in tune with modern times than the left.

A rival journal of the left, the *New Statesman*, complained that the intellectuals of *Marxism Today* give 'no blueprint, outline or plan of what might be done. Hobsbawm and Hall quote a number of economists and financiers, but most of them assume the continuing primacy of the free market and recommend controls only temporarily.'[48] The ultra-left *Socialist Worker* endorsed the criticisms of the intellectuals from *Marxism Today*. It pointed to the irony that it was those same intellectuals who led 'the stampede to the right' in the 1980s and who 'pioneered the notion that the left should 'modernise' because the working class was a dying force.' The same group had even argued that the workers were so attached to Thatcherism that Labour should have an electoral pact with the Liberals. *Socialist Worker* was particularly scornful about *Marxism Today*'s pretensions at an alternative radicalism since it amounted simply to wishing that global capitalism could be regulated. 'It argues for measures little different to what is being discussed by the world's top businessmen . . . It argues for controls on the movement of capital and for more government intervention to stop wild market swings.' There is no conception that capitalism should be removed and one columnist even declares that capitalism is 'an incredibly robust system' and that 'capitalism is natural'.[49]

If *Marxism Today* was distinctly vacuous in its policy proposals some of its analysis was persuasive. Barnett described New Labour's project as populist-corporatism. The populism was evident in its desire to remain in touch with public opinion and to take soundings from 'focus groups'. Its corporatism rests on the fact that its constitutional reforms are less about devolution of power and more about administrative decentralisation. While setting up assemblies in Scotland and Wales and permitting elected mayors in local government, Blair still wished to control the personnel and the decisions of these organisations. The comparison was less with a democratised and devolved state, therefore, and more with a vast corporation which allows managerial independence to its various branches, but controls their activities very tightly.[50] This could explain Blair's desire to limit the tax-raising powers of the Scottish Assembly and to influence the choice of the Mayor of London. While welcoming the thrust of constitutional reform undertaken by the Labour government since 1997 Barnett argues against Blair's comment that 'the choice is either his form of government or a return to the Tories . . . He is wrong. There is an alternative for Britain. Its name is democracy, its manners are decentralised . . . and its home is Europe.'[51]

Many left-wingers defend the government from within the social democratic tradition. Mulgan, formerly of the think-tank Demos, who is closely involved in advising Blair, attacked the *Marxism Today* intellectuals. Expressing his disappointment about their lack of engagement in political activity, he denied that New Labour rejected the social democratic tradition. It still believed in 'the role of active government' while understanding that governments can be more effective if the public sector does not become a vested interest in its own right . . . [New Labour politicians] believe in liberty, although they are also 'sensitive that their electors' concerns about family and crime were not taken seriously enough' previously. 'They believe in citizenship but want to enrich it . . . with a strong sense of responsibility and mutual commitment.'[52] Mulgan added that Blair had launched the debate about the Third Way in an open manner to encourage maximum discussion about ends and means. The same commentator advanced another common defence of New Labour's methods, that incremental progress was more likely to be successful than rapid reform, as in the past 'governments of the left launched explosive frenzies of reform only to crumble into disappointment and recrimination soon after'.[53] Some of the defences of the government's authenticity as a social democratic administration are unduly confident. Richards argues that New Labour is committed to its traditional and core basic values of community, individual freedom, tolerance, fairness and opportunity for all and a moral objection to poverty, although 'the ways these values are expressed through policy and government action change'.[54] Without a changing application of traditional values, he argues that Labour would still be debating votes for women, temperance, Rhodesia or the National Plan instead of crime, jobs, Europe and the environment. New Labour has rediscovered its roots in ethical socialism with Blair referring to the influence of Keir Hardie, William Temple, John McMurray and R.H. Tawney. Richards attempts to make his case by postulating the Britain of 2007 after a decade of Labour government. Inside the single currency Britain will be prosperous as a result of the work of the Regional Development Agencies, unemployment will be cured, the National Health Service will symbolise Britain's success and Blair will have proved that 'government can make a difference to our lives, that politics still matters in the face of the globalisation juggernaut'.[55]

Gamble's prediction for the future is more plausible as he eschews both Richards' *naïveté* and the vague carping of *Marxism Today*. 'The real radicalism of Blair's project lies in his determination to end the hegemony of the Conservative Party in British politics. If that succeeds, other forms of political radicalism will be back on the agenda in a way they have not been for a generation.'[56] Gamble fully understands the case that Blairism demonstrates the triumph of the Thatcherite impact on British politics.[57] The case is based on the argument that the election of 1997 led only to a change of personnel, that Thatcher's agenda continued, and that neo-liberal economic doctrines as well as social conservatism and moral authoritarianism were maintained. The Labour Party was even able to exploit 'one nation' rhetoric in 1997 because the Conservatives had abandoned it.[58] Gamble's interpretation is more realistic, however, than this overly simplistic view that New

Labour is neo-Thatcherite. He points out that Labour's key components are modernisation of the welfare state and the constitution. New Labour is a coalition of right and left, radical and conservative and it is premature to decide which will prevail. He expects that there will have to be economies in welfare in order to deliver the promises to the electorate on health and education. 'However, the New Labour project, to create a more inclusive society and remedy some of the underfunding of the public services, depends on the success of its strategy for reforming welfare by ending the dependency culture and getting many of those on benefit back into jobs.'[59] Finally, Gamble argues that if Labour can secure the entirety of its constitutional agenda then it will have altered the British state so profoundly that it will prove very difficult for an incoming Conservative government to reverse it. As one MP who is a proponent of the Third Way expresses it, 'Labour has travelled a long way in a short time on the whole constitutional agenda . . . Old Labour would never have found anything wrong with the British political system, as long as it could take turns to run things from time to time.'[60]

Certainly, if Giddens is correct and the old social democratic agenda of 'pervasive state involvement in social and economic life; state domination over civil society; Keynesian demand management; full employment; egalitarianism; comprehensive welfare and low ecological consciousness' has become obsolete, then Blair can not be condemned as a mere Thatcherite for recognising the need to modify it. Old-style social democracy is obsolete because it does not address the issues of globalisation, individualism, the declining salience of the state and the rise of ecology. Giddens defines individualism not in the atomistic sense of neo-liberalism, but as the requirement of contemporary society for people to constitute themselves as individuals to plan, understand and design their own lives.[61] He argues that the state has lost salience to the market and to non-governmental organisations, as Thatcher had always planned, but also to the 'sub-politics' of single-issue groups such as Greenpeace and Oxfam. The challenge of change and modernity requires the Third Way to develop a programme of 'the radical centre; a new democratic state; an active civil society; a democratic family; a mixed economy; equality redefined as social inclusion; positive welfare rather than dependency on benefits; a social investment state and a cosmopolitan democracy'.[62] Giddens stresses that social inclusion is as much about discouraging strata from the top of society from opting out of social involvement, as it is about preventing the exclusion of an 'underclass' from opportunity and social participation. While Giddens is pulling together ideas drawn from the practice of New Labour, from objective social trends regardless of the actions of governments, and even from his own 'wish list', he is ideologically much closer to Blair's government than he is to either traditional social democrats or Thatcherites. He is clear that Thatcherism is fatally flawed by virtue of its lacerating contradiction that devotion to 'the free market on the one hand, and to the traditional family and nation on the other, is self-contradictory . . . nothing is more dissolving of tradition than the "permanent revolution" of market forces'.[63]

While it is premature to be dogmatic about the ideological affinities of New Labour, and it is the choices and events of its entire first term and perhaps beyond which will facilitate a definitive answer, it is apparent that the old differentiation between left and right is being superseded. There are clearly areas of programmatic convergence between Thatcherism and Blairism, and there is some validity in the assessment that in the 1997 election Labour was seeking power simply in order to pursue a 'warmed up' version of 'one-nation' Conservatism.

New Labour was created from many sources, however, including the experience of the Australian Labour Party in government from 1983 to 1996. Essentially, it appears to be a centre party seeking to grapple with the changes in the environment of politics over the previous twenty years, of which Thatcherism was one crucially important element. In short, Thatcher impacted upon, but did not create, New Labour.

POSTSCRIPT

It is difficult to analyse the impact of Thatcherism in a value-free manner. Certain quantitative measures are possible. Britain's economic growth from 1979 to 1997, while higher than the 1970s, was less than in the 'Butskellite' years of the 1950s and 1960s. Rates of growth of 1.9 per cent from 1979 to 1988 and 1.5 per cent from 1988 to 1997 did nothing to arrest Britain's relative decline compared to such competitor countries as Germany and Japan. Nor was the record of inflation impressive when set against Thatcher's declared aim of zero inflation. The high inflation rates produced in 1990 as a result of Thatcher and Lawson's policy decisions were particularly poor. Nor did Thatcher and Major reduce the tax burden. At the end of 1996 taxation stood at 37.2 per cent of a taxpayer's income as against 31.1 per cent in 1979.[1] It was the balance between direct and indirect taxation which was altered and this had been a Thatcherite aim. She pursued the aim both for ideological and political reasons. The taxpayer is more likely to notice the deductions from the pay packet than the hidden supplement added to the price of purchased goods.

While much of the population was more prosperous at the end of the Thatcherite years, inequality had increased. While average real income grew by 37 per cent between 1979 and 1992 the incomes of the poorest 10 per cent declined by 18 per cent. It is clear why commentators commented on the rise of deprivation and of the 'underclass' in the Thatcher years. Employment opportunities also became skewed with 37 per cent of households having no full-time worker at the end of Thatcher's term of office. Deregulation of the labour market also heightened job insecurity and increased the casualisation of the workforce. Social divisions in Britain were replicated in the development of a 'dual labour market' in which some enjoyed good pay, conditions and security, while others were compelled to accept part-time, low wage and insecure employment at the fringes of the labour market. Given the problems of unemployment, an ageing population, the rise of single motherhood, and the rising numbers of in-work poor which Thatcher's policy of deregulating labour markets and abolishing Wages Councils assisted, it is not surprising that Thatcher and Major totally failed to curb welfare spending.

> Expenditure on education as a percentage of GDP fell between 1975 and 1995 from 6.7 per cent to 5.2 per cent. Spending on the health service, however, rose during this period. In 1975 it was equivalent to 3.8 per cent of GDP. By 1995 it had risen to 5.5 per cent (a lower percentage than in most other industrial countries). Public housing experienced the greatest cut, declining from 4.2 per cent of GDP in 1975 to 2.1 per cent twenty years later. As happened elsewhere spending on social security increased most. In 1973–74 it made up 8.2 per cent of GDP. This reached 11.4 per cent by 1995–96. Expenditure on social security went up by more than 100 per cent in real terms over the period.[2]

These and similar quantitative measures underline the interpretation that Thatcherism was a divisive political project with some groups faring well. The interests of domestic and international finance capital were particularly well catered for in the years of Thatcherism. But the economic benefits were spread more widely. Until the recession of 1990 Thatcherism was able to produce a 'contented majority', although the benefits of North Sea oil, the revival of the world economy from 1982 to 1987 and the proceeds of privatisation made this possible. Even in the realm of privatisation the main benefits were enjoyed by the chief executives of recently privatised firms who awarded themselves huge salaries.[3] In short, the perception, still adhered to by many Conservatives, that at a national or macro level Thatcherism transformed Britain does not appear convincing when set against the data. In politics it is perceptions rather than facts which matter most, however, and the view that Thatcher gave Britain a much needed stimulus after decades of relative failure remains entrenched in some quarters. Even sceptics maintain that in 1979 Britain needed 'a dose of innovation, of entrepreneurship, of extended individual choice'.[4] The outcome, however, was that which could have been anticipated from a more rampant capitalism than had existed previously. While some parts of the economy flourished, other parts, together with the lives of the many people attached to them, suffered from capitalism's inherently self-destructive tendencies.

At a qualitative level judgements are necessarily more contentious. It is clear that Thatcher weakened much of civil society, and despite rhetorical intentions of 'rolling back the state', centralised power in Westminster and Whitehall. The diffusion of power to the market as well as to agencies and quangos did nothing to strengthen other levels of government in Britain. Democracy was weakened. The only powerful elected part of British government was 'the elective dictatorship' of Thatcher and Major on the basis of a minority of the popular vote. One constitutional theorist suggested that in the Thatcher years 'the constitution became part of party politics, rather than a set of rules lying above politics'.[5]

Thatcher and Major never converted the intellectual and cultural elites to their cause, apart from a number of academics previously committed to so-called New Right ideas. Oxford University denied her an honorary degree and one philosopher criticised Thatcher as 'packaged together in a way that's not exactly vulgar, just low'.[6] Many intellectuals found it difficult to forgive her for the resonance that she acquired with large segments of society who were immune to their own left-wing, eclectic or even rational alternatives. Much of the arts world was similarly critical, although paradoxically her apparent philistinism encouraged critical creativity, just as youth unemployment assisted some pop and rock bands to develop their creative musical skills. The emergence of 'Cool Britannia' owed much to developments in the Thatcher and Major years.

Thatcher's main impact was political. She was undoubtedly an electoral success, although the change in leadership to Major in 1990 may have facilitated the fourth successive Conservative victory in 1992. While her goal of destroying socialism was always grandiose, as previous Labour governments had tended to be pragmatic in office, she certainly hastened the modernisation of Labour. Her success was almost too great. She helped fashion a Labour Party which, 'stealing some clothes' from the Conservatives, was able to achieve a spectacular victory over her party in 1997. Despite her election victories, however, surveys demonstrated that Thatcher failed to wean the British people away from a preference for a regulated, compassionate capitalism, or from a readiness to defend public services. Her impact on her party in making the European Union deeply unpopular served only to ensure that Major's government unravelled on the issue. She simply ensured that it would be a Labour government which would take the crucial decisions about British membership of a single currency system.

Ultimately she bequeathed a Conservative Party confused about its purpose. Was it primarily a patriotic party determined to pursue a strategy of 'Anglo-Saxon capitalism' distanced from Europe; or was it the party of international free markets, free trade and the unregulated flow of capital, as many of its financial backers had always assumed? Perhaps Letwin is correct. Thatcherism encouraged an 'enterprise culture' and 'vigorous virtues' at a time when they were deficient in Britain, but its long-term historical impact on the country's future development may prove less important.

William Hague, who became party leader in June 1997, has shown some tentative signs of endorsing a more libertarian style of politics than Thatcher in the area of social and personal morality. This will displease such individual Conservative thinkers as Roger Scruton who always insisted on marriage, religion and natural hierarchy in society, in order to soften Thatcher's economic policy with a dose of social order. Both Scruton and Hague can converge on dislike of the 'nanny state', however, with reference to the banning of handguns, beef on the bone, tobacco advertising and field sports. One commentator supports this analysis, describing the New Labour government as 'the most puritan and priggish in living memory'.[7] One Conservative theorist suggests that the party is developing a linkage between a commitment to personal freedom and Euroscepticism. 'Arguing for freedom – a free nation and free individuals – would give the Tories a banner under which to fight.'[8]

There are many problems for the Conservative Party. The scale of its defeat makes it harder to determine the new course that it should take, Blair has captured much of the middle ground of British politics, and the attachment of many in its ageing membership to a vision of an older England which the party wishes to protect from European infection has limited appeal to younger voters. Events may yet come to the rescue of the Conservatives, and all governments ultimately suffer a bout of 'mid-term blues'. The Conservatives were heartened by securing 36 seats and 35.8 per cent of the vote as against Labour's 29 seats and 28 per cent of the vote in the elections to the European Parliament in June 1999 by campaigning on a platform of hostility to the European single currency.[9] The possibility of a recession and certainly of declining economic confidence could undermine the New

Labour government. The intervention of the unexpected, such as the resignation in December 1998 from the cabinet of the arch-moderniser in the Labour Party, Peter Mandelson, as a result of a minor scandal may yet help the Conservatives. Blair's dominance, the massive Labour lead in the opinion polls and, above all, the Conservative Party's continuing lack of a clear positive ideological direction, however, suggest that the Thatcher and Major years may appear, in historical perspective, a more mixed blessing for the future of the party than ever seemed the case in the wake of the electoral successes of 1979, 1983, 1987 and even 1992.

Gamble correctly demonstrates that many of the pillars of the party's previous appeal have been dislodged, and that Thatcherism was a contributory cause. As the erstwhile party of the Union its resistance to devolution has left it bereft of parliamentary representation in Scotland and Wales, although its enforced acceptance of the Scottish Parliament and the Welsh Assembly has enabled it to secure representation in these bodies, through the introduction of proportional representation in Scottish and Welsh elections. The cause of Empire is no longer relevant and, in any event, Thatcher handed Hong Kong over to the Chinese in 1997. Nor can the party convince as the protector of the country's historic constitution. Thatcher's attack on many of the institutions, professions and organisations of the 'establishment' weakened and hollowed the British state. 'The Conservatives . . . have been the gravediggers of the old constitution, and helped create the conditions in which radical reform . . . has become possible.'[10] The final pillar of Conservatism has been the defence of property. The decline of Communism, the weakening of trade unions, the business-friendly style of Blair and the sympathy of segments of business for the single currency have served to lessen the links between the party and the business community. Marquand argues that the Conservatives are no longer the party of business.[11]

Restoration of a balanced competition between the two main parties may take a long time after the debacle of 1997.[12] The party must either soften its stance and revert to competing with Labour on the centre ground as after 1951, or wholeheartedly promote national sovereignty, constitutional conservatism and economic and social libertarianism. The dilemma is that Blair has captured the centre ground, but if the Conservative Party nudges still further to the Right it is open to the charge of the disillusioned Lord (Ian) Gilmour that it would become 'that rare and dismal thing; a doctrinaire sect without charismatic leaders.'[13]

A final area of controversy is that of whether Thatcherism was an aberration, or an integral feature of the development of British Conservatism since the Great Reform Act of 1832. There is a considerable literature which assumes that Thatcherism was a distinct ideology divorced from the essentially non-ideological Conservative tradition. This is the most sterile of academic controversies, as the conclusions of individual writers depend entirely upon their definition of ideology. Since ideology is one of the most elusive and variously defined concepts in the entire social sciences, it just will not suffice for a writer on Thatcherism to assert that she changed the party by introducing ideology where it had been absent previously. Ideology can be defined as a rigorous set of consistent beliefs, a defence of the status quo or even a single political idea. One writer has identified over twenty distinct definitions.[14] In reality all political decisions are necessarily rooted in values, or in an orientation to the status quo, and in that respect Thatcherism was no different from the governments of Peel, Salisbury, Baldwin, Macmillan and Heath. In its orientation towards acquiring power the Conservative Party has historically drawn from an entire delta of beliefs and principles. There were no Thatcherite values which could not be discovered in previous Conservative history. Social conservatism, social order and discipline, the free market, fiscal prudence, patriotism, effective central government, a strong leader, the defence of property and privilege have all been elements of Conservative political history. Only the social libertarianism with which Hague briefly dabbled is a recent strand. Even if Thatcher stressed some elements rather than others, or invoked new defenders of Conservative values such as Hayek and Friedman, she was simply extending the thrust of intra-Conservative party debate which, stimulated by Powell, had taken off from the mid-1960s. Paternalist and 'one nation' Conservatism has normally been the minor key of Conservatism; the three decades after 1945 being the exception. British government from 1979 to 1997 was simply that of the Conservative Party in power under the leaderships of Thatcher and Major. Thatcherism made a substantial impact upon Britain simply because of its unusual longevity.

NOTES

CAB	Cabinet
CCO	Conservative Central Office
CRO	Conservative Research Department
HC Debs	House of Commons Debates
LSC	Leaders Sub-Committee

PREFACE

1. G. Peele, *Governing the UK*, third edn (Oxford, Blackwell, 1995), p. 19.

CHAPTER 1

1. B. Coleman, *Conservatism in the Nineteenth Century* (London, Edward Arnold, 1989); B. Evans and A. Taylor, *From Salisbury to Major: Continuity and Change in Conservative Politics* (Manchester, Manchester University Press, 1997); R. Blake, *The Conservative Party from Peel to Thatcher* (London, Fontana, 1985) and A.J. Davies, *We the Nation* (London, Abacus, 1995).
2. T. Lindsay and M. Harrington, *The Conservative Party 1918–1979*, second edn (London, Macmillan, 1979), p. 3.
3. A. Seldon and S. Ball (eds), *Conservative Century* (Oxford, Oxford University Press, 1994), p. 9.
4. S. Ludlam and M. Smith (eds), *Contemporary British Conservatism* (London, St Martin's Press, 1995), p. 82.
5. N. Gash, *The Age of Peel* (London, Edward Arnold, 1968); N. O'Sullivan, *Conservatism* (London, Dent, 1976), pp. 82–92.
6. A.J. Davies, *We the Nation*, p. 80.
7. *Sunday Telegraph*, 16 May 1993.
8. I. Gilmour, *Dancing with Dogma: Britain under Thatcherism* (London, Simon and Shuster, 1992), p. 219.
9. F. O'Gorman, *British Conservatism: Conservative Thought from Burke to Thatcher* (London, Longman, 1986), p. 148.
10. M. Pugh, *The Tories and the People 1880–1935* (Oxford, Basil Blackwell, 1985), p. 139.
11. F. O'Gorman, *British Conservatism*, p. 177.
12. R. Blake, *The Conservative Party*, p. 133.
13. Ibid., p.140.
14. Ibid., p. 218.
15. B. Harrison, *Peaceable Kingdom: Stability and Change in Modern Britain* (Oxford, Clarendon Press, 1982), p. 357.
16. J. Charmley, *A History of Conservative Politics 1900–1996* (London, Macmillan, 1996), p. 69.

17. B. Evans and A. Taylor, *From Salisbury to Major*, pp. 40–57.
18. B. Evans, 'The Impact of the New Deal on British Politics' (unpublished PhD thesis, 1980), chapter 4.
19. A.J. Davies, *We the Nation*, p. 284.
20. R. Blake, *The Conservative Party*, p. 243.
21. Ibid., p. 245.
22. D. Butler and D. Stokes, *Political Change in Modern Britain* (London, Macmillan, 1969), chapter 3.
23. P. Addison, *The Road to 1945* (London, Cape, 1975), p. 17.
24. A.J. Davies, *We the Nation*, p. 26.
25. R.A. Butler, *Advance*, vol. 1, April 1947.
26. A.J. Davies, *We the Nation*, p. 26.
27. T. Lindsay and M. Harrington, *The Conservative Party*, p. 156.
28. A. Taylor in Seldon and Ball, *Conservative Century*, p. 340.
29. B. Roberts in Seldon and Ball, *Conservative Century*, pp. 253–4.
30. R.A Butler, *The Art of the Possible* (London, Hamish Hamilton, 1971), p. 153.
31. J. Ramsden, *The Making of Conservative Party Policy* (London, Longmans, 1980), pp. 154–5.
32. S. Ludlam and M. Smith, *Contemporary British Conservatism*, p. 8.
33. Earl of Kilmuir (David Maxwell Fyfe), *Political Adventure* (London, Weidenfeld and Nicolson, 1964), p. 160.
34. B. Evans and A. Taylor, *From Salisbury to Major*, p. 90.
35. M. Macmillan, *The Tides of Fortune* (London, Macmillan, 1969), p. 301.
36. Ibid., p. 355.
37. B. Evans and A. Taylor, *From Salisbury to Major*, p. 95.
38. S. Procter, 'Floating Convertability: The Emergence of the Robot Plan, 1951–52', *Contemporary Record*, 7 (1) (1993), pp. 24–43.
39. A. Howard, *RAB* (London, Cape, 1987), p. 194.
40. B. Evans and A. Taylor, *From Salisbury to Major*, p. 96.
41. *The Times*, 14 May 1953.
42. CAB, 129/88 C(57) 195, 7 September 1957.
43. J. Charmley, *A History of Conservative Politics*, p. 204.
44. A. Sked and C. Cook, *British Politics since 1945* (London, Penguin, 1984), p. 162.
45. A. Gamble, *The Free Economy and the Strong State: The Politics of Thatcherism* (Basingstoke, Macmillan, 1988), p. 68.
46. J. Ramsden, *The Making of Conservative Party Policy*, p. 22.
47. A.W. Phillips, 'The Relationship between Unemployment and the Rate of Change in the United Kingdom 1861–1957', *Economica*, November 1958.
48. T. Lindsay and M. Harrington, *The Conservative Party*, p. 235.
49. A.J. Davies, *We the Nation*, p. 364.
50. Ibid., p. 364.
51. H. Macmillan, *At the End of the Day*, (Basingstoke, Macmillan, 1973), p. 365.
52. A. Seldon and S. Ball, *Conservative Century*, p. 249.
53. B. Evans, and A. Taylor, *From Salisbury to Major*, pp. 130–2.
54. E. Powell, Lecture to Manchester University Students Union, October 1963.
55. Quoted from The *Spectator* in R. Shepherd, *Iain Macleod* (London, Pimlico Press, 1994), p. 336.
56. A. Sked and C. Cook, *British Politics*, p. 218.
57. J. Enoch Powell, *Still to Decide* (London, Batsford, 1971), p. *vi*.
58. S. Ingle, *The British Party Systems* (Oxford, Blackwell, 1987), p. 73.
59. J. Ramsden, 'The Conservatives since 1945', *Contemporary Record*, 2(1), 1988, 17–22.
60. A. Seldon, *UK Political Parties Since 1945* (London, Philip Allen, 1980), p. 31.
61. A. Gamble, *The Conservative Nation* (London, Routledge, 1974), p. 91.
62. 'Conservative Party Policy-Making, 1965–70', *Contemporary Record*, (Spring 1990).
63. J. Enoch Powell, *Still to Decide*, p. 22.
64. *Guardian*, 20 August 1998.

65. M. Friedman, 'The Role of Monetary Policy'. *American Economic Review*, April 1968.
66. P. Cosgrave, *The Lives of Enoch Powell* (London, Bodley Head, 1989), p. 139.
67. R. Lewis, *Enoch Powell* (London, Cassell, 1979), p. 187.
68. J. Hillman, *Geoffrey Howe: A Quiet Revolutionary* (London, Weidenfeld and Nicolson, 1988), p. 73.
69. CRD, 3/17/11, 28 May.
70. CRD, 3/7/7/7, Selsdon Park Proceedings.
71. *Swinton Journal*, Autumn 1968, p. 40.
72. There are numerous anecdotes about his insensitivity. One junior minister, for example, had a whole host of serious personal problems and approached Heath in the division lobby of the House of Commons to discuss them. Before he opened his mouth Heath snapped at him, 'If you want to resign put it in writing'. Heath was a man of few words and could not bother with social niceties with MPs or their spouses. One journalist reported that when Heath made an attempt at humour, 'it was no laughing matter'.
73. Some of the discontent led to rebellions on policy which, it has been suggested, were as much about leadership style as about policy. The most serious rebellion was over British membership of the European Economic Community (EEC), which led to fifteen MPs going into the lobby to vote against their party even on a vote of confidence. See Norton, *Conservative Dissidents: Dissent within the Parliamentary Conservative Party, 1970–74*, (London, Temple Smith, 1978), p. 67.
74. D. Kavanagh, *Thatcherism and British Politics: The End of Consensus?* (Oxford, Oxford University Press, 1987), pp. 204–7.
75. A. Seldon and S. Ball, *The Heath Government 1970–1974* (London, Longman, 1996), p. 1.
76. D. Kavanagh in A. Seldon and S. Ball, *The Heath Government*, p. 384.
77. In conversation with the author, 1993.
78. M. Holmes, *The Failure of the Heath Government* (London, Macmillan, 1989), p. 144.
79. J. Campbell, *Edward Heath* (London, Cape, 1993), p. 810.
80. CRO, 3/7/4/3, Proceedings of the Selsdon Park Meeting, January 1970.
81. B. Evans and A. Taylor, *From Salisbury to Major*, p. 152.
82. *The Times*, 12 October 1970.
83. T. Ling, *The British State since 1945* (Cambridge, Polity Press, 1998), p. 60.
84. C. Leys, *Politics in Britain* (London, Heinemann, 1983), p. 90.
85. *The Times*, 3 November 1971.
86. J. Bruce-Gardyne, *Whatever Happened to the Quiet Revolution?* (London, Charles Knight, 1974), p. 1.
87. *Observer*, 4 July 1971.
88. *Hansard*, 8 February 1971, vol. 811, cols. 80–3.
89. D. Kavanagh, *Thatcherism*, p. 94.
90. B. Evans and A. Taylor, *From Salisbury to Major*, p. 200.
91. P. Walker, *Staying Power* (London, Bloomsbury, 1991), p. 142.
92. *The Times*, 16 October 1972.
93. *The Times*, 2 February 1971.
94. S. Ball and A. Seldon, *The Heath Government*, p. 135.
95. N. Ridley, *My Style of Government* (London, Hutchinson, 1992), p. 6.
96. *The Economist*, 30 January 1971, 13 February 1971, and 14 April 1971.
97. D. Kavanagh, *The Reordering of British Politics* (Oxford, Oxford University Press, 1997), p. 42.
98. A. Seldon and S. Ball, *The Heath Government*, p. 185.
99. In conversation 1994.
100. M. Thatcher, *The Downing Street Years* (London, Harper Collins, 1993), p. 232.
101. SC(73)17, 'The Tactical Situation in February 1973', p. 3.
102. D. Butler and D. Kavanagh, *The British General Election of October 1974* (Basingstoke, Macmillan, 1975), p. 132.
103. J. Charmley, *A History of Conservative Politics*, p. 195.
104. *Independent*, 28 February 1994.
105. D. Kavanagh, *The Reordering*, p. 197.

106.   A. Seldon and S. Ball, *The Heath Government*, p. 384.
107.   D. Kavanagh, *The Reordering*, pp. 101–2.
108.   *Contemporary Record*, vol. 1, 1987, pp. 28–9.
109.   P. Walker, *Staying Power*, p. 111.
110.   I. Gilmour, *Dancing with Dogma*, p. 3.
111.   H. Young, *One of Us* (London, Macmillan, 1990), p. 106.
112.   LSC, (74)15, 19 July 1974.
113.   A. Seldon and S. Ball, *The Heath Government*, p. 330.
114.   M. Holmes, *The Failure*, p. 81.
115.   Ibid., p. 129.
116.   Ibid., p. 137.
117.   J. Charmley, *A History of the Conservative Party*, p. 195.
118.   R. Blake, *The Conservative Party*, p. 314.
119.   Ibid., p. 315.
120.   In conversation with the author.
121.   K. Middlemas, *Politics in an Industrial Society: The British Experience* (London, Deutsch, 1979), vol. 2, pp. 442–4.
122.   A. Seldon and S. Ball, *The Heath Government*, p. 344.
123.   Ibid., p. 350.

CHAPTER 2

1.   The idea of the writing on the wall is derived from Philip Whitehead, *The Writing on the Wall*, (London, Michael Joseph, 1986). There is an extensive debate about whether the politics of the period from 1945 to 1979 was one of consensus between the parties, convergence or merely a settlement at elite level which excluded ordinary party members as well as citizens. However this debate is resolved, it is apparent that a new confrontational mood emerged after Thatcher acquired the party leadership, based partly upon a loss of confidence that the established policies were any longer capable of delivering economic prosperity, social stability or a contented electorate.

2.   DuCann was acting in the party's interest, but his personal resentment against Heath and his own interest in becoming party leader gives credibility to the idea of a conspiracy. These events are described in J. Campbell, *Edward Heath*, (London, Cape, 1993), pp. 658–60.

3.   M. Halcrow, *Keith Joseph: A Single Mind*, (Basingstoke, Macmillan, 1989), p. 71.

4.   G. Howe, *Conflict of Loyalty*, (Basingstoke, Macmillan, 1995), p. 89.

5.   E. Evans, *Thatcher and Thatcherism*, (London, Routledge, 1997), p. 7.

6.   J. Prior, *A Balance of Power*, (London, Hamish Hamilton, 1986), p. 99.

7.   B. Castle, *The Castle Diaries*, (Basingstoke, Macmillan, 1990), p. 561.

8.   J. Campbell, *Edward Heath*, pp. 679–81.

9.   A.J. Davies, *We the Nation*, (London, Little Brown and Company, 1975), p. 75.

10.   There are many conventional accounts of the 1975 leadership contests which stress this version of events and regard the election as a largely ideology-free zone. For example, N. Fisher, *The Tory Leaders*, (London, Weidenfeld and Nicolson, 1977); P. Cosgrave, *Margaret Thatcher: A Tory and Her Party*, (London, Hutchinson, 1978), L.P. Stark, *Choosing a Leader*, (London, Macmillan, 1996); N. Wapshott and G. Brock, *Thatcher*, (London, Macdonald and Sydney, 1983); J. Critchley, *Westminster Blues*, (London, Futura, 1985); and H. Young and A. Sloman, *The Thatcher Phenomenon*, (London, BBC, 1986).

11.   N. Tebbitt, *Upwardly Mobile*, (London, Weidenfeld and Nicolson, 1988), p. 141.

12.   Panorama, BBC 1 TV, 10 February 1975.

13.   M. Crick, *Michael Heseltine: A Biography*, (London, Hamish Hamilton, 1997), p. 180.

14.   H. Young and A. Sloman, *The Thatcher Phenomenon*, p. 33.

15.   P. Cosgrave, *Thatcher: The First Term*, (London, Bodley Head, 1985), p. x.

16.   H. Young, *One of Us*, (London, Pan Books, 1989), pp. 64–5.

17.   P. Seuyd and P. Whiteley, 'Conservative Grassroots', in S. Ludlam and M. Smith, *Contemporary British Conservatism*, (London, St Martins Press, 1994), p. 82.

18. D. Kavanagh, *Thatcherism and British Politics*, (Oxford, Oxford University Press, 1987), p. 199.
19. R. Morris, *Tories*, (London, Mainstream, 1991), p. 234.
20. B. Porter, *Plots and Paranoia: A History of Political Espionage in Britain*, (London, Unwin Hyman, 1989), p. 221.
21. C. Challen and M. Hughes, *In Defence of the Party: The Secret State, The Conservative Party and Dirty Tricks*, (London, Medium, 1996), p. 35.
22. A.J. Davies, *We the Nation*, p. 32.
23. R. Shepherd, *Iain Macleod*, (London Pimlico Press, 1994), p. 366.
24. B. Evans and A. Taylor, *From Salisbury to Major: Continuity and Change in Conservative Politics*, (Manchester, Manchester University Press, 1996), chapters 1–6.
25. T.E. Lindsay and M. Harrington, *The Conservative Party 1918–1979*, Basingstoke, Macmillan, 1979), p. 282.
26. *Guardian*, 20 August 1998.
27. Frequent conversations with Conservative party activists between 1974 and 1977. The proximity between counter-inflationary policies and industrial relations is made clear in G. Howe, *Conflict of Loyalty*, p. 99.
28. P. Dorey, *British Politics Since 1945*, (Oxford, Blackwell, 1995), p. 139.
29. H. Legru, *The Conservative Mind*, (London, Mills and Boon, 1924), p. 66.
30. *Crossbow*, Summer 1976, p. 36.
31. I. Clark, 'Test Your Powellism', 'Crossbow', February 1976, p. 13.
32. J. Campbell, *Edward Heath*, p. 682.
33. J. Ranelagh, *Thatcher's People*, (London, Fontana, 1992), passim.
34. BBC TV, 'Tribute to Enoch Powell', 13 February 1988.
35. *Daily Telegraph*, 13 October 1977.
36. In a speech to the University Students Union at Manchester University in 1963 he first expressed his commitment to the free market. His nationalism was stridently expressed in the late 1960s although it was sometimes difficult to determine where his true nationalist convictions lay. Sometimes they appeared to be focused on Britain, but at other times England or even the West Midlands.
37. T. Russell, *The Tory Party: Its Policies, Divisions and Future*, (Harmondsworth, Penguin Books, 1978), p. 12.
38. Ibid, p. 170.
39. R. Behrens, *The Conservative Party from Heath to Thatcher*, (Farnbrough, Saxon House, 1980), p. 3.
40. B. Evans and A. Taylor, *From Salisbury to Major: Continuity and Change in Conservative Politics*, (Manchester, Manchester University Press, 1997), p. 210.
41. Conservative Central Office, *The Right Approach*, October 1976.
42. *Crossbow*, February 1976, p. 4.
43. H. Penniman, (ed.) *Britain at the Polls: 1979*, (Washington, American Enterprise Institute for Public Policy and Research, 1981), p. 71.
44. I. Gilmour, *Inside Right*, (London, Quartet Books, 1977). See T. Utley in the *Daily Telegraph*, 10 October 1997.
45. Quoted in T. Russell, *The Tory Party*, p. 105.
46. *Daily Telegraph*, 3 September 1977.
47. Ibid.
48. *Daily Telegraph*, 12 September 1997.
49. Ibid.
50. P. Whitehead, *The Writing on the Wall*, pp. 210–19.
51. *Daily Telegraph*, 13 September 1977.
52. *Daily Telegraph*, 19 September 1977.
53. Minutes of SC (77) 57, Conservative Party Archives, University of Oxford.
54. P. Dorey, 'Conservatives and the Unions: Thatcherism's Impact', *Contemporary Record*, 4 (4) (April 1991), p. 9.
55. K. Middlemas, *Power, Competition and the State. Threats to the Post-War Settlement: Britain 1961–1974*, (London, Macmillan, 1974), p. 333.

56. SC/75/23, SC 76/51, 27 October 1975.
57. *The Conservative Manifesto 1979*, p. 8.
58. *Daily Telegraph*, 10 October 1977.
59. J. Prior, *A Balance of Power*, (London, Hamish Hamilton, 1986), p. 109.
60. P. Dorey, *British Politics since 1945*, p. 141.
61. V. Gillick, *Sex and Politics: The Family and Morality in the Thatcher Years*, (Basingstoke, Macmillan, 1991), pp. 14 and 167.
62. Ibid., p. 168.
63. D. Cliff, 'Religion, Morality and the Middle Class', in R. King and N. Nugent, *Respectable Rebels: Middle Class Campaigns in Britain in the 1970s*, (London, Hodder and Stoughton, 1979), p. 139.
64. Ibid., p. 136.
65. CCO 75/23, SC/76/51.
66. *World in Action*, Granada Television, 30 January 1978.
67. SC (75) 36, 9 June 1975.
68. *Sunday Telegraph*, 10 September 1978.
69. P. Dorey, *British Politics Since 1945*, p. 153.
70. I. Crewe, B. Sarlvik and J. Alt, 'Partisan Dealignment in Britain 1964–1974', *British Journal of Political Science* 7, pp. 166–8.
71. D. Butler and D. Kavanagh, *The British General Election of 1979*, (Basingstoke, Macmillan, 1979), pp. 138–42.
72. P. Dorey, *British Politics Since 1945*, p. 165.
73. K. Morgan, *The People's Peace*, (Oxford, 1990, Oxford University Press), p. 432–3.
74. I. Crewe, 'Why the Conservatives Won', in H. Penniman, *Britain at the Polls*, p. 302. Such former socialists as Paul Johnson, Hugh Thomas and Kingsley Amis were symptomatic.
75. P. Seyd, 'Factionalism in the 1970s', in Z. Layton Henry, *Conservative Party Policy*, (London, Macmillan, 1980), p. 242.

CHAPTER 3

1. P. Cosgrove, *Thatcher; the First Term* (London, Bodley Head, 1983), chapter 3.
2. J. Ranelagh, *Thatcher's People* (London, Fontana, 1991), p. 284.
3. J. Prior, *A Balance of Power* (London, Hamilton, 1986), p. 115.
4. H. Young, *One of Us* (London, Macmillan, 1989), p. 146.
5. J. Ranelagh, *Thatcher's People*, p. 1.
6. Ranelagh's book which is cited above is built on the idea of a core of advisers and influentials. It is unclear, however, whether Thatcher picked advisers who endorsed her existing views, or whether her views were formed as a result of the impact of the advice which she received. The reality is that she had some limited plans. She knew she wished to weaken the public sector and promote the private, and that she favoured a strict fiscal and monetary stance even if it would remove unproductive jobs and unemployment would follow. She also had the political goal of weakening socialism. Yet her plan was also worked out on the job and this is where her advisers exerted influence. Further, much of the work of any government is reactive and involves dealing with events and challenges unforeseen in opposition. Governments respond to a moving picture, therefore, rather than a still frame. Ultimately, advisers could change her mind but only within the parameters of certain established views and prejudices. It is also likely that Thatcher as a relatively lucky politician could often not believe her luck over the degree of compliance in the country, and so became more 'Thatcherite' as she went along, reaching a state of *hubris* in 1987.
7. J. Charmley, *A History of Conservative Politics 1900–1996* (Basingstoke, Macmillan, 1996), p. 212.
8. M. Holmes, *Thatcherism: Scope and Limits* (Basingstoke, Macmillan, 1989), p. 151. There is a vast and conflicting literature on this theme. It is hard to refute Thatcherism's link with expanding social forces and the Labour Party was increasingly associated with diminishing social groups. A Thatcher apologist, Martin Holmes, notes the growth potential in the

groups to which the party appealed in the 1980s, but he also recognises the growing opposition of 'the public-sector middle-class and intellectual opinion-formers, the hostility of the sizeable claimant class, the regional economic and political distortions and the maverick Scottish vote'.

9.   E. Evans, *Thatcher and Thatcherism* (London, Routledge, 1997), p. 18.
10.   Ibid., p. 18.
11.   N. Lawson, *The View from No. 11: Memoirs of a Tory Radical* (Reading, Corgi Books, 1992), p. 28.
12.   M. Thatcher, *The Downing Street Years* (London, Harper Collins, 1993), p. 43.
13.   N. Lawson, *The View from No. 11*, pp. 36–7.
14.   J. Bruce-Gardyne, *Mrs Thatcher's First Administration* (Basingstoke, Macmillan, 1984), p. 165.
15.   J. Prior, *A Balance of Power*, pp. 119–20.
16.   Many clear 'one nation' Tories remained in Thatcher's first cabinet, albeit outside the crucial economic ministries. They included Lord Carrington at the Foreign Office, Peter Walker at Agriculture, Mark Carlisle at Education, and Norman St John Stevas as Leader of the House, although he had voted for Thatcher in 1975. More ambiguously there was also Francis Pym at Defence, Christopher Soames as Leader of the House of Lords and Michael Heseltine at Environment.
17.   M. Thatcher, *The Downing Street Years*, p. 43.
18.   J. Bruce-Gardyne, *Mrs Thatcher's First Administration*, p. 166.
19.   B. Anderson, *John Major* (London, Fourth Estate, 1991), p. 157.
20.   P. Jackson, 'Economic Policy' in R. Rhodes and D. Marsh, *Implementing Thatcherite Policies: Audit of an Era* (Buckingham, Open University Press), p. 10.
21.   Some of the arcane debates in the early Thatcher years are discussed in H. Stephenson, *Mrs Thatcher's First Year* (London, Jill Norman, 1990), chapter 3: and W. Keegan, *Mrs Thatcher's Economic Experiment* (London, Allen Lane, 1984), chapter 5.
22.   Lord Nigel Lawson in conversation. See also W. Keegan, *Mrs Thatcher's Economic Experiment*, p. 150.
23.   H. Stephenson, *Mrs Thatcher's First Year*, pp. 53–6.
24.   M. Thatcher, *The Downing Street Years*, p. 52.
25.   W. Keegan, *Mrs Thatcher's Economic Experiment*, p. 138.
26.   Lord Lawson in conversation with the author.
27.   M. Thatcher, *The Downing Street Years*, p. 44.
28.   E. Evans, *Thatcher and Thatcherism*, p. 19.
29.   N. Lawson, *The View from No. 11*, pp. 66–7.
30.   Ibid., pp. 68–71.
31.   K. Harris, *Thatcher* (London, Weidenfeld and Nicolson, 1988), p. 71.
32.   H. Young, *One of Us*, p. 203.
33.   W. Keegan, *Mrs Thatcher's Economic Experiment*, p. 147.
34.   Ibid., p. 203.
35.   BBC TV News, 21 August 1980.
36.   P. Riddell, *The Thatcher Government* (Oxford, Blackwell, 1985), pp. 64–8.
37.   Ibid., p. 47.
38.   D. Willetts, *Modern Conservatism* (Harmondsworth, Penguin, 1992), p. 55.
39.   D. Young, *The Enterprise Years: A Businessman in Cabinet* (London, Headline Press, 1990), p. 54.
40.   P. Riddell, *The Thatcher Era and its Legacy* (London, Blackwell, 1991), pp. 46–7.
41.   D. Farnham, 'Trade Union Policy 1979–89: Restriction or Reform?', in S. Savage and L. Robins, *Public Policy Under Thatcher* (Basingstoke, Macmillan, 1990), chapter 3.
42.   C. Leys, *Politics in Britain* (London, Heinemann, 1983), p. 170.
43.   W. Keegan, *Mrs Thatcher's Economic Experiment*, p. 155.
44.   P. Jenkins, *Mrs Thatcher's Revolution* (London, Pan Books, 1988), p. 153.
45.   A. Gamble, *Free Economy and Strong State* (Basingstoke, Macmillan, 1978).
46.   P. Jenkins, *Mrs Thatcher's Revolution*, p. 153.
47.   J. Bruce-Gardyne, *Mrs Thatcher's First Administration*, p. 182.

48. P. Jenkins, *Mrs Thatcher's Revolution*, p. 153.

49. A. Gamble, *Free Economy and Strong State*, pp. 288–9.

50. N. Lawson, *The View from No. 11*, p. 98.

51. P. Walker, *Staying Power* (London, Bloomsbury, 1991), p. 159.

52. J. Prior, *A Balance of Power*, p. 131.

53. Lord Hailsham, *A Sparrow's Flight* (London, Collins, 1990), p. 407.

54. *Hansard*, 10 March 1981, vol. 1000, col. 760.

55. In the speech Thatcher acknowledged the key role of Alan Walters in preparing the budget, although she added that John Hoskyns and David Woolfson also provided advice.

56. I. Gilmour, *Dancing with Dogma* (London, Simon and Schuster, 1992), p. 146.

57. The Manpower Services Commission had been set up by the Heath government in 1973 to engage in manpower planning with the three partners of government, trade unions and employers represented; but since the recession of the mid-1970s it had been reduced to providing job-creation and training schemes. The cabinet meeting coincided with a Central Policy Review Staff (CPRS) prediction that youth unemployment would be particularly serious with unemployment likely to rise to 3 million. John Hoskyns of the Downing Street Policy Unit called for political imagination to deal with the problem. The YTS, supported strongly at the meeting by Prior and John Nott, was the result. See B. Evans, *The Politics of the Training Market: from Manpower Services Commission to Training and Enterprise Councils* (London, Routledge, 1992), p. 67.

58. P. Riddell, *The Thatcher Government*, p. 50. The new Employment Secretary, Norman Tebbit, proposed compulsion with the threat of benefit loss and a low training allowance, simply to get the TUC to sign up. In reality, he offered a higher allowance and had every intention of saving compulsory participation for the future.

59. N. Lawson, *The View from No. 11*, p. 108.

60. P. Dorey, *British Politics since 1945* (Oxford, Blackwell, 1995), p. 170.

61. H. Young, *One of Us*, p. 221.

62. J. Bruce-Gardyne, *Mrs Thatcher's First Administration*, p. 103.

63. C. Johnson, *The Economy under Mrs Thatcher* (Harmondsworth, Penguin, 1991), p. 224.

64. N. Tebbit, *Upwardly Mobile* (London, Weidenfeld and Nicolson, 1988), p. 181

65. R. Morris, *Tories* (London, Mainstream, 1991), p. 215. For the suggestion that there was some sexual awareness of Parkinson on her part see J. Ranelagh, *Thatcher's People*, p. 31.

66. N. Lawson, *The View from No. 11*, pp. 111–13.

67. Ibid., pp. 103–4.

68. P. Dorey, *British Politics since 1945*, p. 171.

69. M. Thatcher, *The Downing Street Years*, p. 154.

70. H. Young, *One of Us*, pp. 240–1.

71. P. Dorey, *British Politics since 1945*, p. 168.

72. J. Bruce-Gardyne, *Mrs Thatcher's First Administration*, p. 104.

73. H. Young, *One of Us*, p. 230.

74. Ibid., p. 314.

75. E. Evans, *Thatcher*, p. 25.

76. The origin of this aphorism is unknown, but it is generally attributed to the Labour front bencher Gerald Kaufmann.

77. Seminar given to the Department of Politics at the University of Sheffield, Spring 1996.

78. M. Thatcher, *The Downing Street Years*, p. 175.

79. Ibid., p. 235.

80. Sir Anthony Meyer, *Stand Up and Be Counted* (London, Heinemann, 1990) pp. 83–101.

81. This was at a time when the Conservatives fought a clever campaign based on the slogan 'Labour isn't Working'.

82. H. Young, *One of Us*, p. 301.

83. *Guardian*, 5 February 1982.

84. B. Evans, *The Politics of the Training Market*, p. 59.

85. Lord D. Young, *The Enterprise Years*, p. 74. 'His measures to counter unemployment led Len Murray, General Secretary of the TUC, to describe his job as "the most important in government".' p. 79.

86. J. Ranelagh, *Thatcher's People*, pp. 215–17 and 244.
87. Lord D. Young, *The Enterprise Years*, p. 200.
88. In conversation with the author, July 1983.
89. M. Thatcher, *The Downing Street Years*, p. 139 and N. Lawson, *The View from No. 11*, p. 155.
90. I. Gilmour, *Dancing with Dogma*, p. 103.

CHAPTER 4

1. M. Holmes, *Mrs Thatcher's First Government: Contemporary Conservatism and Economic Change* (Brighton, Harvester Wheatsheaf, 1985), pp. 154–5.
2. BBC TV 'Question time', 19 May 1983.
3. H. Young, *One of Us* (London, Pan Books, 1990), p. 331.
4. A. Gamble, *The Free Economy and the Strong State* (Basingstoke, Macmillan, 1988), p. 120.
5. M. Heseltine, *Where There's a Will* (London, Hutchinson, 1987), p. 5.
6. Ibid., pp. 54–68.
7. Ibid., p. 96.
8. Ibid., p. 299.
9. H. Young, *One of Us*, p. 486.
10. D. Butler and D. Kavanagh, *The British General Election of 1987* (Basingstoke, Macmillan, 1988), p. 7.
11. *The Times*, 4 August 1983.
12. D. Butler and D. Kavanagh, *The British General Election of 1987*, Appendix 1, p. 312.
13. *Guardian*, 10 October 1983.
14. All these stories were analysed in the press but see particularly The *Guardian*, 10 October 1983.
15. D. Butler and D. Kavanagh, *The British General Election of 1987*, pp. 7 and 13.
16. A leading Conservative politician in conversation.
17. These recollections and judgements are derived from discussions with senior Conservatives at the highest of levels.
18. D. Willetts, 'The Role of the Prime Minister's Policy Unit', *Public Administration*, 65 (4) (1987), pp. 444–54. The members of the Unit were drawn from industry and the civil service.
19. The Royal Institute of Public Administration's Report, 'Appointments and Promotions in the Civil Service', is analysed in *Public Administration*, 65 (Autumn 1987), p. 353. It concludes that Thatcher was more proactive but not partisan in this area.
20. Sir J. Hoskyns, 'Conservatism is not Enough', *Parliamentary Affairs* 55 (1984), p. 4. He argued that where both the personnel and the organisation are wrong only the Prime Minister has the 'clout' to introduce change. He regretted her lack of radicalism, reflecting that in business, radicalism has to be the norm.
21. Sir J. Hoskyns, 'Needed Now: A Tory National Plan', *The Times*, 9 October 1984. He complained that the Prime Minister was not bringing fresh thought to British politics.
22. H. Elcock, *Local Government* (London, Methuen, 1991), p. 39.
23. D. Wilson and C. Game, *Local Government in the United Kingdom* (Basingstoke, Macmillan, 1998), p. 55.
24. S. Savage, *Public Policy under Thatcher* (Basingstoke, Macmillan, 1990), p. 184.
25. D. Wilson and C. Game, *Local Government*, p. 185.
26. E. Evans, *Thatcher and Thatcherism* (London, Routledge, 1997), p. 61.
27. F.A. Hayek, 'Why I am not a Conservative', in *The Constitution of Liberty* (London, Routledge, Kegan and Paul, 1960) Postscript.
28. I. Gilmour, *Inside Right: Conservative Policies and the People* (London, Quartet Books, 1978), p. 114.
29. The Whig philosopher Edmund Burke is often thought of as a major theorist of British Conservatism and he strongly defended established institutions in *Reflections on the Revolution in France*.

30. GMTV, 14 August 1994.
31. See S. Savage and L. Robins, *Public Policy under Thatcher*, chapter 12 for changing central-local relations, and A. Gamble, *Free Economy and Strong State*, p. 118 for a discussion of the government's policy towards civil liberties.
32. Bassey Ekpe, 'The Thatcher Governments and the Growth of the Security Services'. Paper presented to the Politics Research Seminar, University of Huddersfield, October 1998.
33. R. Rhodes, 'The New Governance: Governing without Government', *Political Quarterly* 44 (September 1996), p. 253.
34. P. Dorey, *British Politics since 1945* (Oxford, Blackwell, 1995), p. 175.
35. M. Holmes, *The First Thatcher Government 1979–1983*, p. 46.
36. N. Ridley, *My Style of Government* (London, Fontana, 1992), p. 67.
37. N. Lawson, *The View from No. 11: Memoirs of a Tory Radical* (London, Corgi Books, 1992), chapters 13 and 14.
38. P. Hain, *Political Strikes: The State and Trade Unionism in Britain* (Basingstoke, Macmillan, 1987), p. 10.
39. P. Walker, *Staying Power* (London, Bloomsbury, 1991), p. 172.
40. E. Evans, *Thatcher*, p. 39.
41. M. Thatcher, *The Downing Street Years* (London, Harper Collins, 1983), chapter 13, pp. 416–20.
42. *Hansard*, vol. 90, col. 645, 27 January 1986.
43. H. Young, *One of Us*, p. 499.
44. P. Riddell, *The Thatcher Era* (Oxford, Blackwell, 1991), p. 68.
45. A. Gamble repeated the myth that government stumbled upon privatisation in 'The Thatcher Decade in Perspective', in P. Dunleavy et al. *Developments in British Politics*, (Basingstoke, Macmillan, 1990), vol. 3, p. 337.
46. S. Edgell and V. Duke, *A Measure of Thatcherism* (London, Harper Collins, 1991), p. 40.
47. N. Lawson, *The View from No. 11*, p. 199.
48. M. Holmes, *Thatcherism: its Scope and Limits: 1983–1987* (Basingstoke, Macmillan, 1989), p. 60.
49. Ibid., p. 61.
50. The Maurice Macmillan memorial lecture cited in N. Lawson, *The View from No. 11*, p. 206.
51. M. Thatcher, *The Downing Street Years*, p. 676.
52. Ibid., p. 680.
53. Ibid., p. 681.
54. This was a commonly expressed view by Simon Jenkins in his columns in *The Times*.
55. P. Walker, *Staying Power*, p. 193.
56. J. Ranelagh, *Thatcher's People*, p. 306.
57. 'The Treasury, Privatisations in the United Kingdom, Background Briefing', (London, HM Treasury, 1990), quoted in P. Dorey, *British Politics since 1945*, p. 203.
58. D. Wilson and C. Game, *Local Government in the United Kingdom*, pp. 84–6.
59. Ibid., p. 341. As often happened in the Thatcher years the left and the local authorities adopted the term but used it to justify the role of local government as overseer of a highly comprehensive set of services catering to the needs of the entire local community.
60. Interview with Peter Jay on 'A Week in Politics', Channel 4 Television, January 1985.
61. N. Lawson, *The View from No. 11*, pp. 480–2.
62. Ibid., p. 414.
63. E. Dell, *The Chancellors* (London, Harper Collins, 1997), p. 501.
64. A. Gamble, *The Free Economy and Strong State*, pp. 225–6.
65. In conversation with the author.
66. D. Butler and D. Kavanagh, *The British General Election of 1987*, p. 36.
67. *The Economist*, 7 June 1986.
68. See chapter 7.
69. N. Tebbitt, *Upwardly Mobile*, (London, Futura, 1989), p. 246.
70. These episodes are discussed in various accounts of the period, but most lucidly in Tebbitt's *Upwardly Mobile*.

71. M. Linklater and D. Leigh, *Not with Honour* (London, Sphere, 1986), p. 136.
72. Paul Foot on 'What the Papers Say'. BBC 2, 17 January 1986.
73. Sir Bernard Ingham in conversation with the author.
74. *Guardian*, 10 January 1986.
75. *Guardian*, 25 January 1986.
76. *Hansard*, vol. 90, col. 649, 27 January 1986.
77. Ibid., col. 659.
78. Ibid., col. 660.
79. Ibid., col. 662.
80. Ibid., col. 663.
81. Ibid., cols 676–9.
82. M. Wickham Jones and D. Shell, 'What Went Wrong? The Fall of Mrs Thatcher', *Contemporary Record* 5 (2) (Autumn 1991).
83. A poll undertaken for BBC 2's 'Newsnight' by staff and students in politics at the Polytechnic of Huddersfield straight after the affair demonstrated that she would lose the marginal seat of Halifax by a substantial margin, and that many electors had developed a negative perception of Thatcher personally.
84. Defence Committee of the House of Commons, *The Defence Implications of the Future of Westland plc* (London, HMSO, 1986), cols. 167, 151 and 258.
85. N. Lawson, *The View from No. 11*, p. 308. Lawson was embarrassed by this 'petty and boorish act'.
86. The Church of England, *Faith in the City: The Report of the Archbishop of Canterbury's Commission on Urban Priority Areas*, December 1985.
87. I. Gilmour, *Dancing with Dogma* (London, Simon and Schuster, 1992), p. 139.
88. Ibid., pp. 246–7. Thatcher only makes a brief passing reference to this speech in her memoirs.
89. D. Butler and D. Kavanagh, *The British General Election of 1987*, p. 33.
90. Ibid., p. 28.
91. See chapter 7.
92. M. Thatcher, *The Downing Street Years*, p. 572.
93. D. Butler and D. Kavanagh, *The British General Election of 1987*, p. 45.
94. N. Lawson, *The View from No. 11*, pp. 702–4.
95. The story behind this has not been told previously. The BBC hired staff and students from a number of university departments to conduct constituency surveys. While many departments conducted their poll well and produced unimpeachable outcomes, a few committed methodological errors which produced a distorted and heavily pro-Labour outcome.
96. See M. Thatcher, *The Downing Street Years*, pp. 573 and 584; N. Tebbit, *Upwardly Mobile*, p. 265 and D. Young, *The Enterprise Years* (London, Headline, 1990), p. 235. When Thatcher conveyed her anxiety to him, Young is alleged to have shaken Tebbit by the shoulders and shouted, 'We are going to lose this f. . . . election.' The episode reveals Thatcher's lack of *sang-froid* when confronted with the possibility of defeat.
97. D. Butler and D. Kavanagh, *The British General Election of 1987*, p. 36.
98. E. Evans, *Thatcher*, p. 27.
99. M. Thatcher, *The Downing Street Years*, p. 579.
100. K. Baker, *The Turbulent Years: My Life in Politics* (London, Faber, 1993), p. 194.
101. D. Butler and D. Kavanagh, *The British General Election of 1987*, p. 269.

CHAPTER 5

1. K. Baker, *The Turbulent Years: My Life in Politics* (London, Faber and Faber, 1993), p. 129.
2. B. Pimlott cited in *New Statesman and Society*, 26 August 1994, p. 8.
3. *The Economist*, 25 July 1987.
4. M. Thatcher, *The Downing Street Years* (London, Harper Collins, 1993), pp. 612–13.

5.   See the *Mail on Sunday*, 17 July 1994 for the campaign about dogs. Leading Conservatives in conversation with the author have indicated this as one of their reasons for the declining quality of Thatcher's leadership in her final years.

6.   D. Childs, *Britain Since 1945: A Political History*, third edn (London, Routledge, 1993), pp. 344–5.

7.   J. Ranelagh, *Thatcher's People* (London, Fontana, 1992), p. 252.

8.   D. Butler and D. Kavanagh, *The British General Election of 1987*, pp. 106–7.

9.   K. Baker, *The Turbulent Years*, p. 160.

10.   In conversation with the author. It can be argued that the problem can be traced back to the local government reforms of 1972 which created city-based Labour authorities as a result of back benchers campaigning to remove suburban areas, such as Wilmslow from Greater Manchester, thus ensuring that the metropolitan authorities would normally be Labour.

11.   K. Baker, *The Turbulent Years*, p. 168.

12.   A leading educational administrator in discussion with the author, September 1998.

13.   E. Evans, *Thatcher and Thatcherism* (London, Routledge, 1997), pp. 72–3.

14.   K. Baker, *The Turbulent Years*, p. 238.

15.   The history of this policy is described analytically in, B. Evans, *The Politics of the Training Market* (London, Routledge, 1992), and their subsequent development can be traced in the TEC movement's own journal *Agenda* and the Unemployment Unit's more critical perspective in *Working Brief*.

16.   M. Thatcher, *The Downing Street Years*, p. 607.

17.   S. Savage and L. Robins, *Public Policy Under Thatcher* (Basingstoke, Macmillan, 1990), p. 112.

18.   E. Evans, *Thatcher*, p. 67.

19.   *Guardian*, 3 January 1995.

20.   M. Thatcher, *The Downing Street Years*, pp. 625–7. Also S. Savage and L. Robins, *Public Policy*, chapter 11.

21.   N. Lawson, *The View from No. 11: Memoirs of a Tory Radical* (Reading, Corgi Books, 1992), p. 595.

22.   N. Ridley, *My Style of Government* (London, Hutchinson, 1991), p. 91.

23.   P. Dorey, *British Politics Since 1945* (Oxford, Blackwell, 1995), p. 204.

24.   I. Gilmour, *Dancing with Dogma*, p. 121.

25.   P. Walker, *Staying Power* (London, Bloomsbury, 1991), p. 198.

26.   N. Lawson, *The View from No. 11*, p. 170.

27.   C. Parkinson, *Right at the Centre* (London, Weidenfeld and Nicolson, 1992), p. 260.

28.   Ibid., p. 266.

29.   J. Richardson, 'The Policies and Practice of Privatisation in Britain' in V. Wright (ed.), *Privatisation in Western Europe* (London, Pinter, 1994), p. 75.

30.   K. Theakston, 'The Party and the Civil Service' in A. Seldon and S. Ball (eds), *Conservative Century* (Oxford, Oxford University Press, 1994), p. 399.

31.   P. Hennessy, *Whitehall* (London, Fontana, 1990) p. 621.

32.   P. Greer, *Transforming Central Government: The Next Steps Initiative* (Buckingham, Open University Press, 1994), p. 6.

33.   K. Theakston, 'The Party and the Civil Service', p. 399.

34.   Sir Peter Kemp in conversation with the author at the Reform Club, 1993.

35.   D. Kavanagh, *British Politics: Continuities and Change*, third edn (Oxford, Oxford University Press, 1998), p. 327.

36.   I. Budge, et al., *The New British Politics* (Harlow, Longman, 1998), pp. 252–3.

37.   This judgement is based upon extensive discussions with chief executives of agencies.

38.   C. Foster and F. Plowden, *The State Under Stress* (Buckingham, Open University Press, 1996), p. 167.

39.   D. Kavanagh, *British Politics*, p. 328.

40.   In discussion with the author.

41.   Discussion at the conference, 'Towards a Radical Century', London School of Economics, September 1988.

42. H. Heclo and A. Wildavsky, *The Private Government of Public Money* (Basingstoke, Macmillan, 1981), passim.
43. Conversations with leaders of Marxist groups.
44. A. Seldon and S. Ball (eds), *Conservative Century* (Oxford, Oxford University Press, 1994), p. 681.
45. M. Thatcher, *The Downing Street Years*, p. 618.
46. Ibid., p. 150.
47. E. Evans, *Thatcher*, p. 64.
48. A. Clark, *Diaries* (London, Phoenix, 1993), p. 195.
49. N. Lawson, *The View from No. 11*, p. 151.
50. A. Clark, *Diaries*, p. 289.
51. K. Baker, *The Turbulent Years*, p. 338.
52. N. Ridley, *My Style of Government*, p. 124.
53. Ibid., p. 134.
54. Ibid., p. 125.
55. M. Thatcher, *The Downing Street Years*, pp. 658–9.
56. I. Gilmour, *Dancing with Dogma*, p. 219.
57. D. Wilson and C. Game, *Local Government in the United Kingdom*, (Basingstoke, Macmillan, 1998), second edn p. 187.
58. D. Kavanagh, *Continuities and Change*, p. 354.
59. For a fuller discussion and justification of this view see D. Butler, A. Adonis and T. Travers, *Failure in British Government* (Oxford, Oxford University Press, 1995).
60. *Guardian*, 26 October 1998.
61. Interviews with cabinet ministers in Conservative governments between 1979 and 1990.
62. *Guardian*, 26 October 1998.
63. M. Thatcher, *The Downing Street Years*, pp. 727–8.
64. *Guardian*, 24 October 1998.
65. Extracts from the Bruges speech are cited in M. Thatcher, *The Downing Street Years*, pp. 744–5.
66. Discussed in H. Young, *The Blessed Plot* (Basingstoke, Macmillan, 1998).
67. I. Gilmour, *Dancing with Dogma*, p.323.
68. P. Riddell, *The Thatcher Era and its Legacy* (Oxford, Blackwell, 1991), p. 231.
69. *The Economist*, 25 July 1987.
70. K. Baker, *The Turbulent Years*, p. 379.
71. M. Thatcher, *The Downing Street Years*, pp. 700–1.
72. N. Lawson, *The View from No. 11*, p. 788.
73. E. Dell, *The Chancellors: A History of Chancellors of the Exchequer, 1945–1990* (London, Harper Collins, 1996), p. 515.
74. N. Lawson, *The View from No. 11*, p. 800.
75. Ibid., p. 168.
76. J. Ranelagh, *Thatcher's People* (London, Fontana, 1991), p. 281.
77. E. Dell, *The Chancellors*, pp. 509–10.
78. N. Lawson, *The View from No. 11*, pp. 932–3.
79. H. Young, *One of Us* (Basingstoke, Macmillan, 1989), p. 588.
80. A. Meyer, *Stand Up and be Counted* (London, Heinemann, 1990), pp. 170–4.
81. M. Thatcher, *The Downing Street Years*, p. 830.
82. N. Fowler, *Ministers Decide* (London, Chapmans, 1991), p. 344.
83. D. Smith, *From Boom to Slump* (Harmondsworth, Penguin, 1992), p. 171.
84. D. Butler and D. Kavanagh, *The British General Election of 1992* (Basingstoke, Macmillan, 1992), p. 10.
85. K. Baker, *The Turbulent Years*, p. 327.
86. M. Thatcher, *The Downing Street Years*, p. 831.
87. This is not to say that they do not count at all for there are other opportunities to discern the mood of activists before the conference at regional conferences, women's conferences and above all the central council meeting in the spring. See R. Kelly, *The Conservative Party Conferences: The Midden System*, (Manchester, Manchester University Press, 1989).

88. *Hansard*, vol. 180, col. 461.
89. Ibid., col. 465.
90. N. Lawson, *The View from No. 11*, pp. 998–1001.
91. K. Baker, *The Turbulent Years*, pp. 364–78.
92. Ibid. p. 368.
93. B. Anderson, *John Major* (London, Fourth Estate, 1991), pp. 108–10.
94. C. Parkinson, *Right at the Centre* (London, Weidenfeld and Nicolson, 1992), p. 13.
95. Ibid., p. 15.
96. M. Wickham-Jones and D. Shell, 'What Went Wrong? The Fall of Mrs Thatcher' in *Contemporary Record 5* (2) (Autumn 1991), p. 331.
97. A. Clark, *Diaries*, p. 289.
98. For example, Sir Bernard Ingham and Sir Charles Powell.
99. A. Clark, *Diaries*, pp. 342–3.
100. J. Ranelagh, *Thatcher's People*, p. 279.
101. A. Clark, *Diaries*, p. 346.
102. J. Ranelagh, *Thatcher's People*, p. 295.
103. M. Wickham-Jones and D. Shell, 'What Went Wrong'?, pp. 338–9.
104. J. Ranelagh, *Thatcher's People*, p. 214.
105. BBC TV, 'The Downing Street Years', November 1993.
106. C. Leys, *Politics in Britain* (London, Heinemann, 1983), pp. 164–70.

CHAPTER 6

1. A. Seldon and S. Ball (eds), *Conservative Century* (Oxford, Oxford University Press, 1994), p. 63.
2. BBC TV 'Newsnight', 27 November 1990.
3. A. Seldon, *Major, A Political Life* (London, Weidenfeld and Nicolson, 1997), p. 131.
4. P. Junor, *The Major Enigma* (London, Joseph, 1993), p. 2.
5. B. Anderson, *John Major* (London, Fourth Estate, 1991), p. 290.
6. M. Seliger, *Ideology and Politics* (London, Allen and Unwin, 1976), p. 105.
7. P. Junor, *The Major Enigma*, p.
8. A. Seldon, *Major*, p. 131.
9. V. Bogdanor, 'the Selection of the Party Leader', in A. Seldon, *Conservative Century*, p. 96.
10. P. Junor, *The Major Enigma*, p. 23.
11. A. Seldon, *Major*, p. 16.
12. P. Junor, *The Major Enigma*, p. 38.
13. D. Butler and D. Kavanagh, *The British General Election of 1992* (Basingstoke, Macmillan, 1992), p. 130.
14. A. Seldon, *Major*, p. 32.
15. P. Junor, *The Major Enigma*, p. 80.
16. A. Seldon, *Major*, p. 74.
17. P. Junor, *The Major Enigma*, pp. 80–5.
18. J. Charmley, *A History of Conservative Politics: 1900–1996* (Basingstoke, Macmillan, 1996), p. 228.
19. Matthew Parris quoted in A. Seldon, *Major*, p. 69.
20. A. Seldon, *Major*, p. 53.
21. *Guardian*, 28 November 1990.
22. A. Seldon, *Major*, p. 132.
23. *Guardian*, 28 November 1998.
24. I. Crewe, 'Values: the Crusade that Failed', in A. Seldon (ed.), *The Thatcher Effect* (Oxford, The Clarendon Press).
25. D. Butler and D. Kavanagh, *The British General Election*, p. 47.
26. John Gray, *Beyond the New Right: Markets, Government and the Common Environment* (London, Routledge and Kegan Paul, 1993), Passim.
27. *Guardian*, 4 October 1993.

28. *Spectator Annual*, 1982, pp. 1–2.
29. A. Gamble, *The Free Economy and the Strong State: The Politics of Thatcherism* (Basingstoke, Macmillan, 1988) p. 210.
30. A. Seldon, *Major*, p. 154.
31. J. Charmley, *A History of Conservative Politics*, p. 239.
32. J. Ramsden, *The Making of Conservative Party Policy* (London, Longman, 1980), p. 311.
33. J. Charmley, *A History of Conservative Politics*, p. 239.
34. K. Baker, *The Turbulent Years: My Life in Politics* (London, Faber, 1993), pp. 281–2.
35. D. Butler and D. Kavanagh, *The British General Election*, p. 29.
36. J. Lovenduski, P. Norris and C. Burness, 'The Party and Women', in A. Seldon and S. Ball, *Conservative Century*, p. 634.
37. A. Seldon, *Major*, pp. 139–41.
38. Ibid., p. 145.
39. *Daily Telegraph*, 3 December 1990.
40. Ibid., 30 November.
41. D. Butler and D. Kavanagh, *The British General Election*, p. 39.
42. B. Evans and A. Taylor, *From Salisbury to Major: Continuity and Change in Conservative Politics* (Manchester, Manchester University Press, 1996), p. 252.
43. W. Bagehot, 'Selling a New Spirit', *The Economist*, 8 December 1990.
44. A. Seldon, *Major*, p. 163.
45. D. Butler and D. Kavanagh, *The British General Election*, p. 29.
46. A. Clark, *Diaries* (London, Phoenix, 1993), p. 377.
47. D. Butler and D. Kavanagh, *The British General Election*, p. 29.
48. A. Duncan et al., *Bearing the Standard: Themes for a Fourth Term* (London, Conservative Political Centre, 1992), p. 22.
49. M. Portillo, *A Vision for the 1990s* (London, Conservative Political Centre, 1992), p. 6.
50. Ibid.
51. D. Butler and D. Kavanagh, *The British General Election*, p. 32.
52. *Financial Times*, 31 December 1991.
53. A. Seldon and S. Ball, *Conservative Century*, p. 63.
54. *Daily Telegraph*, 29 April 1991.
55. See later discussion.
56. *The Times*, 19 June and 9 March 1991.
57. B. Evans and A. Taylor, *From Salisbury to Major*, p. 255.
58. *Hansard*, vol. 199, col. 271, 20 November 1991.
59. Ibid., col. 274, 20 November 1991.
60. Ibid., col. 279, 20 November 1991.
61. Ibid.
62. Richard Kelly, 'The Party Conferences', in A. Seldon and S. Ball, *Conservative Century*, p. 256.
63. N. Lawson, *The View from No. 11*, second edn (London, Corgi Books, 1992), p. 1013.
64. Ibid.
65. Lord Lawson in discussion with the author.
66. *Independent*, 16 November 1991.
67. S. Hogg and J. Hill, *Too Close to Call* (London, Warner Books, 1995), p. 77.
68. A. Seldon, *Major*, p. 246.
69. *Independent*, 16 November 1991.
70. HC Debs, 6th series, vol. 199, cols. 293–8.
71. *The Times*, 20 December 1991.
72. S. Hogg and J. Hill, *Too Close to Call*, p. 157.
73. A. Seldon, *Major*, p. 249.
74. Ibid., p. 251.
75. S. Hogg and J. Hill, *Too Close to Call*, p. 182.
76. Ibid., p. 184.
77. Ibid.
78. A widely expressed view by car salesmen to the author at the time.
79. S. Hogg and J. Hill, *Too Close to Call*, p. 191.

80. *Daily Telegraph*, 24 February 1992.
81. Ibid., 23 February 1992.
82. *Guardian*, 22 April 1992.
83. D. Butler and D. Kavanagh, *The British General Election of 1992*, p. 95.
84. A. Seldon, *Major*, p. 270.
85. Ibid., p. 271.
86. HC Debs. 6th series, vol. 188, cols. 630–7.
87. S. Ludlam and M. Smith, *Contemporary British Conservatism*, p. 5.
88. Ibid., p. 115.
89. S. Hogg and J. Hill, *Too Close to Call*, p. 57.
90. W. Hutton, *The State We're In*, second edn (London, Vintage, 1996), p. 37. Hutton asserts that the combined costs of switching from the domestic rates to the Poll Tax and then reverting to the Council Tax was 0.5 per cent of GDP or £3 billion.
91. D. Butler and D. Kavanagh, *The British General Election*, p. 121.
92. W. Hutton, *The State We're In*, p. 184.
93. S. Hogg and J. Hill, *Too Close to Call*, pp. 57–8.
94. A. Seldon, *Major*, p. 171.
95. *Guardian*, 20 March 1991, p. 63.
96. K. Walsh, 'Local Government', in P. Catterall, *Contemporary Britain: An Annual Review* (Oxford, Blackwell, 1992), p. 57.
97. P. Hennessy, *Whitehall*, second edn (London, Fontana, 1990), p. 302.
98. S. Hogg and J. Hill, *Too Close to Call*, p. 63.
99. Ibid., p. 69.
100. Ibid., p. 70.
101. Sir Peter Kemp in conversation with the author, 1993.
102. *Sunday Times*, 24 March 1991.
103. F. Hirschman, *Exit, Voice and Loyalty* (Cambridge Massachusetts, Harvard University Press, 1970).
104. B. Evans, *The Politics of the Training Market: From Manpower Services Commission to Training and Enterprise Councils* (London, Routledge, 1992), p. 177.
105. *Financial Times*, 25 March 1991.
106. A widely held view at a conference, 'Towards a Radical New Century', organised for politicians and academics at the London School of Economics, by the *New Statesman*, the City of London and Shell UK.
107. *Daily Telegraph*, 7 October 1991.
108. *Sunday Times*, 23 December 1990.
109. *Sunday Telegraph*, 2 February 1992.
110. For example, Cyril Townsend MP in Bexley Heath.
111. M. Pinto-Duschinsky, Political Parties in P. Catteral (ed.), *Contemporary Britain: An Annual Review* (Oxford, Blackwell, 1992), p. 37.
112. D. Butler and D. Kavanagh, *The British General Election*, p. 39.
113. A. Seldon, *Major*, p. 257.
114. D. Butler and D. Kavanagh, *The British General Election*, p. 42.
115. S. Hogg and J. Hill, *Too Close to Call*, p. 219.
116. D. Butler and D. Kavanagh, *The British General Election*, p. 257.
117. A. King et al. (eds), *New Labour Triumphs; Britain at the Polls* (New Jersey, Chatham House, 1997), p. 177.

CHAPTER 7

1. D. Butler and D. Kavanagh, *The British General Election of 1997* (Basingstoke, Macmillan, 1997), p. 46.
2. A. Seldon, *Major* (London, Phoenix, 1997), p. 292.
3. D. Denver, 'The Government That Could Do No Right', in A. King et al. (eds) *New Labour Triumphs; Britain at the Polls* (New Jersey, Chatham House, 1992), pp. 16–17.

4. Quoted in A. Seldon, *Major*, p. 290.
5. Interview with the author.
6. *Financial Times*, 7 September 1992.
7. *Guardian*, 17 September 1992.
8. E. Dell, *The Chancellors: A History of the Chancellors of the Exchequer, 1945–1990* (London, Harper Collins, 1997), pp. 554–5.
9. A.J. Davies, *We The Nation: The Conservative Party and the Pursuit of Power* (London, Little Brown, 1995), p. 299.
10. D. Denver, 'The Government That Could Do No Right', p. 18.
11. S. Hogg and J. Hill, *Too Close to Call* (London, Warner Books, 1995), pp. 187–8.
12. *Daily Telegraph*, 18 September 1992.
13. *Sun*, 17 September 1992.
14. This is evident in The *Express, Mail, Mirror, Financial Times* and *Guardian*.
15. *The Times*, 17 September 1992.
16. *Independent*, 17 September 1992.
17. D. Butler and D. Kavanagh, *The British General Election*, p. 12.
18. The nature of the traditional Tory lead in these areas is multi-faceted. It had its origins in the deference of the poor towards the rich and the assumption by poorer people that Tories are necessarily richer and better able to manage money. Postwar austerity after 1945, the devaluation of 1967 and the forced resort to the International Monetary Fund for a loan in 1976 were also events which Conservatives exploited to suggest Labour's tendency to generate economic hardship.
19. A. King et al. (eds), *New Labour Triumphs; Britain at the Polls* (New Jersey, Chatham House, 1992), p. 20.
20. A. Seldon, *Major*, p. 325.
21. See the discussion in A. Seldon, *Major*, pp. 325–30.
22. In informal discussion with guests at a dinner at the University of Cambridge in November 1992.
23. *Daily Telegraph*, 19 October 1992.
24. Jeremy Paxman interviewing Heseltine on BBC TV 'Newsnight', October 1992.
25. *Guardian*, 22 October 1992.
26. A. Seldon, *Major*, p. 336.
27. *The Economist*, 11 April 1992.
28. *Sunday Times*, 25 October 1992.
29. S. Baker, A. Gamble and S. Ludlam, 'Whips or Scorpions', in *Parliamentary Affairs* 47, (1) (1993).
30. E. Nicholson, *Secret Society* (London, Cassell, 1996), pp. 183–4.
31. H. Wallace, 'At Odds with Europe', in *Political Studies* 45 (4), p. 681.
32. Ibid.
33. A. Seldon, *Major*, p. 341.
34. C. Challen and M. Hughes, *In Defence of the Party: The Secret State, the Conservative Party and Dirty Tricks* (London, Medium Press, 1996), p. 148.
35. *Independent*, 23 July 1991.
36. This view is explained in K. Judge and B. New, *Health* (Oxford, Blackwell, 1993), pp. 280–93.
37. The Citizen's Charter: First Report, CM 201 (London, HMSO, 1992).
38. K. Theakston and G .Fry, 'The Party and the Civil Service', in A. Seldon and S. Ball, *Conservative Century* (Oxford, Oxford University Press, 1994), p. 400.
39. *Working Brief*, Unemployment Unit, November 1991, p. 3.
40. Simon Heffer constantly referred disparagingly to the 'Pooterism' of the Charters, implying that they were the conception to be expected of a Mr Nobody.
41. A. Gamble, 'In Government, but not in Power', in *New Statesman*, 1 October 1993.
42. The Right Honourable Lord Wakeham and Giles Chichester, *The Carlton Lectures 1993*, Foreword.
43. Ibid., p. 14.
44. Ibid., pp. 16–17.

45. A. Seldon, *Major*, p. 361.
46. Ibid., p. 362.
47. *Guardian*, 25 April 1993.
48. *Independent on Sunday* quoted in A. Seldon, *Major*, p. 370.
49. S. Foster, *Political Parties: Thatcherism Abandoned?* (Sheffield, Hallam University, 1994), p. 84.
50. *Sunday Telegraph*, 10 October 1993.
51. *Sunday Telegraph*, 3 October 1993.
52. *Sunday Telegraph*, 10 October 1993.
53. *Guardian*, 4 October 1993.
54. *Sunday Telegraph*, 27 April 1997.
55. Peregrine Worsthorne, *Sunday Telegraph*, 26 September 1993.
56. S. Foster, *Political Parties*, p. 86.
57. A.J. Davies, *We the Nation* (London, Little Brown, 1995), p. 320.
58. S. Ludlam and M. Smith (eds.), *Contemporary British Conservatism* (London, St Martins Press, 1995), p. 63.
59. BBC Radio 4, 'The World at One', 16 September 1993.
60. D. Butler and D. Kavanagh, *The British General Election of 1997*, pp. 25–6.
61. C. Challen, *Price of Power*, pp. 105–6.
62. A. Seldon, *Major*, p. 383.
63. C. Challen, *Price of Power*, pp. 109–10.
64. D. Butler and D. Kavanagh, *The British General Election of 1997*, p. 26.
65. D. Denver, 'The Government that Could Do No Right', in D. Denver et al. *New Labour Triumphs*, p. 22.
66. S. Foster, *Political Parties*, p. 80.
67. Party workers in one northern constituency say that this was the only policy, in their experience, which led to people coming in off the streets to abuse them while they were working.
68. Simon Heffer in the *Spectator*, 17 July 1993.
69. *Independent*, 1 March 1993.
70. *Independent*, 15 March 1993.
71. Charles Moore in the *Spectator*, 26 September 1992.
72. B. Evans and A. Taylor, *From Salisbury to Major: Continuity and Change in Conservative Politics* (Manchester, Manchester University Press, 1996), p. 265.
73. D. Butler and D. Kavanagh, *The British General Election of 1997*, p. 8.
74. HC Debs, vol. 226, cols, 284–5, 9 June 1993.
75. *Sunday Telegraph*, 27 June 1993.
76. Simon Heffer in the *Spectator*, 17 July 1993.
77. Ibid.
78. A. Seldon, *Major*, p. 402.
79. *Spectator*, 4 July 1992.
80. A. Seldon, *Major*, pp. 384–9.
81. *Sunday Telegraph*, 25 July 1993.
82. *The Times*, 26 July 1993.
83. M. Holmes, *The Conservative Party and Europe* (London, Bruges Group, 1994), paper 17, p. 1.
84. BBC TV News, 2 July 1994.
85. A. Seldon, *Major*, pp. 431–2.
86. Ibid., p. 434. Many other scandals followed including the discovery of the body of Tory MP Stephen Milligan in bizarre circumstances which suggested sexual games.
87. *Independent*, 8 October 1994, summary of a report published by P. Seyd and P. Whiteley on the membership of the Conservative Party.
88. P. Seyd and P. Whiteley, 'Conservative Grassroots', in S. Ludlam and M. Smith, *Contemporary British Conservatism*, pp. 62–8.
89. C. Pattie and R. Johnston, 'Paying Their Way: Local Associations, the Constituency Quota Scheme and Conservative Party Finance', in *Political Studies* 44 (5) (December 1996), p. 934.

90.   *Sunday Times*, 13 November 1994.
91.   *Sunday Times*, 10 July 1994.
92.   A. Seldon, *Major*, p. 476.
93.   D. Butler and D. Kavanagh, *The British General Election of 1992*, p. 16.
94.   *The Times*, 7 April 1994.
95.   *Guardian*, 31 March 1994.
96.   *Guardian*, 13 June 1994.
97.   D. Baker, I. Fountain, A. Gamble and S. Ludlam, 'The Blue Map of Europe: Conservative Parliamentarians and European Integration', in C. Rallings et al., *British Elections and Parties Yearbook 1995* (London, Cass, 1995), p. 51.
98.   *Guardian*, 31 March 1994.
99.   *Sunday Telegraph*, 26 June 1994.
100. BBC TV News, 27 June 1994.
101. Helen Wallace, 'At Odds with Europe', *Political Studies* 45 (4).
102. A. Seldon, *Major*, p. 486.
103. *Independent*, 15 October 1994.
104. BBC Radio 4, 'The World This Weekend', 3 July 1994.
105. *Financial Times*, 5 April 1994.
106. *New Statesman*, 8 July 1994.
107. A. Seldon, *Major*, p. 475.
108. *Financial Times*, 1 June 1993.
109. *Independent*, 5 November 1994.
110. R. Morris, *Tories* (London, Mainstream, 1991), p. 247.
111. E. Nicholson, *Secret Society*, p. 221.
112. This discussion is elaborated further in Stephen Wilks, 'Conservative Governments and the Economy, 1979–1997', in *Political Studies* 45 (4), pp. 689–704.
113. *Guardian*, 4 February 1995.
114. A. Seldon, *Major*, p. 535.
115. D. Butler and D. Kavanagh, *The British General Election of 1997*, p. 11.
116. *Daily Telegraph*, 7 December 1998.
117. A. Seldon, *Major*, p. 546.
118. Ibid., p. 542.
119. A. Seldon, *Major*, p. 557.
120. P. Norton, 'The Conservative Party' in A. King et al., *New Labour Triumphs; Britain at the Polls* (New Jersey, Chatham House, 1992), p. 100.
121. *Sunday Times*, 2 July 1995.
122. *Sunday Times*, 9 July 1998.
123. M. Gove, *Michael Portillo: The Future of the Right* (London, Fourth Estate, 1995), p. 330.
124. Ibid., p. 306.
125. *Sunday Telegraph*, 9 July 1995.
126. *Sunday Telegraph*, 16 July 1995.
127. N. Barry, 'Conservative Thought and the Welfare State', in *Political Studies* 45 (2), p. 345.
128. *Sunday Telegraph*, 16 July 1995.
129. *Sunday Times*, 10 September 1995.
130. Cited in A. Seldon, *Major*, p. 603.
131. *Daily Telegraph*, 14 December 1995.
132. D. Butler and D. Kavanagh, *The British General Election of 1997*, p. 20.
133. D. Kavanagh, *British Politics: Continuities and Change* (Oxford, Oxford University Press, 1997), p. 297.
134. P. Norton, 'The Conservative Party', pp. 91–3.
135. D. Baker, 'Collaborative Research and the Members of Parliament Project', in *Politics* 17 (1), p. 63.
136. *Sunday Telegraph*, 17 December 1995.
137. *Sunday Telegraph*, 7 January 1996.
138. Ibid.

139. P. Norton, 'The Conservative Party', pp. 106–7.
140. D. Denver, 'The Government that Could No No Right', p. 29.
141. See, D. Leigh and E. Vulliamy, *Sleaze: The Corruption of Parliament* (London, Fourth Estate, 1997) for a full account of the Hamilton affair.
142. D. Denver, 'The Government that Could Do No Right', p. 30.
143. *New Statesman*, 22 March 1996.
144. A. Seldon, *Major*, p. 641.
145. D. Denver, 'The Government that Could Do No Right', p. 44.
146. *Huddersfield Daily Examiner*, 17–19 July 1996.
147. A. Seldon, *Major*, p. 642.
148. *Daily Telegraph*, 10 October 1996.
149. Ibid., p. 644.
150. D. Butler and D. Kavanagh, *The British General Election of 1997*, p. 11.
151. The conference proceedings are described and analysed in A. Seldon, *Major*, pp. 672–6.
152. C. Challen, *Price of Power*, pp. 113–15.
153. D. Butler and D. Kavanagh, *The British General Election of 1997*, p. 38.
154. T. Keswick and E. Heathcott-Amery, *A Conservative Agenda: Proposals for a Third Term* (London, Centre for Policy Studies, 1996), Prologue.
155. Ibid., pp. 14–29.
156. *The Times*, 24 January 1997.
157. D. Butler and D. Kavanagh, *The British General Election of 1997*, p. 11.
158. S. Dorrell, *How to Win the Next Election* (London, Conservative Political Centre, 1996), pp. 6–9.
159. J. Patten, *Things to Come: The Tories in the Twenty-First Century* (London, Sinclair Stevenson, 1995), p. 4.
160. Ibid., pp. 25–7.
161. D. Willetts, *Why Vote Conservative?* (Harmondsworth, Penguin, 1997).
162. Ibid., pp. 89–106.
163. Ibid., pp. 39–40.
164. D. Butler and D. Kavanagh, *The British General Election of 1997*, p. 44.
165. A. Seldon, *Major*, p. 702.
166. Ibid., p. 705.
167. Talk Radio News, 16 March 1997.
168. D. Butler and D. Kavanagh, *The British General Election of 1997*, p. 101.
169. *Sun*, 18 March 1997.
170. A. Seldon, *Major*, p. 723.
171. D. Butler and D. Kavanagh, *The British General Election of 1997*, p. 233.
172. A. King, 'Why Labour Won At Last', in A. King et al. (eds), *New Labour Triumphs; Britain at the Polls* (New Jersey, Chatham House, 1992), pp. 177–206.

Chapter 8

1. R. Levitas, (ed.) *The Ideology of the New Right* (Cambridge, Polity Press, 1986), pp. 1–4.
2. S. Brittan, *The Economic Consequences of Democracy*, (London, Temple Smith, 1977), p. 45.
3. *The Times*, 4 January 1975.
4. D. King, *The New Right: Politics, Markets and Citizenship* (Basingstoke, Macmillan, 1987), p. 111.
5. Ibid., chapter 7.
6. J. Aitkin, MSC, TVEI and Education in Perspective', *Political Quarterly*, 57 (1986), p. 231.
7. D. King, 'The Conservatives and Training Policy 1979–1992: From a Tripartite to a Neoliberal Regime', *Political Studies* 41, (June 1993), pp. 221–7.
8. In discussions with the author.
9. A. Brown, 'Labour Market Policy in Britain: A Critical View', (Edinburgh, Waverly papers Politics Series), p. 2.

10. Local TEC Annual Reports suggest this pattern and Sir Geoffrey Holland who was Permanent Secretary at the Department of Employment informed the author that TECs would have to re-establish local networking which the MSC had uprooted.

11. P. Riddell, *The Thatcher Government* (London, Martin Robertson, 1983), p. 7.

12. See for example, M. Seliger, *Ideology and Politics* (London, Allen and Unwin, 1976).

13. R. Levitas, (ed.) *The Ideology of the New Right* (Cambridge, Polity Press, 1986), pp. 12–16.

14. D. Winch, *Economics and Policy* (London, Fontana, 1972), pp. 303–4.

15. D. Willets, *Modern Conservatism* (Harmondsworth, Penguin, 1972), p. 420.

16. R. Skidelsky, 'Introduction' in R. Skidelsky (ed.) *Thatcherism*, (Oxford, Blackwell, 1988), p. 18.

17. A. Vincent, 'British Conservatism and the Problem of Ideology', *Political Studies*, 42 (2) (June 1994), p. 206.

18. S. Letwin, *The Anatomy of Thatcherism*, (London, Fontana, 1992), pp. 303–4.

19. Ibid., pp. 45–6.

20. Ibid., p. 3.

21. David Howell MP in conversation.

22. Review in the *Sunday Express* of I. Gilmour, *Dancing with Dogma: Britain under Thatcherism*, (London, Simon and Schuster, 1992). Cited on dust jacket publicity.

23. Robert Harris, Review in the *Sunday Times* of I. Gilmour, *Dancing with Dogma*. Cited on dust jacket publicity.

24. B. Evans, 'Political Ideology in Britain', in L. Robins, (ed.) *Understanding British Politics*, (London, The Politics Association, 1984), p. 131.

25. I. Gilmour, *Dancing with Dogma*, pp. 338–9.

26. F. Pym, *The Politics of Consent*, (London, Hamish Hamilton, 1994).

27. J. Bulpitt, 'The Discipline of the New Democracy: Mrs Thatcher's Domestic Statecraft', *Political Studies*, 34 (1986), p. 26.

28. S. Jenkins, *Accountable to None*, (Harmondsworth, Penguin, 1992), p. 1.

29. Ibid., pp. 210–11.

30. Ibid., p. 14.

31. S. Hall, *The Hard Road to Renewal: Thatcherism and the Crisis of the Left* (London, Verso Books, 1988), p. 7.

32. Ibid., p. 6.

33. A. Gamble, *The Free Economy and the Strong State* (London, Macmillan, 1989), p. 144.

34. Ibid., p. 226.

35. Ibid., p. 236.

36. D. Marsh, 'Explaining Thatcherism: Beyond Uni-Dimensional Explanation', Round Table: 'The Politics of Thatcherism', Political Studies Association Conference, (1994).

37. A. Gamble, *The Free Economy and the Strong State*, p. 236.

38. See J. Larrain, *The Concept of Ideology* (London, Hutchinson, 1979), pp. 79–83. Thatcher frequently resorted to platitudes of common sense to communicate with a mass electorate. She was fond of such aphorisms as 'managers must be allowed to manage' and 'a country must live within its means'. As she expressed it herself, 'we had also taken apprenticeships in advertising and learnt how to put a complex and sophisticated case in direct, clear and simple language . . . our agenda would, with luck, strike people as familiar common sense'. M. Thatcher, *The Downing Street Years*, (London, Harper Collins, 1993), p. 5

39. B. Jessop and K. Bonnet et al., *Thatcherism*, (London, Polity Press, 1988), pp. 59–65.

40. Ibid., pp. 120–1.

41. B. Jessop, *The Capitalist State* (London, Martin Robertson, 1982), p. 244.

42. The concept of the dual labour market has been thoroughly analysed, in B. Evans, *The Politics of the Training Market: From Manpower Services Commission to Training and Enterprise Councils* (London, Routledge, Kegan and Paul, 1992); P. Ainley and M. Corney, *Training for the Future: The Rise and Fall of the MSC*, (London, Cassell, 1990); C. Benn and J. Fairley, *Challenging the MSC*, (London, Pluto Press, 1986).

43. N. Lawson, *The View from Number 11*, pp. 40–2.

44. B. Evans and A. Taylor, *From Salisbury to Major*, p. 236.

45. B. Jessop, *Thatcherism*, pp. 180–3.
46. J. Ramsden, 'Thatcher and Conservative History', *Contemporary Record*, 4 (4) (April 1991), pp. 2–3.
47. M. Bentley, 'Is Mrs Thatcher a Conservative?' *Contemporary Record*, 4 (3) (February 1991), p. 2.
48. D. Marsh and R. Rhodes, *Implementing Thatcherite Policies: Audit of an Era*, (Buckingham, Open University Press, 1992), p. 3.
49. J. Moon, 'Evaluating Thatcher', *Politics* 14 (2) (September 1994), p. 44.
50. Ibid.
51. In conversation with the author.

CHAPTER 9

1. *Guardian*, 'Think-tank Running on Empty', 31 July 1997.
2. D. Kavanagh, *The Reordering of British Politics*, p. 170.
3. Leader's speech at the 1996 Labour Party conference.
4. D. Butler and D. Kavanagh, *The British General Election of 1992*, (Basingstoke, Macmillan, 1992) p. 44.
5. D. Butler and D. Kavanagh, *The British General Election of 1992*, p. 45.
6. Ibid., pp. 52–3.
7. I. Crewe, 'Has the Electorate Become Thatcherite', in R. Skidelsky, *Thatcherism*, p. 38.
8. See C. Hughes and P. Wintour, *Labour Rebuilt: The New Model Party*, (London, Fourth Estate, 1990). This provides a detailed account of the intra-party changes between 1987 and 1990 although it tends to overestimate the role of organisations such as the party's Shadow Communications Agency and the work of the various Policy Review Groups which were set up, and to underestimate the extent to which the process was managed by the party leadership, and so produced the policy proposals which the party's leaders would accept.
9. D. Kavanagh, *The Reordering of British Politics* (Oxford, Oxford University Press, 1997), p. 186.
10. J. Rentoul, *Tony Blair* (London, Little Brown, 1995), p. 182.
11. A. Downs, *An Economic Theory of Democracy*, (New York, Harper and Row, 1957).
12. J. Rentoul, *Tony Blair*, p. 180.
13. Ibid., p. 180.
14. Quoted in D. Butler and D. Kavanagh, *The British General Election of 1987*, p. 54.
15. M. Smith and J. Spear, *The Changing Labour Party* (London, Routledge, 1992), p. 228.
16. Ibid.
17. J. Rentoul, *Tony Blair*, pp. 236–40.
18. *Independent*, 8 August 1991.
19. M. Smith and J. Spear, *The Changing Labour Party*, p. 229.
20. J. Rentoul, *Tony Blair*, p. 261.
21. A. Giddens, *The Third Way: The Renewal of Social Democracy* (Cambridge, Polity Press, 1988), p. 16.
22. D. Kavanagh, *The Reordering of British Politics*.
23. Will Hutton, Editor-in-Chief, the *Observer*, 20 September 1998.
24. A. Gamble, 'After the Watershed', in A. Coddington and M. Perryman, *The Moderniser's Dilemma*, (London, Lawrence and Wishart, 1998), p. 23.
25. *The Economist*, December 1996, p. 48.
26. *The Economist*, December 1996, p. 47.
27. Speech delivered to the conference 'Towards a Radical New Century', The London School of Economics, 17 September 1998.
28. Ibid.
29. Ibid.
30. Ibid. This theme was taken up by officials from the Regional Government Office for Yorkshire and Humberside at the opening of the Halifax Careers Centre, 11 December 1998.

31. Tony Blair, 'Today', BBC Radio 4, 30 September 1998.
32. J. Gilbert, 'Blurred Vision' in A. Coddington and M. Perryman, *The Modernisers Dilemma: Radical Politics in the Age of Blair*, (London, Lawrence and Wishart, 1998), p. 78.
33. *The Economist*, December 19, p. 48.
34. S. Hall and M. Jacques (eds), *New Times: The Changing Face of Politics in the 1990s* (London, Lawrence and Wishart, 1990), p. 449.
35. P. Mandelson and R. Liddle, *The Blair Revolution: Can Labour Deliver?* (London, Faber, 1996).
36. D. Kavanagh, *The Reordering of British Politics*, pp. 218–21.
37. A. Giddens, *The Third Way*, pp. 18–20.
38. Ibid., pp. 147–53.
39. Alan Simpson MP, *New Statesman*, 16 November 1997.
40. T. Bewes, 'Who Cares Who Wins? Post-Modernism and the Radicalism of Indifference', in A. Coddington and M. Perryman, *The Modernisers Dilemma: Radical Politics in the Age of Blair* (London, Lawrence and Wishart, 1998), pp. 194–5.
41. K. Davey, 'Anxiety and Identification on the British Left', in A. Coddington and M. Perryman, *The Modernisers Dilemma*, p. 266.
42. M. Jacques, 'Good to be Back', in *Marxism Today*, November/December 1998, p. 3.
43. E. Hobsbawm, 'The Big Picture: the Death of Neo-Liberalism', in *Marxism Today*, October 1998.
44. S. Hall, 'The Great Moving Nowhere Show', *Marxism Today*, October 1998, p. 11.
45. Ibid.
46. A. Kaletsky, 'The Market Myth', in *Marxism Today*, October 1998.
47. D. Held, 'Globalisation: the Timid Tendency', in *Marxism Today*, October 1998.
48. *New Statesman*, 30 October 1998, p. 11.
49. *Socialist Worker*, 31 October 1998, p. 11.
50. Paper delivered to Sheffield University, Department of Politics, November 1998.
51. A. Barnett, 'All Power to the Citizens', in *Marxism Today*, October 1998.
52. G. Mulgan, 'Whinge and a Prayer', *Marxism Today*, October 1998.
53. Ibid.
54. P. Richards, 'The Permanent Revolution of New Labour', in A. Coddington and M. Perryman, *The Modernisers Dilemma: Radical Politics in the Age of Blair* (London, Lawrence and Wishart, 1998), p. 33.
55. Ibid.
56. Gamble, 'After the Watershed', p. 30.
57. See also *Political Quarterly* 68 (4) (1997).
58. A. Gamble, 'After the Watershed', pp. 15–16.
59. Ibid., p. 29.
60. T. Wright MP, 'Electoral Reform: A Challenge to New Labour', *Representation* 33, (Summer/Autumn 1995), p. 33.
61. A. Giddens, *The Third Way*, p. 7.
62. Ibid., p. 70.
63. Ibid., p. 15.

POSTSCRIPT

1. E. Evans, *Thatcher and Thatcherism* (London, Routledge, 1997), pp. 116–17.
2. A. Giddens, *The Third Way: The Renewal of Social Democracy* (Cambridge, Polity Press, 1998), pp. 113–14.
3. *Guardian*, 15 November 1996.
4. R. Dahrendorf, 'Changing Social Values Under Mrs Thatcher', in R. Skidelsky (ed.) *Thatcherism*, (Oxford, Blackwell, 1988), p. 200.
5. V. Bogdanor, in D. Kavanagh and A. Seldon (eds) *The Thatcher Effect* (Oxford, Oxford University Press, 1989), p. 142.

6. H. Young, *One of Us*, (London, Macmillan, 1989), p. 411.

7. *Sunday Independent*, 7 December 1997.

8. M. Gove, 'War on the Vague: Towards the New Tories' in A. Coddington and M. Perryman, *The Modernisers Dilemma: Radical Politics in the Age of Blair* (London, Lawrence and Wishart, 1998), p. 260.

9. *The Economist*, 19 June 1999.

10. A. Gamble, 'After the Watershed', in A. Coddington and M. Perryman, *The Modernisers Dilemma*, p. 25.

11. D. Marquand, *Must Labour Win?* (Fabian Society, 1998), p. 6. Despite the better European election vote than anticipated, the polls revealed the Conservatives trailing Labour by 51 per cent to 28 per cent, *The Times*, 24 June 1999.

12. D. Kavanagh, *The Reordering of British Politics* (Oxford, Oxford University Press, 1997), p. 116.

13. *The Economist*, 19 June 1999.

14. M. Hamilton, 'The Elements of the Concept of Ideology', *Political Studies* 35 (1987), p. 18.

INDEX